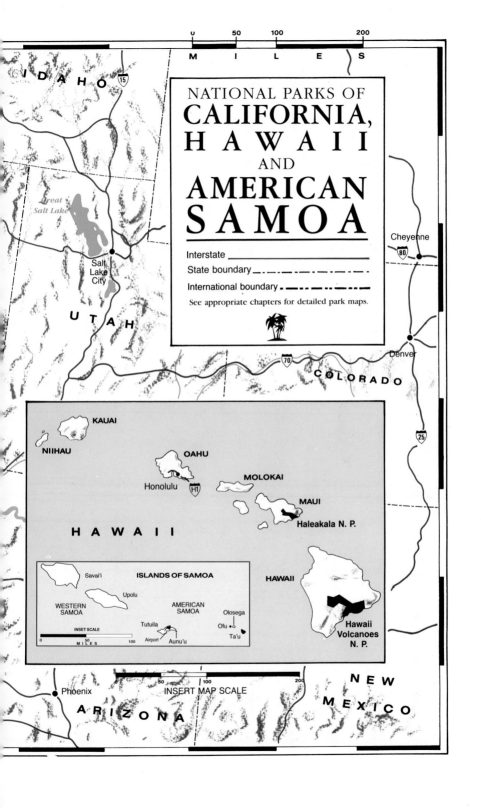

MILES

0   50   100   200

NATIONAL PARKS OF
CALIFORNIA,
HAWAII
AND
AMERICAN
SAMOA

Interstate _____

State boundary _ _ . _ . _ . _ . _ .

International boundary . _ . _ . _ . _ .

See appropriate chapters for detailed park maps.

IDAHO

UTAH

Great Salt Lake

Salt Lake City

COLORADO

Cheyenne

Denver

Phoenix

ARIZONA

NEW MEXICO

KAUAI

NIIHAU

OAHU

Honolulu

MOLOKAI

MAUI

Haleakala N. P.

HAWAII

HAWAII

Hawaii Volcanoes N. P.

ISLANDS OF SAMOA

Savai'i

Upolu

WESTERN SAMOA

AMERICAN SAMOA

Tutuila

Aunu'u

Olosega

Ofu

Ta'u

Airport

INSET SCALE

0   50   100

MILES

INSERT MAP SCALE

0   50   100   200

THE SIERRA CLUB GUIDES
TO THE
NATIONAL PARKS
OF
CALIFORNIA, HAWAII, AND
AMERICAN SAMOA

Published by
Stewart, Tabori & Chang

Distributed by

R A N D O M   H O U S E

Library of Congress Cataloging-in-Publication Data

The Sierra Club guides to the national parks of California, Hawaii, and American
Samoa / (text by Joseph E. Brown . . . et al.). — Rev. and updated.

p. cm. — (Sierra Club guides to the national parks)
Rev. ed. of: The Sierra Club guides to the national parks of the Pacific Southwest
and Hawaii, c1984.
Includes Index.
ISBN 0-679-76497-6 (pbk.)
1. National parks and reserves—California—Guidebooks.
2. National parks and reserves—Hawaii—Guidebooks. 3. National parks and
reserves—American Samoa—Guidebooks. 4. California—Guidebooks. 5.
Hawaii—Guidebooks. 6. American Samoa—Guidebooks. I Brown, Joseph E.,
1929- . II. Sierra Club. III. Sierra Club guides to the national parks of the
Pacific Southwest and Hawaii. IV. Series.
F859.3.S55 1996
917.3—dc20
96-11450
CIP

TEXT BY:
Joseph E. Brown: Channel Islands and Redwood
Michael Collier: Death Valley*
Barbara B. Decker & Robert W. Decker: Haleakala,
Hawaii Volcanoes, Lassen Volcanic
David Lavender: Kings Canyon and Sequoia
Susanna Margolis: American Samoa*
William Truesdell: Joshua Tree*
*New in the revised edition.

Text revisions throughout this edition by the Project Editor.

Photo credits can be found on pp. 339–340

PROJECT EDITOR: Donald Young (Revised Edition); Irene Pavitt (First Edition)
CONSULTING EDITOR: James V. Murfin (First Edition)
DESIGNER: J.C. Suarès
PHOTO EDITOR: Amla Sanghvi (Revised Edition); Christine A. Pullo (First Edition)
COPY EDITOR: Randy Blunk (Revised Edition)
ART AND PRODUCTION: Alice Wong, Lisa Vaughn, Melanie Random,
Evangeline Yao, Christopher Young (Revised Edition)

Created by Stewart, Tabori & Chang, Inc., 575 Broadway, New York, NY 10012

Printed in Singapore

24689753

Revised Edition

Cover Photographs: Cathedral Peak, Yosemite (© Donna Dannen); Joshua Tree
(© Jeff Foott); Island Fox (© Robert Gildart); Illustration and Map
(© Bill Russell). Frontispiece: Coast view, Redwood National Park (© Ed Cooper).
Back cover: Redwood forest, Redwood National Park (© David Muench)

T The fifty-four national parks of the United States contain many glorious natural splendors. Each year, tens of millions of Americans and growing numbers of visitors from around the world contemplate the beauty of snow-capped mountains, cascading waterfalls, groves of soaring trees, glistening surf-kissed beaches, and deep and mysterious red-rock canyons. Herds of large mammals enhance the setting in some parks, and uncounted numbers of other animals, birds, crawly things, and plants occupy their own niches as participants in nature's grand design.

The National Park System contains about 375 units, but the five volumes of *The Sierra Club Guides to the National Parks* feature only those units designated as a "national park" or as a "national park and preserve." An act of Congress is required for the establishment of a park. The world's first national park—Yellowstone—was created in 1872. The list has grown steadily, as the American people, through their elected representatives, demonstrated many times their commitment to preserving parks for the enjoyment of themselves and of generations yet to come. In 1994 alone, three more parks were added to the list.

The Sierra Club was founded in California in 1892 by the naturalist John Muir and some of his friends. One of the oldest and largest conservation organizations, the Club, which now has more than 550,000 members, has been in the forefront of many efforts to create new parks.

This series has been produced with the cooperation of the Sierra Club and with the participation of the National Park Service and Random House. Leading nature writers and photographers have contributed to the guides. This revised edition contains new chapters on the six parks established since the mid-1980s. As well, the chapters on the forty-eight other parks have been thoroughly reviewed and completely updated.

We hope you will enjoy exploring the parks, and we know these guides will enhance your experience.

—Donald Young, Editor

M A P S

C O N T E N T S

NATIONAL PARK OF
AMERICAN
SAMOA

Waterfall in a deep gorge on Ta'u island, American Samoa.

NATIONAL PARK OF AMERICAN SAMOA
PAGO PAGO, AMERICAN SAMOA 96799
TEL.: (684) 633-7082*

*Use prefix code 011 if phoning from the United States.

HIGHLIGHTS: Undisturbed Paleotropical rain forest • Clear water and living reefs • 3,000-year-old culture • Pacific flying foxes (fruit bats)

ACCESS: Commercial flights to Pago Pago from Hawaii; frequent commercial small-plane service from Pago Pago to Ta'u and Ofu islands.

Hours: Dawn to dusk.

FEES: No park entrance fees; fees likely if private guiding services are arranged.

PARKING: Limited, at trail heads.

GAS: Ample supply on Tutuila, limited on both Ofu and Ta'u.

FOOD, LODGING: Private restaurants, hostelries, on the island of Tutuila; limited facilities on Ta'u and Ofu. Village stays may be possible—contact the NPS office, Pago Pago.

VISITOR CENTER: Visitor contact station at the NPS office, Pago Pago; apply there for local guides, information, etc.

MUSEUM: No in-park museum; Jean M. Haydon Museum, Pago Pago, offers diverse exhibits.

GIFT SHOP: None within park boundaries; commercial shopping available in Pago Pago, and crafts may be purchased in villages.

PICNICKING: No facilities; picnicking permitted anywhere within the park—all trash to be carried out.

HIKING: Tutuila unit—trail along Alava Ridge, rough bushwhacking in the interior; Ofu unit—coastline and reef walking; Ta'u unit—coastline walking, extremely rough bushwhacking in the interior.

BACKPACKING: Day-use areas only at present; inquire at NPS office, Pago Pago, for updates.

CAMPGROUNDS: No overnight use of the park is allowed; day use only.

TOURS: Commercial tour operators, fishing and diving operators, car rental agencies.

OTHER ACTIVITIES: Swimming, snorkeling, diving, fishing, bird- and bat-watching, village life.

FACILITIES FOR DISABLED: None at present.

For additional information, see also Sites, Trails, and Trips on pages 26–32 and the map on pages 14–15.

THE LURE OF THE SOUTH PACIFIC HAS ALWAYS held a dual promise—of undisturbed and spectacular scenery, and of an untrammeled and tranquil way of life. As much as anywhere in the Pacific—perhaps as much as anywhere on earth—these promises hold true in the National Park of American Samoa.

Here are high rain forests poking up through clouds, surf-beaten cliffs and quiet coves where seabirds nest, lush vegetation from coastline to mountaintop, pristine water curling to foam atop a fringing reef that is home to brilliant coral and extravagant marine life. Here too are the artifacts and sacred precincts of an ancient culture and the villages where that culture—*fa'a Samoa*, the Samoan way—persists today.

The National Park of American Samoa comprises separate units on three of the seven islands of this U.S. territory. The three island units total some 8,000 acres, 1,000 of them offshore waters and reefs. The acreage includes a major expanse of untouched native rain forest on Tutuila, the main island of American Samoa; a beautiful stretch of beach with coral reef on Ofu, some 60 miles east of Tutuila; and another undisturbed rain forest and cliff-bound coast—the biggest unit in the park—on Ta'u, east of Ofu.

There are many "onlys" about the National Park of American Samoa. It represents the only U.S. soil south of the equator. It contains the only Paleotropical rain forest on U.S. territory. It is perhaps the only park in the National Park System that even rangers on patrol get to by commercial airliner, albeit a small island-hopper.

What truly makes the park unique, however, is the system of land tenure and jurisdiction under which it is managed. For this is leased land, owned by local villages that regulate its use according to "custom"—a catchall word that embraces history, tradition, and local culture. Acting on behalf of the villages, the governor of American Samoa has rented the land of the park to the National Park Service. And while the land within the authorized park is to be managed like any other unit of the National Park System, its true owners, the Samoan villagers and their chiefs, may continue to carry out on it certain traditional subsistence and gathering activities, as they always have.

HISTORY

Like all of the islands of Oceania, Samoa was settled, probably around 1300 B.C., by migrants who had originally come from southeast Asia. These proto-Malay people, as they are denoted, sailed

AMERICAN SAMOA

NATIONAL PARK

Road _____

Unpaved Road _ _ _ _ _ _ _ _ _ _

Trail ....

Coral Reef _____

N

VICINITY MAP I

ISLANDS OF SAMOA

Savai'i

Upolu

WESTERN
SAMOA

AMERICAN
SAMOA

Olosega

Ofu

Ta'u

Tutuila

Airport

Aunu'u

INSET SCALE

| 0 | 50 | 100 |

M I L E S

Tutuila Unit

INSET SCALE

| 0 | 1/2 | 1 |

M I L E S

Matalia Pt.

Vatia
Bay

Vatia

Trail to
Vatia

Afono

Mt. Alava
El.1610'

Ridge Trail

TO VATIA

North
Pioa
Mtn.

Pago
Pago

South Pioa Mtn.
(Rainmaker Mtn.)

Aerial
Tramway

Pago Pago
Harbor

Fagasa

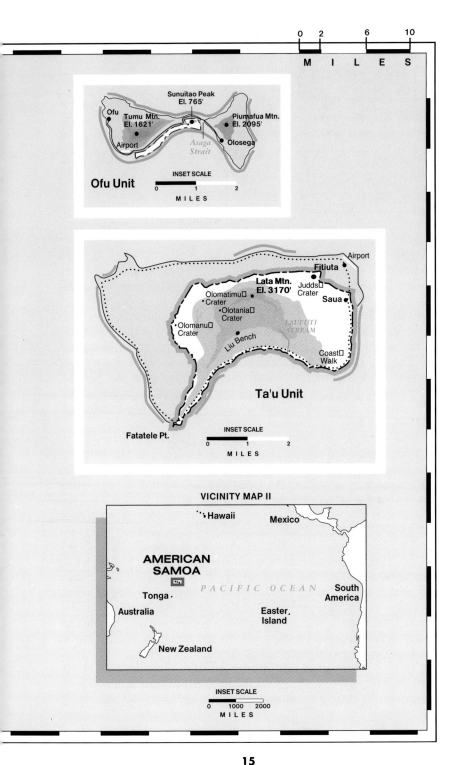

0 2   6   10

M   I   L   E   S

Ofu Unit

Sunuitao Peak
El. 765'

Ofu

Tumu Mtn.
El. 1621'

Piumafua Mtn.
El. 2095'

Airport

*Asaga
Strait*

Olosega

INSET SCALE

0   1   2

M I L E S

Airport

Fitiuta

Lata Mtn.
El. 3170'

Judds☐
Crater

Olomatimu☐
Crater

Saua

•Olotania☐
Crater

•Olomanu☐
Crater

*LAUFUTI
STREAM*

Liu Bench

Coast☐
Walk

Ta'u Unit

Fatatele Pt.

INSET SCALE

0   1   2

M I L E S

VICINITY MAP II

Hawaii

Mexico

**AMERICAN
SAMOA**

PACIFIC OCEAN

South
America

Tonga

Australia

Easter
Island

New Zealand

INSET SCALE

0   1000   2000

M I L E S

first to the islands of Melanesia, then to Fiji, and from there to Samoa, bringing with them ingredients of the culture and language we today call Polynesian. Indeed, Samoa and the islands of nearby Tonga are considered the cradle of Polynesia, from which early Polynesians ranged outward to settle every habitable island in the triangle created by Hawaii, New Zealand, and Easter Island.

Archeological evidence and oral tradition concur that the millennia preceding contact with Europeans were marked by tribal and interdistrict warfare that only occasionally yielded to eras of peace under a strong ruler—the most famous being Queen Salamasina, who unified Samoa in about A.D.1500 and ruled peacefully for fifty years. Descended from the four paramount families and holder of the four highest titles, Salamasina personified a persistent Samoan cultural fact—the consolidation of power in families and its transfer through titles defining lineage.

Dutch explorer Jacob Roggeveen is credited as the first European to make contact with Samoa. Sighting the islands in 1722, he (incorrectly) charted the chain. Roggeveen was followed by French, English, and Russian explorers. In their wake came whalers and traders and missionaries. Then came the governments protecting the interests of their whalers and traders and missionaries, and with the governments came the guns and ships to back up the claims of protection.

The German and American governments clashed over Samoa, settling their differences in a 1900 treaty that ceded Western Samoa to Germany and left the seven islands to the east as American Samoa. In fact, the United States Navy had been using the harbor at Pago Pago—pronounced *Pango Pango*—on the island of Tutuila as a provisioning station since 1872. In that year, a New York shipbuilder's report described Pago Pago as "the most perfectly land-locked harbor that exists in the Pacific Ocean."

The Navy remained in charge throughout World War II, when the Samoan islands became a staging area for the United States Marine Corps. Troops and supplies poured in—and roads, airstrips, docks, and medical facilities were built to accommodate them. The island—and its economy—were transformed, only to suffer a stunning blow when the troops departed, and again in 1951, when the naval station was closed.

The Department of the Interior now assumed administrative responsibility for American Samoa, bringing in federal aid for public works. In 1966, a new constitution established laws protecting fa'a Samoa and prohibiting foreigners from owning customary land. In 1976, after three times rejecting home rule, the people of

Top: In 1927, the lovely harbor at Pago Pago remained nearly in a pristine state.
Above: By the 1980s, western civilization had discovered this exotic location.

American Samoa voted to elect their own governor. American Samoa sends a nonvoting delegate to the U.S. Congress, and its citizens are U.S. nationals who have free entry to the United States but may not vote in U.S. elections.

Fiction and Fact

The Navy was still in charge when two of the most famous visitors to American Samoa made their appearance. Somerset Maugham passed through Pago Pago en route to Tahiti in 1916, lodging in rooms above the grocery in a building that still stands. Here he was inspired to write the story "Rain," about the prostitute Sadie Thompson and the missionary Davidson and what happened between them in the shadow of Mount Pioa, Rainmaker Mountain. Maugham's story became an instant classic; it has since mutated numerous times—into a play, a movie, and a musical, and it made its author a rich man.

Margaret Mead published *Coming of Age in Samoa* in 1928, based on research in three villages on the coast of Ta'u. This study, a classic of cultural determinism, tells how the conditions of adolescence that then prevailed in Samoa—few choices, few contradictions, free and open attitudes toward sex—produced far less stress than that suffered by American adolescents and equipped Samoan children "particularly well for passing through life without nervous instability."

A dramatic portrait of how culture shapes experience, *Coming of Age in Samoa* thrust Mead into the front ranks of anthropologists and, by reaching a wide popular audience, brought her enormous personal celebrity. Mead's work has since been both vociferously criticized and vigorously defended, but the book has never been out of print, and it continues to persuade readers that the islanders of the Pacific may know secrets about how to live that elude the rest of us.

Establishment of the Park

In 1988, Congress authorized the National Park of American Samoa "to preserve and protect the tropical forest and archeological and cultural resources of American Samoa, and of associated reefs, to maintain the habitat of flying foxes, preserve the ecological balance of the Samoan tropical forest, and, consistent with the preservation of these resources, to provide for the enjoyment of the unique resources of the Samoan tropical forest by visitors from around the world."

Passage of the bill was the signal for National Park Service

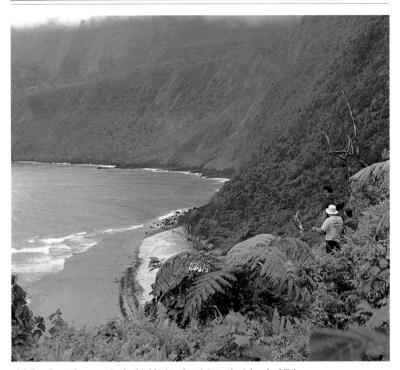
A hike along the coast is the highlight of a visit to the island of Ta'u.

personnel to solidify earlier "general" agreements allowing public use of the land. Doug Cuillard, superintendent of the proposed park, began lease negotiations with the landowners of the territory projected for the park, the government of American Samoa, and the *matai* (chiefs) in nine villages—four on Tutuila, three on Ta'u, and two on Ofu. The parties agreed that the governor of American Samoa would act as agent for all the landowners. Then, based on an amount determined by the High Court of American Samoa, the governor disbursed rental compensation to the villages in accordance with court orders. The lease agreement was drawn up in final form in September 1993, but the final details, such as provisions protecting the Samoans' traditional activities, will be worked out on a case-by-case basis with village committees.

Concurrent with all this work was the commissioning of studies on traditional uses of the land and on vegetation and topography. These studies establish a baseline for the preparation of the park's General Management Plan and for the ecotourism, sought by both the National Park Service and the matai, that can achieve economic development in a manner compatible with traditional culture and in harmony with the natural environment.

Fire and Fractures

The islands of the National Park of American Samoa are classic examples of high volcanic islands. They sit along the Pacific Ring of Fire, a chain of volcanic activity that has been forming arcs of islands for millions of years and that is still active today.

The volcanic activity is a function of plate tectonics—specifically, of the movement of the Pacific Plate. It underlies the largest single geographical feature on earth, the Pacific Ocean, which occupies more than one-third of the globe. The plate is produced at the East Pacific Rise, a mound that parallels the west coast of South America. Along the rise, the earth continually emits crust that creeps northwestward, sinking as it goes, until it is subducted into trenches at the northern and western borders of the ocean floor.

Other plates resist this subduction, and the ocean floor heaves and creaks until earthquakes relieve the pressure, shattering the

Fagatele Point, on Tutuila; the islands are the tops of volcanoes that grew underwater.

crust around the trenches. Volcanoes form in these fractures; this boiling edge in the ocean floor, paralleling the line of trenches formed by Pacific Plate subduction, is the Ring of Fire. Wherever enough molten lava has escaped through a vent in the ocean floor to break through the surface of the water along this ring, an island has formed.

In American Samoa, Tutuila's mountains are the eroded remnants of four volcanoes. Ta'u is the remnant of a single volcanic shield. Ofu and its companion, Olosega (to which it is today connected by a road bridge), were formed by at least six volcanic cones.

The harbor of Pago Pago, which nearly bisects Tutuila, is actually a submerged crater whose southern wall collapsed millions of years ago, leaving what is today the mouth of the harbor. On Ta'u, four craters—all within the park boundary—have yet to sink quite so low. An undersea eruption northwest of Ta'u in 1868 is evidence that volcanic activity in the Samoan chain may not be over.

Wind and Wave

Once an island has been formed, it almost immediately begins to sink, as the ocean floor settles into the earth's mantle. At the same time, the protruding island is a barrier to waves and wind that erode its slopes and pulverize debris into sediment and sand. Air currents blocked by mountaintops form intense heat, causing clouds and rain. The rain cuts streams down the slopes; plants grow there and slow the erosion of the mountains. The streams also carry debris; they carve ridges and valleys. Bays form where the valleys meet the sea, and in the trapped debris in the bays, coral reefs begin to grow.

As the reefs rise toward the surface of the water, they lessen the impact of waves on the shoreline and thus slow the formation of cliffs. The waters clear, and the coral grows even higher—and wider afield, until the reef fringes the island. Only where fresh water runs off the island's mountains into the sea is there a break, or pass, through the coral skeleton of the reef.

The islands of American Samoa are young islands. They contain numerous plant communities—littoral, lowland, montane, ridge, and cloud forest. Their cone-shaped mountains rise steeply. Their southern windward slopes are typically gentler than those on the northern leeward side and lushly carpeted with vegetation, while the leeward sides tend to be cliff-bound. Fringing reefs are common in these islands; stretches of fringing reefs are included within the boundaries of the national park in all three island units.

Rain Forests

The Tutuila and Ta'u units of the National Park of American Samoa offer a prime example of Paleotropical rain forest. These forests are the "end point" for numerous species that find refuge in such a habitat, and that makes the park of critical significance for the region. In this environment are more than 450 plant species, over sixty-five bird species, and two species of native bats—the Pacific flying foxes so essential to the health of the forest. One of these species, *Pteropus samoensis*, is a candidate for protection under the Endangered Species Act.

The forest vegetation runs from the coast along sloping lowlands to ridges to the highly diverse forests of the foothills to cloud forests at elevations above 2,000 feet to mountain scrub on the highest summits.

The islands are home to twenty-four species of seabirds including petrels, shearwaters, tropic birds, boobies, frigate birds, noddies, and terns. The twenty-eight species of waterfowl, marsh, and land birds include Pacific herons, rails, swamp hens, fruit doves, pigeons, lories, owls, swiftlets, kingfishers, honeyeaters, curlews, egrets, and herons.

Pacific flying foxes are the only terrestrial mammals native to American Samoa. They are an Old World group that probably reached Samoa along the same route as humans did, via Melanesia and Fiji, except that the flying foxes, which are fruit bats, arrived by air. Two species—*samoensis* and *tonganus*—range throughout the islands. They are similar in size, with wingspans of up to 3 feet, and in feeding habits, eating fruits and sometimes blossoms. The two species differ in neck color and behavior. The *samoensis* bats, greatly depleted by the numerous destructive hurricanes of the late 1980s, are mostly diurnal; the *Pteropus tonganus* roost by day, usually suspended from trees in sleeping colonies, and feed at night.

Flying foxes are considered a food delicacy in the Pacific and have been heavily exploited as such.

Reefs

The reefs of Samoa are home to clams, snails, octopus, mullet, jacks, mackerel, scad, surgeonfish, and parrotfish. They are also home to one of the most interesting species in the Pacific, *palolo*, or reefworm (*Eunice viridis*). Seven days after the full moon in

Opposite: Branches of the banyan tree send down shoots that take root and form secondary trunks.

October or November, the worms emerge from the reef to propagate the species. Awaiting this rising of the palolo, which occurs at night, is a large contingent of Samoans, for whom this so-called caviar of the Pacific is a great delicacy. Using baskets and nets and cheesecloth, they scoop up a portion of the palolo for feasting.

Ofu's reef—more than 2 miles of which form the Ofu unit of the park—is pristine, and close to shore in shallow water. In fact, the Ofu unit of the park is virtually a reef preserve. The coral here has been growing for centuries, long enough in some cases to qualify as micro-atolls.

Cultural Resources

Samoan culture plays a significant role in what the visitor to the national park will experience. The archeological sites and sacred places attest to a 3,000-year-old culture, to a rich legendary cosmogony, and to an ancient network of trade that clearly required the most extraordinary skills of sailing and navigation.

Traditions and rituals guide behavior in Samoa—fa'a Samoa, the Samoan way. Fa'a Samoa is based on collective life, and its central unit is the *aiga* (pronounced ah-*ing*-ah), the extended family of blood relatives, in-laws, and adopted members. A matai, or chief, has authority over the aiga's lands and assets, and he or she is responsible first and foremost for aiga welfare. Several aiga constitute a village or subvillage, each with its own matai, creating a complex social structure.

The traditional Samoan home is the *fale*, open-sided, set on a platform of coral, with wooden pillars supporting a roof of thatch or pandanus. Mats covering the pebble floor of the platform are the traditional furniture. Today, traditional fales have mostly given way to enclosed fales with corrugated tin roofs and jalousie windows—although in some cases an open fale serves as the "front porch" of an enclosed home.

The round fales in the center of villages are guest fales. Traditionally, any traveler could take rest or shelter in a guest fale. He could count on complete hospitality from the villagers, and they could count on receiving a gift in return. If the guest had nothing to give, he was in debt to the village and owed a favor.

Oblong fales belong to the talking chiefs, the *tulafeles*. They sit on the long sides, while the *ali'i*, the final decision-makers, sit on the round ends. The ali'i are outnumbered but more powerful.

Economic and political power is traditionally shared between men and women in village life, while labor is divided according to gender or talent. For example, the women's council may decide that a new health facility is needed; because health is the province

*Clockwise, from top: Mile-a-minute vine;
giant clam; hawksbill turtle; Tonganus
fruit bat, or flying fox.*

of women, the decision to build is theirs. But building is the province of men, so they will be asked to implement the decision for the welfare of the village.

Along with the power of tradition in fa'a Samoa is the power of religion, which is ubiquitous, predominantly Protestant Christian, and taken quite seriously. In concert with the churches, fa'a Samoa enforces a code of behavior all visitors should follow:

•In a Samoan village: ask permission for just about anything—from taking a photo to taking a swim; stop and wait if you are passing through the village during evening *sa*, the dusk curfew when families stop for prayer; if you pass a fale where a meeting is going on, lower anything you may be carrying to hip level; don't eat while walking through a village; if you are asked to share *kava* (made from the dried root of the pepper plant), spill a few drops on the ground or mat in front of you before drinking; be extra quiet on Sundays.

•In a Samoan home: sit with your legs folded under you, not stretched straight out; don't speak or eat while standing; if you are invited to stay, present a gift before leaving—and make a ceremony out of the presentation.

SITES, TRAILS, AND TRIPS

As this guidebook goes to press, Park Superintendent Chris Stein and Chief Ranger Leota Vaea Ainu'u are drafting a General Management Plan for the park. This entails working with matai and village committees to create infrastructure, to manage or reestablish native biota, to develop the unique combination of human and natural history that can make the National Park of American Samoa a model of ecotourism.

Today's pioneering visitors, however, can nevertheless expect a diversity of options and activities.

Tutuila

Tutuila is the main island of American Samoa, home to all but perhaps 1,000 of the island nation's 46,000 population, and gateway to the national park. Pago Pago is headquarters for most of the park's hotels and restaurants, for commercial tour operators and car rental agencies, for purchasing supplies and making arrangements.

The first stop for any visitor to the park should be the National

A chick of the white tern, one of twenty-four speices of seabirds in the islands.
Overleaf: Samoan men row a longboat in the harbor at Pago Pago.

Park Service office in Pago Plaza, Pago Pago. The office is open from 8:00 A.M. to 5:00 P.M. Monday through Friday. Here, the visitor can pick up a brochure as well as directions and information on trails and trail conditions, village accommodations, and more.

The Tutuila unit of the park contains approximately 2,500 acres. The park's boundaries ride along the top of the center of the island, above Pago Pago harbor and the towns that surround it, running about 5 miles from west to east and about a mile from north to south at the widest point—plus another mile north along the spit of land to Matalia Point.

This is primarily undisturbed native rain forest, including coastal, lowland, montane, and ridge forest vegetation. At its western border and all along the northern coast, the park area contains significant seabird nesting sites. Look for varieties of noddy, booby, tern—even frigate, shearwater, and petrel. Park territory skirts the village of Vatia on the north coast.

Because the steep interior of Tutuila is so overgrown, access on foot is difficult. As of this writing, a ridgeline trail offers a walk of some 3 miles from the trail head at Fagasa Pass to the top of Mount Alava, just above Pago Pago Harbor. Mount Alava is the site of American Samoa's television transmitter as well as terminus of the aerial tramway that was built in 1965 to transport personnel and equipment for the transmitter's construction. Currently in disuse, the tramway is one of the longest nonsupported cable spans in the world; the plan is to refurbish it as a park facility.

In the meantime, there is the ridgeline trail. From Fagasa, the walk proceeds first through the lush vines, climbers, and epiphytes of montane rain forest on up to the ridge forest of Alava, where shallow soils and wind exposure leave a lower canopy and dense trees. In time, this ridgeline trail may be extended another 2 miles or more to Afono Pass on the eastern edge of the park.

For the present, Afono, the north coast, and the village of Vatia can be reached by car—a drive of only about 30 minutes.

The only way to access the other two units of the park, however, is by Twin Otter plane, the workhorse of Pacific travel.

Ta'u

Ta'u has the park's biggest unit—about 5,400 acres, plus about 250 acres of offshore waters out to the reef. Indeed, most of Ta'u island is national park, which dominates the island's east and southeast.

The numerous daily flights from Pago Pago land at Fitiuta, on Ta'u's eastern coast, where lodging can also be found. A trail leads from Fitiuta southward along the coast into park territory.

Red mangrove, Pala Lagoon on Tutuila island.

Most of the park territory on Ta'u is high cloud forest—particularly important for endemic species and watershed protection—and it is mostly inaccessible. Hurricanes have downed many trees, making much of the interior uplands nearly impassable. Hiking in the interior thus means strenuous bushwhacking. At lower elevations on Ta'u there is still much traditional small-plot agriculture, which is an approved land use within the park.

The coast walk—down the east coast of Ta'u through small forest-farming areas, then west along the south coast to Fatatele Point, about 10 miles in all—is the highlight of a visit to the park here. It takes the hiker along a steep, cliff-bound coast to the falls of Laufuti Stream, then on underneath the high Liu Bench outcropping and along a fringing reef. The cliffs of the south coast drop in two or three steps from the top of Lata Mountain, which sits in the middle of the island and in the center of the park and is American Samoa's highest peak (3,170 feet).

Lata Mountain's environment—undisturbed cloud forest, dense montane rain forest, and montane scrub—provides the perfect conditions for highly successful breeding of many seabirds, and they abound: shearwater, petrel, tropic bird, tern, noddy.

As the ridge descends, vegetation changes from cloud forest to rain forest to littoral forest. Laufuti Stream is the island's only freshwater perennial; it contains fish that are very likely endemic—if not, where did they come from? The falls drop 1,500 feet and are very beautiful.

Native flying foxes are also evident on Ta'u. And the island contains the only snake found in American Samoa, the rare Pacific boa. The boa, typically brown in color with darker spots, can grow to nearly six feet in length. This Pacific version has a distinctive triangular head ending in a straight snout. It is found in the littoral vegetation along Ta'u's south shore, where it feeds on small mammals, birds, and lizards. It is also semiarboreal—a good climber.

Near the village of Saua on the east coast, the walker can see remains of a large village dating back to prehistory.

Ofu

The approximately 70 acres of national park on Ofu were an afterthought for park planners, but a very happy afterthought, for here is the quintessential white-sand beach of the South Pacific. In fact, Ofu's portion of the national park is just that—2.5-mile strip of beach with road, a coral reef, and the water between the two.

The airport in the southwest of the island is next to the island's lodging, which is a 10-minute walk from park territory. There is lodging as well on Olosega, the small island east of Ofu and attached to it by a road bridge. From the westernmost point of Ofu to the easternmost point of Olosega is a distance of some 4 miles, so exploration of villages, numerous grave sites, beach, reef, and hills is not difficult. Tumu Mountain (1,621 feet) on Ofu is a possible climb, but Sunuitao Peak is virtually inaccessible.

The coral reef, however, is eminently accessible, although great care should be taken whether walking or snorkeling. The reef is pristine, diverse, healthy, and growing. It has been so for a long time. Several of its porite corals are big enough to constitute micro-atolls—in one case, as much as 18 feet long. One of these has been identified as being at least 300 years old.

The Ofu unit of the park that separates this reef from the subsistence agriculture behind the road stands as a line of defense against potential damage to the reef. The metaphor can be extended to the park as a whole. Too often in Oceania, development initiatives masterminded from abroad have served to undermine and even destroy the very things that lured people to Pacific islands in the first place. As subsistence agriculture recedes throughout these islands, development may be sought to take its place; as the "leisure industry" looks for newer locations for resorts, it looks farther afield—maybe to Ofu, Ta'u, Tutuila. The park designation can help the people of American Samoa preserve and protect their piece of paradise for everyone.

Opposite: The pristine coral reef along the shore of Ofu island has been growing for several centuries.

CHANNEL ISLANDS NATIONAL PARK

California sea lions are one of six species of seals and sea lions on San Miguel Island.

CHANNEL ISLANDS NATIONAL PARK
1901 SPINNAKER DRIVE
VENTURA, CALIFORNIA 93001
TEL.: (805) 658-5700

HIGHLIGHTS: Anacapa Island • Santa Barbara Island • San Miguel Island • Arch Rock • Signal Peak • Landing Cove • Santa Rosa Island • Santa Cruz Island

ACCESS: To park headquarters, drive from Ventura (no public transit available). To islands, take private or charter vessels from Ventura, Oxnard, or Santa Barbara.

HOURS: Visitor Center, daily, 8 A.M.–5 P.M.; longer hours between Memorial Day and Labor Day. Closed Thanksgiving and Christmas. Access to islands is subject to weather and permit restrictions.

FEES: None.

PARKING: At park headquarters.

GAS, FOOD, LODGING: In Ventura, Oxnard, and Santa Barbara.

VISITOR CENTER: At Ventura harbor. Offers exhibits and films; postcards, books, and posters for sale.

MUSEUM: Exhibits in Visitor Center.

PETS: Not permitted in park headquarters or ashore on Anacapa, San Miguel, Santa Rosa, and Santa Barbara islands.

PICNICKING: On all five park islands, and at park headquarters.

HIKING: Permitted on Santa Barbara and East Anacapa islands without permit; on San Miguel, Santa Cruz, and Santa Rosa islands with permit.

BACKPACKING: Permitted on all park islands with permit. Carry water.

CAMPGROUND: Tent camping with permit on Anacapa, Santa Rosa, San Miguel, and Santa Barbara islands. Primitive only: no gas, food, electricity, or water.

TOURS: Guided tours on islands by arrangement; contact park headquarters for further information. In English.

OTHER ACTIVITIES: Scuba diving, swimming (generally requires a full wet suit), fishing (license required), and kayaking.

FACILITIES FOR DISABLED: At park headquarters: parking, restrooms, theater, exhibits, and observation tower.

For additional information, see also Sites, Trails, and Trips on pages 48–49 and the map on pages 38–39.

ONE OF THE MOST RECENT ADDITIONS TO the national park system, Channel Islands National Park is a striking and awe-inspiring contrast to the teeming southern California megalopolis that appears to be but a stone's throw away. Reached only by boat, the five islands are a primitive anachronism in the Space Age, a refuge where seals and whales and sea birds enjoy freedom from human influences, and where the ever-changing drama of the relentless ocean constantly unfolds before the visitor.

Four of the five islands are related geologically; all are related historically. Yet each exhibits its own features and its own specialized habitats for wildlife. Covering only a little more than 127,000 acres of land area, the islands are constantly exposed to the sea's influence. Surf pounds rocky shoreline; winds funneled through the Santa Barbara Channel can be a mariner's nightmare in winter or a weekend sailor's delight in summer. In season, great stands of yellow coreopsis—one of the island's most noted plants—form a vivid backdrop for birdwatching and nature studies. Trails lead to high points with incredible vistas of the other islands, the mainland to the east, and the Pacific to the west. The island shoreline reveals ragged, surf-carved caves that echo to the din of colonies of barking seals and sea lions.

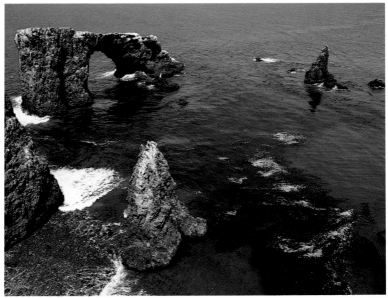

Arch Rock rises from the surf off East Anacapa Island, which is 11 miles from the California mainland.

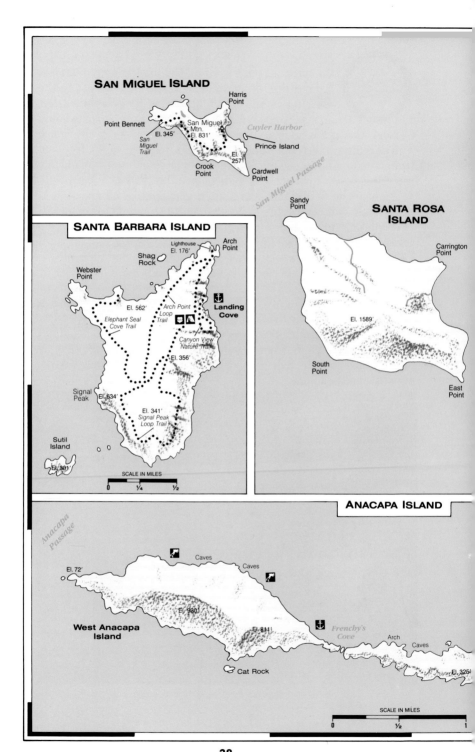

SAN MIGUEL ISLAND

Harris Point

Point Bennett

San Miguel Mtn.
El. 831'

El. 345'

San Miguel Trail

Cuyler Harbor

Prince Island

El. 257'

Crook Point

Cardwell Point

San Miguel Passage

SANTA BARBARA ISLAND

Lighthouse
El. 176'

Arch Point

Shag Rock

Webster Point

El. 562'

Arch Point Loop Trail

Landing Cove

Elephant Seal Cove Trail

Canyon View Nature Trail

El. 356'

Signal Peak

El. 634'

El. 341'
Signal Peak Loop Trail

Sutil Island

El. 301'

SCALE IN MILES

0   ¼   ½

SANTA ROSA ISLAND

Sandy Point

Carrington Point

El. 1589'

South Point

East Point

ANACAPA ISLAND

Anacapa Passage

El. 72'

Caves

Caves

El. 930'

El. 811'

Frenchy's Cove

Arch

Caves

West Anacapa Island

Cat Rock

El. 325'

SCALE IN MILES

0   ½   1

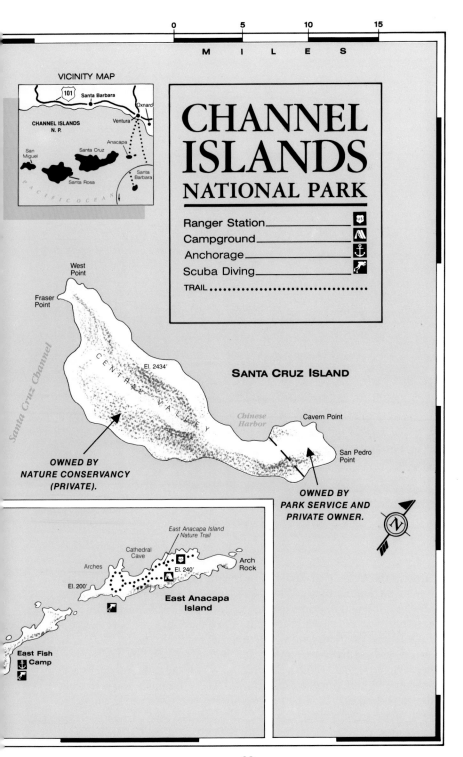

0   5   10   15

M I L E S

VICINITY MAP

101 Santa Barbara
Oxnard
CHANNEL ISLANDS
N. P.
Ventura
Anacapa
San
Miguel
Santa Cruz
Santa Rosa
Santa
Barbara
PACIFIC OCEAN

CHANNEL ISLANDS
NATIONAL PARK

Ranger Station _____ US
Campground _____
Anchorage _____
Scuba Diving _____
TRAIL ••••••••••••••••••••••••

West
Point

Fraser
Point

CENTRAL VALLEY

El. 2434'

SANTA CRUZ ISLAND

Santa Cruz Channel

Chinese Harbor

Cavern Point

San Pedro
Point

**OWNED BY
NATURE CONSERVANCY
(PRIVATE).**

**OWNED BY
PARK SERVICE AND
PRIVATE OWNER.**

N

East Anacapa Island
Nature Trail

Cathedral
Cave

Arches

El. 240'

Arch
Rock

El. 200'

**East Anacapa
Island**

East Fish
Camp

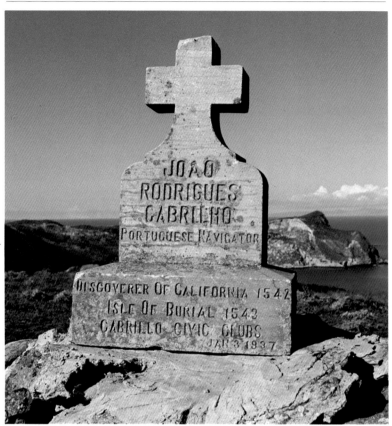

A memorial to Portuguese explorer Joao Rodrigues Cabrilho, who is believed to have been buried on San Miguel Island.

HISTORY

Early History

Among the Channel Islands' first inhabitants were coastal Indians known as the Chumash. When they first arrived remains questionable, but it was sometime between 11,000 and 30,000 years ago. The Chumash crisscrossed the Santa Barbara Channel between the islands and the mainland in sturdy boats called tomols. They subsisted on shellfish and other marine organisms as well as on berries, nuts, roots, bulbs, and plants, which they obtained through trading with mainland populations. The Chumash were a well-developed society and had an extensive trade network when the first white explorers arrived.

The first European explorer to see the Channel Islands, in 1542, was Joao Rodrigues Cabrilho, a Portuguese navigator who sailed under the flag of Spain. He may be buried on San Miguel, where he died from injuries early in that year.

A succession of other explorers and visitors followed, including sealers and whalers whose trail of exploitation is evident even today. Fur seals were their particular victims, and by the late 1800s the sea otter was hunted to near extinction. A few ranchers and farmers settled on the islands in the late nineteenth century.

Establishment of the Park

In 1938, President Franklin D. Roosevelt proclaimed two of the islands—Anacapa and Santa Barbara—a national monument. Their status was elevated in 1980 to that of a national park, and the islands of San Miguel, Santa Cruz, and Santa Rosa were added. (Santa Catalina, San Clemente, and San Nicolas are not part of Channel Islands National Park.)

But ownership is complex. The U.S. Navy owns San Miguel, but it is administered by the National Park Service. Landing permits are required. For some years after the park was established, all of Santa Cruz and Santa Rosa, the largest islands, were privately owned. Ninety percent of Santa Cruz is now owned by the Nature Conservancy, a private, not-for-profit organization. However, the eastern end is co-owned by the Park Service and a private owner. A permit is required for landing on the eastern portion; contact the Nature Conservancy for access to the rest of Santa Cruz. No permit is needed to visit Anacapa and Santa Barbara islands. Santa Rosa is owned by the Park Service; a permit is required to land or hike on the island.

In addition, a 1-mile area around all of the National Park Service-administered islands is designated, as are all features—natural, archeological, and historic—within the 250,000-acre park. A national marine sanctuary extends 6 nautical miles around each of the islands that compose Channel Islands National Park.

GEOLOGY

The four northern Channel Islands are the seaward extension of the Santa Monica Mountains. Fossil remains found on Santa Rosa, Santa Cruz, and San Miguel indicate that these islands probably were joined to one another and to the mainland until about 600,000 years ago. At that time, intense earthquakes, accompanied by fault folding, caused this seaward expanse to separate from the mainland.

Overleaf: Channel Islands' tidepools, such as this one at Point Bennett on San Miguel Island, are part of a national marine sanctuary. Collecting specimens is forbidden.

Climate and Precipitation

During the summer, days are usually sunny, although sometimes the islands are veiled in fog. Swimming is possible in 68° F ocean water, and air temperatures seldom exceed 80° F. Winter is the season of rainfall (about 12 inches), the highest winds, and the fiercest seas.

Wildlife

Channel Islands' wildlife mixes species of the ocean, land, and air. The largest mammal is the California gray whale, which swims past the islands in winter toward calving grounds in Mexico. In spring, large numbers of pinnipeds haul out of the ocean to form breeding colonies, and playful porpoises frolic just past the surf. Elsewhere in the coastal waters is a teeming variety of life, ranging from the microscopic to the largest creature on earth, the whale: plankton, sharks, succulent abalone, lobsters, many game fish, and the infinite variety

The island fox is found only on the Channel Islands.

of animals such as starfish and the flowerlike anemone that are found in tidepools alternately exposed and covered by changing tides.

Of the islands' birds, the western gull is perhaps the most familiar resident, along with many of its sea-bird cousins such as the Brandt's cormorant, brown pelican (an endangered visitor), and sandpiper. Wildlife ashore consists of smaller animals and birds, mostly rodents, songbirds, and the distinctive island fox, which is endemic to the Channel Islands.

Flora

Channel Islands' plants are generally hardy species, because they must be tolerant of salt water and wind. Morning glory, buckwheat, exquisite lotuses, mallows, and locoweeds are examples. The "tree sunflower" (giant coreopsis) is found on all five islands, and the Santa Barbara ice plant is an example of an exotic species. Tree species are few in number, but three—the ironwood tree, the Torrey pine, and the Santa Cruz Island pine—are found only on the Channel Islands and in a few isolated sections on the mainland.

Checkermallow.

Brown pelican.

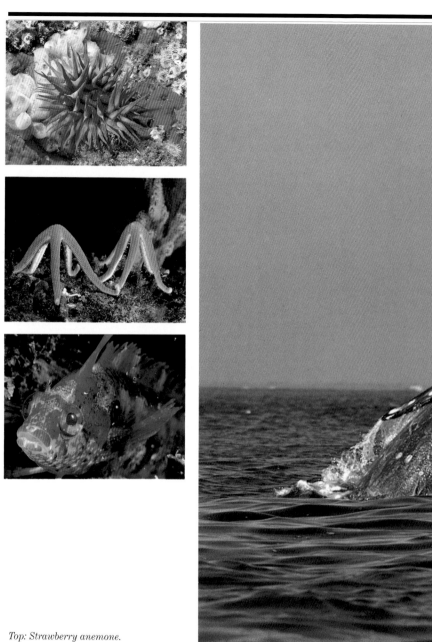

Top: Strawberry anemone.
Center: Spawning starfish.
Bottom: Kelp fish.
Right: California gray whale.

There are small Visitor Centers on the islands, but it is wise to check well in advance with the National Park Service Visitor Center in mainland Oxnard, California, for specifics. Camping is permitted, but even on a day trip, the visitor always should come "self-contained."

Anacapa Island

Closest of the five islands to the California mainland (11 miles), 700-acre Anacapa is actually three small islets, the highest of which rises to an elevation of 930 feet. East and Middle Anacapa are made up of rolling plateaus sandwiched between steeply rising cliffs. Vegetation is scrubby and brownish most of the year, but ablaze in wildflower color a few days after spring rains. Birds are seen in profusion: gulls, scoter ducks, black oyster catchers, and brown pelicans. Whales swim by offshore in winter. California sea lions and harbor seals haul ashore during the breeding season and prefer rocky ledges.

Santa Barbara Island

Santa Barbara Island, only 640 acres in area, is almost entirely surrounded by high cliffs that rise to two hilltops, the higher of which is 635-foot Signal Peak. The only safe landing is at Landing Cove, which is protected from prevailing westerly winds. An easy, .25-mile self-guiding nature trail introduces visitors to the island's resources. There are also 5 miles of trails for visitors to explore on their own and a primitive campground near the ranger station. Because of past farming and grazing practices, plant growth is sparse, consisting mainly of introduced grasses and ice plant. Both animals and plants are making a comeback, however, notably the once-threatened, 6,000-pound elephant seal, which forms breeding colonies in winter. Sharp eyes will spot land birds such as the American kestrel, burrowing owl, horned lark, and meadow lark, as well as land animals such as the deer mouse.

San Miguel Island

Westernmost of the islands, 10,000-acre San Miguel has a history of shipwrecks, battered as it constantly is by ocean swells that roll thousands of miles across the Pacific. Its isolated location, however, seems ideal for five of the major colonizing sea-bird species of southern California: auklets, cormorants, gulls, guillemots, and snowy plovers. American kestrels, red-tailed hawks, and barn owls hunt smaller prey over fields of buckwheat, live-forever, and rose mallow. No visitor should miss the island's barren forests of wind-carved caliche, the fossilized remains of ancient vegetation strewn across a lunarlike landscape amid drifting sands. At Point Bennett, six species of seals and sea lions may be seen; five of these species breed here.

Santa Rosa Island

Santa Rosa Island has been called an "archeological and zoological treasure." Buried remains of a 6-foot dwarf mammoth, carbon-dated at 30,000 to 40,000 years, have been found associated with possible man-made tools. This find has touched off a scientific debate over when humans actually arrived in North America. Deeply eroded gullies, sea caves, and a few beaches are noted features of this 53,000-acre island.

Santa Cruz Island

The western part of Santa Cruz is owned by the Nature Conservancy. At 65,000 acres, it is the largest Channel Island. It has several rugged peaks and a pastoral central valley. Gently flowing fresh-water creeks and streams feed an abundant biotic community.

TRAILS OF CHANNEL ISLANDS NATIONAL PARK

ANACAPA ISLAND

EAST ANACAPA ISLAND NATURE TRAIL: Starts and ends at the information station; 1.5 miles; figure-eight loop with fourteen observation points winds through unique wildflowers and plant life; excellent opportunities to see wildlife.

SANTA BARBARA ISLAND

CANYON VIEW NATURE TRAIL: Starts and ends at information center near Landing Cove; .25 mile; .33 hour; introduces the island's resources; leads by one of the more interesting of the island's canyons; picturesque views of the ocean; superb bird-watching.

There are 5 miles of other trails available for explorers: Arch Point Loop Trail, Elephant Seal Cove Trail, and Signal Peak Loop Trail; all trails lead by sea gull rookeries and unique plant communities; outstanding opportunities to observe seals and sea lions.

SANTA ROSA ISLAND

Several miles of trail are available, with or without a ranger; check at Visitor Center for more information.

SAN MIGUEL ISLAND

SAN MIGUEL TRAIL: Starts at the ranger station overlooking Cuyler Harbor; ends at Point Bennett; 14 miles round trip; tour meets at beach area and is under the guidance of a park ranger (there are no self-guided tours); permits required; passes remains of old ranch complex and a unique caliche forest.

Overleaf: Yellow coreopsis, or "tree sunflowers," flourish on all of the islands.

DEATH VALLEY
NATIONAL PARK

Death Valley, a land of bizarre sights: a boulder inches its way across the "Racetrack."

DEATH VALLEY NATIONAL PARK
DEATH VALLEY, CALIFORNIA 92328
TEL: (619) 786-2331

HIGHLIGHTS: Artist's Drive • Badwater • Saratoga Spring • Zabriskie Point • Dante's View • Sand Dunes • Titus Canyon • Scotty's Castle • Ubehebe Crater • Racetrack • Aguereberry Point • Eureka Dunes

ACCESS: From the east, California 190 into Furnace Creek, and from the west into Stovepipe Wells; from the south, California 178 into Furnace Creek.

FEES: For automobiles and for individuals by bicycle and bus.

CAMPING: At Furnace Creek, Mesquite Springs, Stovepipe Wells, Wildrose.

GAS, FOOD, AND GIFT SHOPS: Furnace Creek, Stovepipe Wells, Panamint Springs, and Scotty's Castle, all open year-round.

LODGING: Furnace Creek, Stovepipe Wells, Panamint Springs, all open year-round.

VISITOR CENTER: At Furnace Creek, open year-round.

MUSEUMS: Death Valley Museum at Visitor Center, Borax Museum at Furnace Creek Ranch.

PETS: Permitted on leash, but not allowed on trails or in public buildings. Extreme heat is dangerous, especially when pets are left in vehicles.

PICNICKING: At Furnace Creek, Sand Dunes, Scotty's Castle, Wild Rose Station, Dante's View.

HIKING: Opportunities exist throughout the park; carry adequate water and sun protection.

BACKPACKING: No permits required at this time; check with rangers at Visitor Center for update. Backpack camping allowed at least 1 mile from established roads, not at water sources.

MOUNTAIN BICYCLES: Must remain on routes opens to all vehicles.

TOURS: At Furnace Creek, Stovepipe Wells, Scotty's Castle.

FACILITIES FOR THE DISABLED: Wheelchair access at Death Valley Museum, Salt Creek, Scotty's Castle, Harmony Borax Works.

For additional information, see also Sites, Trails, and Trips on pages 82–91 and the map on pages 56–57.

EATH VALLEY BECAME ONE OF THE NATION'S newest and largest national parks when it was expanded in 1994 to 3,350,000 acres, and advanced from national monument to park status. That status is well deserved. Death Valley has long been a destination for those fascinated by extremes of climate and topography. The valley and its surrounding mountains hold a lifetime of canyons to explore, peaks to climb. Its rocks are an open book, waiting to be read by anyone with curiosity and a big enough canteen. The valley's plants and animals are a study in survival under fire. And everywhere are the traces of those people who went these ways before—early Native Americans, the forty-niners, and the host of "one-blanket jackass" prospectors of the late 1800s.

Death Valley can live up to its name with brutal summertime heat and intense dryness. But its flanks can also be carpeted with golden flowers in springtime. Or a winter storm may shroud the mountains' shoulders in a blanket of snow. The white salt-pan on the valley floor shimmers in summer with mirages, promising water where there is only heat. And yet a hundred real springs bless the mountainsides with water, and pools of water dot the canyons below. It is a land of extremes.

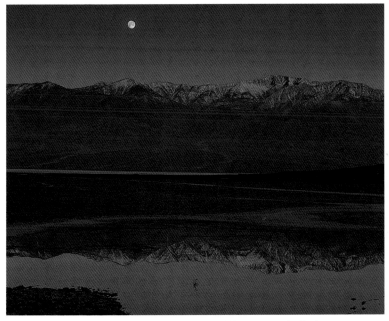

Badwater, a pool near the lowest point in the United States (-282 ft. elev.).

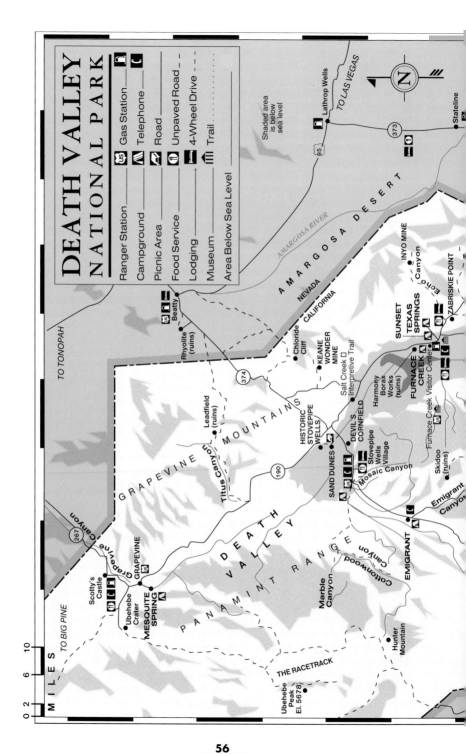

DEATH VALLEY
NATIONAL PARK

Ranger Station
Campground
Picnic Area
Food Service
Lodging
Museum
Area Below Sea Level

Gas Station
Telephone
Road
Unpaved Road
4-Wheel Drive
Trail

TO TONOPAH

TO BIG PINE

TO LAS VEGAS

AMARGOSA RIVER

AMARGOSA DESERT

NEVADA
CALIFORNIA

Shaded area
is below
sea level

Lathrop Wells

95

373

Stateline

Beatty

Rhyolite
(ruins)

374

Chloride
Cliff

KEANE
WONDER
MINE

Salt Creek
Interpretive Trail

INYO MINE

Echo Canyon

ZABRISKIE POINT

SUNSET
TEXAS
SPRINGS

FURNACE
CREEK

Harmony
Borax
Works
(ruins)

Furnace Creek Visitor Center

Leadfield
(ruins)

GRAPEVINE   MOUNTAINS

Titus Canyon

HISTORIC
STOVEPIPE
WELLS

DEVIL'S
CORNFIELD

SAND DUNES

Stovepipe
Wells
Village

Mosaic Canyon

190

Skidoo
(ruins)

Emigrant
Canyon

EMIGRANT

DEATH
VALLEY

Marble
Canyon

Cottonwood Canyon

PANAMINT RANGE

Hunter
Mountain

THE RACETRACK

Ubehebe
Peak
El. 5678

Scotty's
Castle

Ubehebe
Crater

MESQUITE
SPRING

GRAPEVINE

Grapevine Canyon

267

N

MILES

0   2   6   10

56
DEATH VALLEY

Amargosa River

Death Valley
Junction

TO LAS VEGAS

Shoshone

Saratoga
Spring

GREENWATER VALLEY

BLACK MOUNTAINS

Amargosa River

Twenty
Mule
Team
Canyon

NATURAL
BRIDGE

Dante's
View
El. 5475'

Split Butte

Shoreline Butte

Ashford Mill
(ruins)

OWLSHEAD
MOUNTAIN

FORT IRWIN MILITARY
RESERVATION

ST'S DRIVE

BADWATER

Lowest Elevation
in U.S.: -282'

Eagle Borax
Works (ruins)

RANGE

Warm Springs Canyon

DEVIL'S GOLF COURSE

PANAMINT

DAYTON-HARRIS
GRAVES

AGUEREBERRY POINT

THORNDIKE

MAHOGANY FLAT

Wildrose
Peak

WILDROSE

CHARCOAL
KILNS

Wildrose Canyon

Panamint City
(ruins)

Sentinel
Peak
El. 9636'

U.S. NAVAL RESERVATION

Telescope
Peak
El. 11049'

Ballarat
(ruins)

PANAMINT VALLEY ROAD

PANAMINT VALLEY

Panamint
Springs

PANAMINT VALLEY

TO LONE PINE

VICINITY MAP

Shoshone

Beatty

Nev.
Calif.

DEATH
VALLEY
N.P.

Trona

INSET SCALE

0 15 30

MILES

THE CALIFORNIA DESERT PROTECTION ACT

Above all, the California desert is a silent place—peaceful and serene, but hardly deserted. Some 2,000 kinds of plants and animals flourish here. The desert harbors some of the world's oldest trees, the state's only dinosaur tracks, singing dunes, creatures of rare dignity like the desert tortoise, deep and narrow gorges, craggy mountains, thousands of archeological sites, and—hardly to be overlooked—the world's largest living organism, a creosote ring.

Native Americans and "European Americans" in small numbers passed through the area for centuries, gathering food, hunting, prospecting, sometimes settling. As coastal California, a few hours by car to the west, surged in population in the mid-twentieth century, growing numbers of people sought out the desert for many kinds of recreation, not all of which were compatible with preserving the fragile environment. A catalyst for alarm was the annual Barstow-to-Vegas motorcycle race, which attracted up to 3,000 riders who plowed across many miles of fragile desert land, crunching all in their path, including carapaces of the endangered tortoise.

By the 1970s, Sierra Club activists, joined by other groups and individual citizens, had organized to fight for congressional rescue of the desert. Jim Dodson, Judy Anderson, Elden Hughes, Peter Burk, Vicky Hoover, and George Barnes were among the volunteers who worked tirelessly for a California Desert Protection Act, lobbying local governments, leading media opinion-makers into the wilds, mapping remote areas, displaying tortoises on nationwide tours, monitoring off-road vehicle abuse, packing legislative hearings wearing bright yellow T-shirts. Sierra Club staff coordinated the strategy in the nation's capital.

Many members of Congress supported the Desert Act, but credit for ultimate success belongs first of all to Senator Dianne Feinstein (D-CA), who in 1994, in an impressive demonstration of will and legislative adroitness, overrode all obstacles, including a last-ditch Republican filibuster, to win final approval in the Senate.

Despite inevitable compromises, the act, which brings federal protection to 6 million acres, was a tremendous victory and accomplishes a lot, upgrading and expanding two national monuments to national park status, establishing the Mojave National Preserve (where hunting will be allowed), and creating sixty-nine federal wilderness areas.

—Donald Young

People have called Death Valley home (by whatever name) since the end of the ice age, thousands of years ago. To those of us accustomed to kinder climates, this seems improbable. The heat, the dryness, the barrenness all appear to conspire to drive out life. But these qualities of the land serve to focus our attention on those who have chosen to live here. A single soul standing in the middle of a desert is much more memorable than one amid countless others.

Traces of a Distant Past

Our glimpses of the earliest people are mere wisps of archeologic insight: a semicircle of stones here, a pointed projectile there. People of the Nevares Spring culture (7000–6000 B.C.) clustered around the shores of a retreating ice-age lake that filled Death Valley. They were hunters who moved on as the temperatures rose and the game disappeared. Those of the Mesquite Flat culture (3000–0 B.C.) hunted game and gathered plants around springs adjacent to the valley's floor. The Saratoga Springs culture (0–A.D. 1100) was the first to hunt here with the bow and arrow; these people had time to turn at least some of their attention to

The twenty-mule-team rigs hauled 12 million tons of borax out of Death Valley.

matters beyond mere survival. They scratched petroglyphs into desert varnish; they arranged great patterns of stone on the desert floor. We look and listen, but the ancient voices remain mute to our modern ears.

Sometime around A.D. 1100, the first historic-era inhabitants arrived in Death Valley. The Southern Piute people occupied the northern end of the valley; the Death Valley Shoshone lived to the south, camping around springs through the remainder of the valley. These Shoshone, in no dietary position to be fastidious, were known to other bands as the *Tsagwaduka,* or "chuckwalla eaters," after their predilection for the 14-inch lizard with whom they shared their home. The Piutes referred to their Shoshone neighbors as the *Panumunt.* The term survives as the name of the Panamint Mountains, which the Shoshone frequented in the fall to harvest pinyon nuts and hunt bighorn sheep. A few Shoshone continue to occupy Death Valley, making fine baskets from willow and rush shoots.

Through the Valley of Death

New Mexican horse traders were the first Europeans known to penetrate Death Valley, sometime in the winter of 1829–30. Their Spanish Trail included an inhospitable trek, the *jornada del muerto,* through the southern end of the valley. The lucrative early trade to southern California quickly drew the attention of enterprising interstate horse thieves, as well as hungry local Piutes and Shoshones.

Two decades later, a number of forty-niners tried a shortcut to reach the California gold fields on the western slopes of the Sierras. The Bennett, Brier, and Arcan families, joined by a group of bachelors who were variously known as the Jayhawkers and Bugsmashers, rolled into Death Valley in December 1849 with twenty-nine wagons. A month later they escaped. Richard Culverwell had died in the interim, and two of the Jayhawkers were to die while crossing Searles Lake to the south. All but one of the wagons had been abandoned. Upon leaving, Asabel Bennett, John Arcan, and William Lewis Manly turned around and one of them uttered, "Good-bye, Death Valley!" The name stuck.

For the most part, the early survivors of Death Valley were happy to have got through with their lives, let alone their possessions. But some would return years later, convinced that, in their passage, they had stumbled somewhere across the gold ore that evaded them in California. One of the Jayhawkers was certain that he had found silver there; another forty-niner recalled gold that he

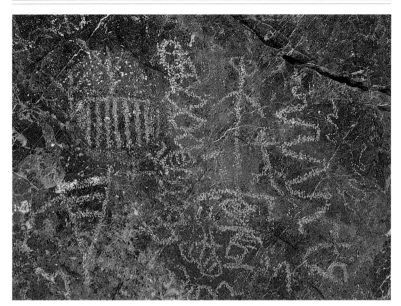

Petroglyphs at Klare Springs: fading messages from the distant past.

knew was in Goler Wash. In 1860, Asabel Bennett returned to the southern end of the Panamints, where he found ore; he then built a small furnace (down in the valley at the mouth of what is now called Furnace Creek) to test his samples; they contained unprofitable lead rather than a bonanza of silver.

It turned out that Bennett was 15 miles too far south and thirteen years too early. In the spring of 1873, prospector Richard Jacobs staked claim to his Wonder of the World vein in the Panamint Mountains. Around it sprung Panamint City—2,000 excited miners, assayers, butchers, bakers, bankers, saloon keepers, and of course, dance-hall girls. Four years and a third of a million dollars in silver bullion later, Panamint City was a ghost town. Other boomtowns would blossom and fade around hard-rock mines in the Death Valley area: Chloride City and the Keane Wonder in the Funeral Mountains; Skidoo and Harrisburg in the northern Panamints; Rhyolite and the Bullfrog District to the east of the Grapevine Mountains.

The Twenty-Mule-Team Era

Gold and silver can certainly spark a prospector's imagination. But so can soap. Borax, a boron salt now used in everything from laundry products to aircraft alloys, had been discovered in 1873 at a

Keane Wonder Mine, Funeral Mountains: gold was discovered here in 1903.

site very near one of the abandoned Jayhawker wagons. But Death Valley was so remote that little attention was paid to the deposit. Nine years later, William T. Coleman knew a good thing when he saw it, and bought a borax claim from Aaron and Rosie Winters for $20,000. He built the Harmony Borax Works, which can now be seen just north of the Visitor Center at Furnace Creek.

Coleman needed more than just confidence to get his product to market. He had tried eight- and then twelve-mule teams in transporting borax to Mojave, California, the nearest railhead, 165 miles away. But the results were disappointing. Coleman then decided to hitch twenty animals together—eighteen mules and two horses. This team could pull two 4 x 6 x 16-foot loaded wagons as well as a 1,200-gallon water tank. The team stretched 100 feet in front of the wagons. In order to roll smoothly through a turn, mules in the middle were trained to pull in the direction opposite the turn, lest the wagons be yanked onto their sides. Each trip to Mojave took ten days. Thus began the twenty-mule-team era. Between 1883 and 1888, these wagons hauled 12 million tons of borax out of Death Valley without ever breaking down. Borax production in Death Valley ceased in 1927, one year after vastly more productive mines were discovered to the south.

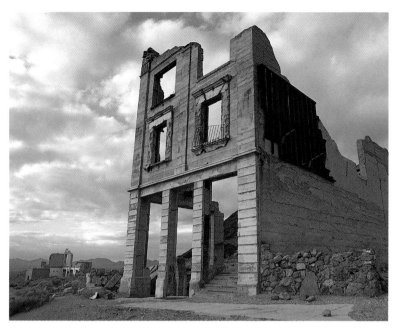

Rhyolite, Nevada once boasted a stock exchange, churches, and an opera house.

Establishment of the Park

In his youth, Stephen Mather had worked as a publicist for the borax industry. Later, as founder and first director of the National Park Service, he was anxious to seek protection of the valley for which he cared so much. He revisited Death Valley in 1927 with Horace Albright, his Park Service colleague; their efforts culminated in the establishment of Death Valley National Monument in 1933. Mather and Albright had to settle for national monument status, realizing that the mining interests in Death Valley could block the congressional approval required for a park but not a presidential mandate necessary to establish a monument. But times change and people have come to appreciate the true value of this desert. In October 1994, the California Desert Protection Act was approved by Congress and signed into law by President Bill Clinton. It created Death Valley National Park, now expanded to 3,350,000 acres.

Overleaf: A steep trail leads to what is left of the Keene Wonder Mine and mill. Following overleaf: Ruins, Harmony Borax Works, in operation 1882-89.

The Rocks Speak

The rocks of Death Valley have millions of years of stories to tell. Theirs is a history born of water and fire, rent by faults, and bent by folds. These rocks have been slowly lifted up and inexorably worn back down by processes that still shape this land.

Death Valley is part of the Basin and Range Province, which encompasses most of Nevada and large portions of Utah, Oregon, and eastern California. The Basin and Range is a region unique for its having been pulled apart like taffy, stretched 150 miles in a west–northwest and east–southeast direction in the vicinity of Death Valley. The ranges are mountain blocks that all align roughly north–south; the basins are low areas that are gradually filled with debris washed down from the uplifted ranges. Seismic studies at Death Valley estimate that the true valley floor is 8,000 to 9,000 feet beneath the surface, now covered with sediments and salt.

Telescope Peak, at the top the Panamint Mountains, looms 11,331 feet above Badwater on the floor of the valley; the two locations are separated by only 18 miles as the crow flies. Indeed, the impact of Death Valley, with its floor 282 feet below sea level, is enhanced by the surrounding ranges—the Panamints and Cottonwoods on the west, the Black, Furnace, and Grapevine Mountains on the east. By one well-accepted interpretation, the valley was created when the mountains on the west side began to slide and pull apart from their counterparts on the east side of the valley. Movement along this fault zone apparently began some 14 million years ago.

Tipsy Mountains

As the mountains around Death Valley pull apart and rise above the valley floor, they have also tipped eastward. As a result, the underlying floor is asymmetric, the east side being quite a bit deeper than the west. One result is that low spots in the valley, such as Badwater, are predominantly nestled up against the Black Mountains.

Evidence of this great tug-of-war litters every corner of the valley. Fault scarps are present along the road just south of Furnace Creek; these are the low linear traces of vertical offset,

Opposite: Breccia—sharp rock fragments in a matrix of sandstone—in Mosaic Canyon.
Overleaf: Fault scarp marks plane where land rose relative to the valley floor.

aligned north–south along the foot of the Black Mountains. The scarps were created as the mountains spasmodically rose relative to the valley floor. Other scarps are visible at the foot of Hanaupah Canyon and along the road north to Scotty's Castle. South of Badwater, a volcanic cinder cone named Split Butte that erupted 690,000 years ago has been surgically cleaved by a segment of the Death Valley Fault Zone. The two sides of the cone have since been separated by a few hundred yards.

The Impact of Water

The mountains surrounding Death Valley are gouged everywhere by the erosion of rainfall that carves canyons back into their flanks. As dry as this country is, when moisture does arrive, it can come by the canyonful. Floods roar down onto the valley floor, disgorging tremendous quantities of sediment. The sediments build up in semicircular alluvial fans at the foot of the canyons. When fans from adjacent canyons converge, they grow into a continuous *bajada*; one can be seen mantling the lowest reaches of the Panamints opposite Furnace Creek.

The Amargosa River drains an 8,700-square-mile area, sluggishly reaching its final destination on the floor of Death Valley. Any water that runs into the valley is trapped. Once here, the only means of escape is by evaporation. But any material brought in by the river—either visible sediments or dissolved salts—will remain behind after the water has gone. Death Valley's floor is a salt pan composed of many thousands of feet of calcite, gypsum, and good old table salt. In places, the erosion of nearby volcanic rocks resulted in a suite of boron-rich minerals like ulexite, colemanite, and borax.

This region has not always been so dry. Near the end of the moist Pleistocene epoch 10,000 years ago, a 600-foot-deep body of water occupied the valley. This lake, referred to as Lake Manly by geographers, was one of a string of connected lakes that stretched from the east side of the Sierras, probably linked all the way to the Colorado River. Remnant shorelines can be seen carved into alluvial fans scattered throughout Death Valley. Particularly good examples are found ringing Shoreline Butte, south of Badwater.

Opposite: The valley floor is a salt pan, composed of calcite, gypsum, and table salt.

Life in the Valley of Death

Many people first come to Death Valley hoping that it will live up to their expectations: mirages wavering over utterly barren expanses, neither bush nor bunny as far as the eye can see. We're all fond of our preconceptions, cultivated by years of not-quite-accurate depictions both in books and on film. J. Ross Browne, writing in 1868, reported, "I have heard complaint that the thermometer failed to show the true heat because the mercury dried up. Everything dries, wagons dry; men dry; chickens dry; there is no juice left in anything, living or dead, by the close of summer."

It is true that Death Valley imposes a unique set of environmental constraints on those that would try to make this their home. The brines of Badwater have been so concentrated by evaporation that only a handful of plants can survive there. Pickleweed is able to grow despite the water's 6 percent salinity. Arrowweed, tolerant of up to 3 percent salinity, establishes strong roots that resist erosion; at the Devil's Cornfield near Stovepipe Wells, arrowweed can be seen growing atop unlikely mounds that remain after the surrounding ground has blown away. Mesquite grows in thin bosks around springs on the valley floor; its tap root can extend 60 or more feet down in search of the fresh water it needs.

Desert holly, well adapted to the demands of the desert, can survive for two, perhaps three years, without any rainfall. Indeed, it is unable to survive if too much water is present. The holly leaves actively secrete a white coating of salt in order to reflect away as much of the summer sun's heat as possible. Creosote bush is able to grow at elevations ranging from the lowest alluvial fans well below sea level, up to an altitude of 4,000 feet within the mountains. When creosote does receive rain, it releases a fragrance that embodies everything that is good about this land. Rain that arrives in November and December, followed by a couple of winter months with mild temperatures, can bless the springtime hillsides of Death Valley with a lavishly colored carpet of wildflowers.

Elevation is an all-important determinant of life zones. With altitude, temperatures decrease and precipitation increases. Climbing out of Death Valley, one leaves behind the spare plant life of the salt pan and alluvial fans and enters an environment

Opposite: Spines of the cottontop cactus.
Overleaf: Bighorn sheep rams near Lake Mead, east of Death Valley.

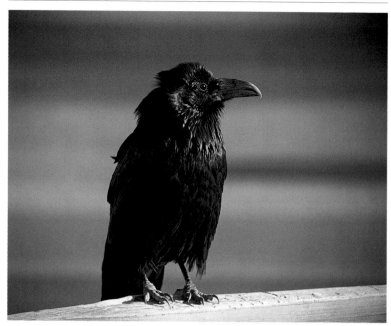
The raven is often seen looking for food in a garbage dump.

above 1,000 feet that supports cactus like the beaver-tail and a barrel cactus called cottontop. Joshua trees—strange Dr. Seuss-like characters—are yuccas that appear in the Cottonwood Mountains at elevations of 4,000 to 5,000 feet above sea level. Farther up grow communities of pinyon and juniper, succeeded still higher by limber pine and bristlecones atop Telescope Peak.

Animal Survival Against All Odds

Death Valley imposes its environmental demands on animals as well as plants. Some adaptations are relatively simple. For instance, most animal activity occurs at nighttime rather than during the heat of the day. The coyote's eerie song adds enchantment to most Death Valley nights, assuring us that there is indeed movement out there in the dark. Lizards like the zebra-tail race around the scorching desert on their toes, extended just that much farther away from the 200° F ground. Other adaptations are much more complex. The kangaroo rat does not need to drink any water, obtaining its moisture instead from the metabolic breakdown of seeds that it eats. Its kidneys are able to concentrate and excrete urine at levels that would make any other mammal dry up and blow away.

A "coyote chorus" of barks, yelps, howls, and yaps may be heard at dusk or at night.

The waters of Death Valley host a surprising array of life. A unique species of fairy shrimp populates the *tinajas* around Death Valley Buttes, and a particular water snail is adept in its ability to survive the cell-popping salinity of the brines at Badwater. A number of species and subspecies of pupfish live in isolated bodies of water scattered around Death Valley. All share common ancestors dating back to the days of Lake Manly and its multitude of interconnected waterways stretching from the Sierras east toward Las Vegas and the Colorado River. As post-Pleistocene dryness isolated each area, its population of pupfish began to evolve into what now are nine individual species. Each is slightly different from the others, and each is found only in its particular pool or spring—and nowhere else on earth.

Larger mammals can be found throughout Death Valley, though they are not always out during the middle of the day. The kit fox pursues rabbits. White-tailed squirrels scurry beneath mesquite trees. Desert bighorn sheep move with confidence across the cliffs of the Panamints. Burros, now feral, have by and large long outlived the prospectors who turned them loose a century ago. These animals are tough survivors; because they outcompete native species like the bighorn sheep, they have been removed from most of the park.

And Now, the Weather

The Death Valley visitor must be prepared for extremes, not only of heat but sometimes of cold. Furnace Creek holds the Western Hemisphere record for high temperature, set on July 10, 1913, at 134° F. Summertime highs can consistently break 120° F for weeks at a stretch; nighttime readings can stay above 100° F. But on the other hand, snow can occasionally dust even the fans extending down from the mountains. And a mantle of white usually covers the shoulders of the Panamints from December to March. Rainfall averages 1.75 inches a year on the valley floor. Most is delivered either by December-through-February storm systems or isolated afternoon thunderstorms in July and August. Summertime humidity can approach zero on the lowest deserts.

Above: Blossoms of the golden evening primrose carpet the desert in April.
Opposite: The roadrunner seldom flies; its diet: lizards, snakes, rodents, scorpions.

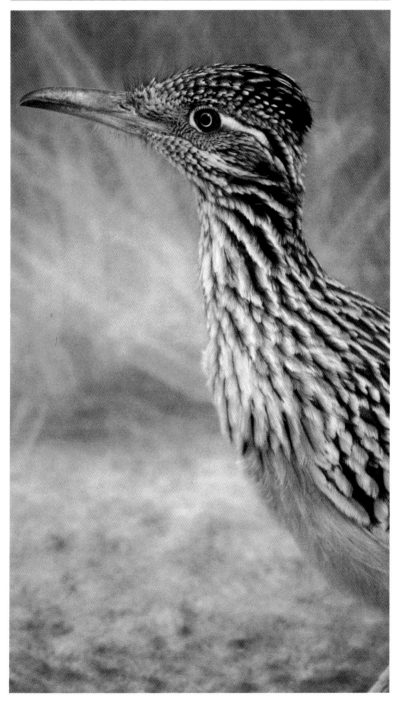

Death Valley offers opportunities for exploration at any time of year. But you must take the valley on its own widely varying terms. Temperatures at ground level on the salt pan reach 200° F in July; an ice ax and crampons may be necessary for ascent of Telescope Peak in January. Always carry water; a couple of quarts may be sufficient for a cool-weather day hike, but summertime hiking can easily require 2 gallons per day per person. Be attentive to your vehicle's condition; if you break down in some parts of the park, you are every bit as isolated and endangered as the Jayhawkers a century and a half ago. Back roads often require high-clearance four-wheel drive.

Furnace Creek is effectively the heart of Death Valley. The Visitor Center and its Death Valley Museum are a good introduction to the park. Nearby is the Furnace Creek Ranch with its lodging, meals, store, pool, and golf course—all nestled into the inviting shade of the date-palm orchard and hundreds of shade-bearing athel trees. The Borax Museum is on the ranch grounds, with its excellent displays describing the natural and human history of Death Valley. The Furnace Creek Inn sits half a mile to the east, preserving an era of pampered accommodations created by the Pacific Coast Borax Company with the help of the Union Pacific Railroad in 1927. Just north of Furnace Creek is the Harmony Borax Works with its twenty-mule-team wagon and the ruins of one of the early borax mills.

South of Furnace Creek

California 178 provides access to the hottest part of Death Valley and the lowest point in the Western Hemisphere. The road leads south, first to Golden Canyon. This narrow canyon is cut through the soft Furnace Creek Formation, with walls that have been sculptured by erosion into soft flowing forms. A trail leads from the parking area into the canyon; its continuation to Zabriskie Point offers a pleasant one-way hike if you have parked a car at the other end. Farther south is the turnoff to the Devil's Golf Course. Here, a 1-mile dirt road leads into the heart of the salt pan. The salt is wedged up and worn down into impossibly contorted shapes. On a quiet morning (as most are), you can sometimes hear the tiny crackling of salt crystals expanding with the day's heat. In other places the salt pan has been diced into a mosaic of polygons, each interlocking with its neighbors.

Artist's Drive is a twisting 8-mile one-way loop that leads into the Black Mountains. Along the way you can stop at the Artist's Palette, where the Furnace Creek Formation assumes especially bright hues of yellow, red, and even turquoise. At the top of the loop, the road is pushed up against the fault that forms the western face of the Black Mountains.

Badwater is 19 miles south of Furnace Creek Ranch. At 282 feet below sea level, it is within inches of being the lowest spot in the hemisphere; the very lowest point actually lies a few miles out into the salt pan. The steep face of the Black Mountains offers an extra hour or two of morning shade at Badwater; at first light, the Panamint Mountains across the valley's salt pan are especially beautiful when seen with their accompanying reflection in the Badwater pool.

Continuing south on California 178, one can contemplate the ruins of the Ashford Mill, which processed gold ore briefly after its construction in 1915. The mill site overlooks the usually dry Amargosa River and Shoreline Butte, carved by the lapping waves of Lake Manly during the Pleistocene epoch. A dirt road, usually two-wheel drive, leads 28 miles from the mill site to Saratoga Spring. The springs are home to a species of pupfish found nowhere else on earth. The surrounding rushes and cattails are alive with bird life.

The playa at the Racetrack: a ship of rock sails on a sea of silt.
Overleaf: The Panamint Range, at sunrise, and its reflection in the Badwater pool.

East of Furnace Creek

California 190 climbs east up Furnace Creek 5 miles to Zabriskie Point. Here, a short walk leads to a breathtaking overlook of sculptured badlands beneath Manly Tower. One mile farther east is the beginning of the 3-mile one-way road through Twenty Mule Team Canyon. The road leads through the badlands of the Furnace Creek Formation, with its deposits of concentrated borax. The hillsides are punctuated with a number of shallow tunnels dug by miners around 1900. The hills live up to the starkest perceptions of a barren desert—for the most part, they are utterly devoid of plant life.

A turnoff 12 miles east of Furnace Creek Ranch passes the Billie and Ryan mines, and continues south to Dante's View. The road climbs steadily up into Greenwater Valley and then crests the Black Mountains at 5,475 feet, looming directly above Badwater. The air is usually 15 to 25 degrees cooler than on the valley floor. The view is apocalyptic. Mountains bristle through a 360° panorama—the Owlshead, Slate, Panamint, Cottonwood, Last Chance, Black, Grapevine, Greenwater, Yucca, Shoshone, Nopah, Spring, and Sierra Nevada. Death Valley lies below, stretching 100 miles north to south. This is a fine perspective from which to consider the alluvial fans that spread out from canyon mouths to cover the foot of the Panamints. During storms, water can burst down the canyons and spray sediment, first left and then right, like an out-of-control fire hose, gradually building the fans into their semicircular shape.

West of Furnace Creek

The Devil's Cornfield lies adjacent to the sand dunes near Stovepipe Wells. Both the cornfield and the sand dunes are the product of winds that regularly howl up Death Valley and down Emigrant Canyon, eddying out around Tucki Mountain. The strong roots of the arrowweed plant anchor them to the fine soil of the Devil's Cornfield; the wind steadily deflates soil from ground not protected by the roots of arrowweed, leaving the plants perched on pillars 8 feet high. The nearby sand dunes are also a product of the wind, having been created by the deposition of sand rather than erosion.

Stovepipe Wells was originally sited at a spring a few miles out in the sand dunes. Herman Eichbaum took a mind to build a resort here in 1926. But his delivery truck broke down a dozen miles short of the stovepipe that marked the well, so he just built his "Bungalette and Bungalow City" on the spot that has now appropriated the name Stovepipe Wells. It currently sports a motel, restaurant, store with gas, and an airstrip. A dirt road strikes south 1 mile up the alluvial fan toward the mouth of Mosaic Canyon. This affords an opportunity for a peaceful 1- to 2-mile hike between polished walls of marble.

From sea level at Stovepipe Wells, westbound California 190 climbs almost 5,000 feet up to Towne Pass; halfway up is the turnoff for *Wildrose Road*, which struggles up Emigrant Canyon to Harrisburg Flats. Vehicles more than 25 feet long or 9 feet wide are prohibited. The first spur from this road leads 9 dirt miles to the abandoned mining town of Skidoo. Once a bustling town of 700 souls, this was the home of one of the few Death Valley-area mines that actually produced more gold than broken promises.

Aguereberry Point lies 6 miles by dirt from the paved road; this is generally passable in a two-wheel-drive vehicle, and always worthwhile. At 6,433 feet above sea level, the point commands a perspective of Death Valley that nicely complements that of Dante's View, projecting out between Trail and Blackwater canyons. Ephedra and sagebrush are interspersed throughout the quartzite outcrop that must have intrigued a hard-rock miner like Pete Aguereberry.

Iron oxides bring color to the clay hills of Golden Canyon.

Beyond Wildrose Spring, Ranger Station, and Campground, the road narrows, then turns to dirt as you encounter the first juniper and pinyon pines. The ten Wildrose Charcoal Kilns are 2 miles up. These were built in 1877 to supply mills of the Modoc mining district in the Argus Mountains, west across the Panamint Valley. Each kiln is 25 feet tall with a floor diameter of about 36 feet. The insides still smell of creosote and are caked with the residue of firings that took a week to reduce thirty-five cords of wood to charcoal.

North of Furnace Creek

At just about the point where the northbound road out of Furnace Creek climbs above sea level, one can turn off to the *Salt Creek Interpretive Trail*. Here, water that had flowed just beneath the ground is forced onto the surface by a low structural rise in the valley floor. A boardwalk leads .5 mile along the creek through a pickleweed marsh. The pickleweed is extremely salt-tolerant; salt grass waves at the water's edge. This brief stretch of water is the only home to every member of the species known as Salt Creek pupfish.

The Keane Wonder Mine lies 4 dirt miles off the Beatty Cutoff. Gold was discovered here in 1903 and a processing mill was constructed in 1907. The tramway that transported ore 1 mile from the mine down to the mill is still in place, shadowing the trail that climbs up to the mine; it continues to the even older mining community of Chloride Cliff along the crest of the Funeral Mountains. The Keane Wonder Mine produced ore in fits and starts until closing for good in 1916.

The road to Titus Canyon starts close to Beatty, Nevada, and the 1905 boomtown of Rhyolite. The bumpy one-way dirt road winds 28 miles through the heart of the Grapevine Mountains. It passes the small ghost town of Leadfield and the petroglyphs at Klare Springs. In the last few miles before emerging onto the valley floor, the road winds through canyon walls so narrow that the route must be limited to one-way traffic only.

Scotty's Castle is 54 miles north of Furnace Creek, at the mouth of Grapevine Canyon. This oasis was constructed in 1922 by a Chicago millionaire, Albert Johnson, under the watchful eye of his colorful prospecting partner, Walter Scott. Two million dollars were spent creating the main house, with its great hall, chime

Opposite, top: Teakettle Junction, a whimsical point of interest deep in the backcountry. Right: Scotty's Castle has antiques, paintings, a pipe organ, and an indoor waterfall.

tower, powerhouse, and 270-foot swimming pool. The grounds are shaded with cottonwoods and outlined with grapevine hedges.

Back down at the mouth of Grapevine Canyon, a road spurs off to the north, leading 7 miles to Ubehebe Crater and then 27 dirt miles farther to the Racetrack. Ubehebe Crater is the .5-mile-diameter product of a tremendous explosion that rocked this end of Death Valley many thousands of years ago when volcanic magma rose into a perched water table. This small pocket of water, lying close to the surface, was quickly heated and flashed to steam. It exploded with a force far greater than that of any man-made device. The 500-foot-deep crater was instantly excavated, as rock and cinders were blown for miles in all directions. A .5-mile trail leads south to Little Ubehebe Crater through scattered desert holly and creosote bushes.

The Racetrack is utterly flat, 3 miles long and 1 mile wide. Like the bottom of Death Valley, the Racetrack is an enclosed basin. Its floor is made up of fine silt; rainfall can sporadically turn it into an inches-deep lake. Rocks littering the Racetrack are blown like toy ships across its surface (perhaps when they are partially buoyed up on a raft of ice), leaving gouges in the silt that mark their voyage.

New Acquisitions

With passage of the California Desert Protection Act in 1994, a number of significant additions were made to the park. Greenwater Valley was added, thus protecting the sites of ghost towns at Greenwater and Furnace. The northern end of Panamint Valley was also included within the park, with its playa and sand dunes. A pleasant restaurant and motel are now within the park at Panamint Springs on the valley's west side.

Saline Valley lies at the foot of the Inyo Mountains, at what is now the northwest side of Death Valley National Park. Its enclosed basin is encircled by the 11,000-foot Inyo Mountains on the west, Hunter Mountain on the south, and the Last Chance Range on the east. The remote Eureka Dunes can be reached by a dirt road that leaves Big Pine–Death Valley Road. The dunes are 400 feet high, sitting astride another landlocked playa. Some people have been fortunate enough to be here when the temperature was just right and the wind just strong enough out of the right direction, and heard the dunes "sing."

Desert Holly, Mosaic Canyon: a white coating of salt reflects away the sun's heat.

TRAILS OF DEATH VALLEY NATIONAL PARK

HARMONY BORAX WORKS: .25-mile loop. Ruins of 1880s borax works. Twenty-mule-team wagon.

NATURAL BRIDGE CANYON: .3 mile one way. Easy climb up the canyon floor to a natural bridge within the narrow canyon.

GOLDEN CANYON: 1 mile one way. Gradual climb along the bottom of an initially narrow canyon that later opens out into beautiful golden walls. Can continue 2 miles to Zabriskie Point.

MOSAIC CANYON: 1 mile one way. Easy walk between water-polished walls.

KEANE WONDER MINE: 1–3 miles one way. Steep climb from the mill site to mines, following the tramway that brought ore to the mill. Trail continues to Chloride Cliff. Gain 1,500 feet from parking area to the mine, and another 2,500 feet to Chloride Cliff.

UBEHEBE PEAK: 3 miles one way. Switchbacks ascend 2,000 feet from the Racetrack to Ubehebe Peak with its sweeping vistas of the Cottonwood Mountains and Saline Valley.

WILDROSE PEAK: 4.2 miles one way. Trail climbs 2,200 feet from the Charcoal Kilns to Wildrose Peak through pinyon and juniper with tremendous views into Death Valley along the entire second half of the walk.

TELESCOPE PEAK: 7 miles one way. Excellent day or overnight hike on good trail from Mahogany Flat Campground. 2,850-foot climb yields views of Death Valley as well as the surrounding country from the Sierra Nevada well into Nevada.

COTTONWOOD AND MARBLE CANYONS: 26-mile loop. Hike begins at the end of an 8-mile four-wheel-drive road in from Stovepipe Wells. Rewards include the narrow canyon walls, the chance to see bighorn sheep on their own terms, and the unsurpassed quiet of true wilderness.

HALEAKALA
NATIONAL PARK

HALEAKALA NATIONAL PARK
P.O. BOX 369, MAKAWAO, HAWAII 96768
TEL.: (808) 572-9306 OR (808) 572-7749
(PARK WEATHER TAPE)

HIGHLIGHTS: Silversword Hosmer Grove• Leleiwi Overlook • Kalahaku Overlook • Puu Ulaula • Pele's Paint Pot • Kipahulu • Oheo • Waimoku Falls • Hawaiian Planting Area • Makahiku Falls

ACCESS: To park entrance (on way to summit): 19 miles from Pukalani: 27 miles from Kahului. To Kipahulu District: 9 miles from Hana; 61 miles from Kahului and airport.

HOURS: Daily 24 hours, year-round. Portions of the park closed during disasters, ice on road, and so on.

FEES: None.

PARKING: At Kipahulu, Red Hill, Haleakala Visitor Center, Kalahaku, Leleiwi, Halemauu, park headquarters, and Hosmer Grove. For campers at Kipahulu and Hosmer Grove.

FOOD, LODGING: Not available in park. Summit area: available 12 miles below park entrance. Kipahulu District: in Hana.

GAS: Not available in park. Summit area: in Pukalani. Kipahulu District: in Hana.

VISITOR CENTER: In summit area, on rim. Offers hourly interpretive talks until noon.

PETS: Permitted on leash, except on trails and in back country.

PICNICKING: At Hosmer Grove, park headquarters in summit area, Oheo Gulch in Kipahulu District.

HIKING: On designated trails. Carry water.

BACKPACKING: Permit required, see campground entry. Check with park headquarters before going into crater.

CAMPGROUNDS: Summit area: Hosmer Grove, no permit required, up to 25 campers/night, fires in grills only; Paliku and Holua, permits required, up to 25 campers/night, no open fires. Kipahulu District: up to 50 campers/night, fires in grills only, no drinkable water available.

TOURS: Summit area: at volcano rim, wilderness trails, and Hosmer Grove. Kipahulu District: at trail side. All tours depend on availability of staff. In English.

FACILITIES FOR DISABLED: Water fountains, restrooms, parking stalls with ramps, and paved walkways.

OTHER ACTIVITIES: Swimming and horseback riding.

Please be aware that the high elevation of the summit may pose problems for people with certain medical conditions. All visitors to the summit should bring a jacket or sweater.

For additional information, see also Sites, Trails, and Trips on pages 112–118 and the map on pages 96–97.

HAWAII'S MASSIVE HALEAKALA VOLCANO rises 10,023 feet into the tropical sky from a sea-level base 33 miles in diameter. Haleakala National Park encompasses the huge crater at the top of the mountain—an immense bowl that is 7.5 miles long, 2.5 miles wide, and .5 mile deep—with an unearthly but strangely beautiful panorama of stark cliffs, multihued cinder cones, and jumbled lava flows on a scale almost impossible to comprehend. This stark, barren place is the home of the Haleakala silversword, a unique plant that had been vandalized and grazed almost into extinction, and the rare Hawaiian goose, the nene.

In spite of the impression of long-dead volcanic fires, Haleakala is still considered to be active; it is the only Hawaiian volcano that is still alive except for those on the much younger Big Island of Hawaii. Its last eruption was around 1790.

Haleakala National Park extends from the summit down Kipahulu Valley on the southeastern flank of the mountain to the coast near Hana. This verdant, mist-shrouded valley with sheer cliffs and shimmering waterfalls descends in just 7.6 miles from a subalpine zone with frequent frosts to a subtropical rain forest and a section of the lovely Maui coast.

Lava formations circa 1860.

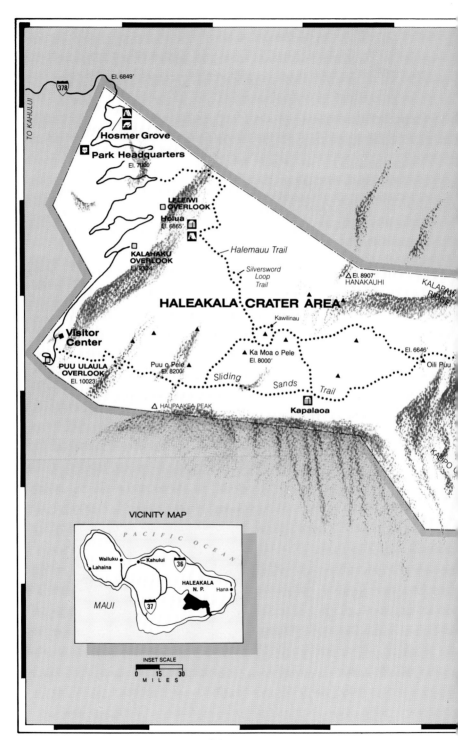

TO KAHULUI

378

El. 6849'

Hosmer Grove

Park Headquarters
El. 7000'

LELEIWI OVERLOOK

Holua
El. 6865'

Halemauu Trail

KALAHAKU OVERLOOK
El. 9324

Silversword Loop Trail

△ El. 8907'
HANAKAUHI

KALAPAW. RIDGE

HALEAKALA CRATER AREA

Kawilinau

Visitor Center

Ka Moa o Pele
El. 8000'

PUU ULAULA OVERLOOK
El. 10023'

Puu o Pele
El. 8200'

Sliding   Sands   Trail

El. 6646'

Oili Puu

KAUPO

△ HAUPAAKEA PEAK

Kapalaoa

VICINITY MAP

PACIFIC OCEAN

Wailuku
Lahaina
Kahului

36

HALEAKALA N. P.

Hana

MAUI

37

INSET SCALE
0   15   30
M I L E S

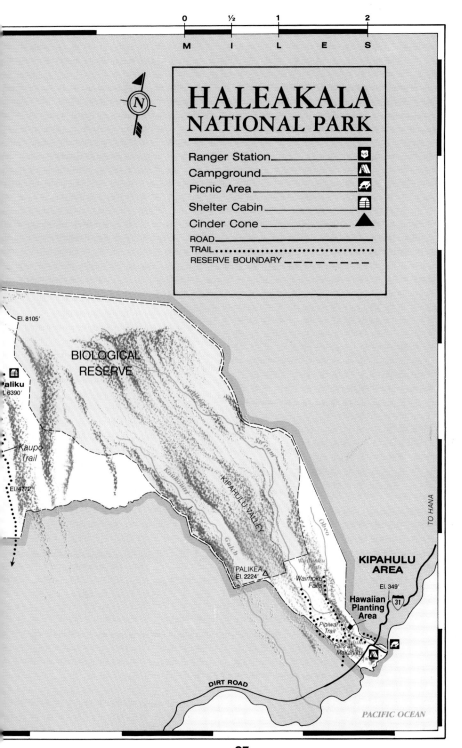

HALEAKALA
NATIONAL PARK

Ranger Station _____ 🛡
Campground _____ ⛺
Picnic Area _____ 🍽
Shelter Cabin _____ 🏠
Cinder Cone _____ ▲

ROAD _____
TRAIL ·····································
RESERVE BOUNDARY _ _ _ _ _ _ _

El. 8105'

BIOLOGICAL
RESERVE

aliku
6390'

Kaupo
Trail

El. 4772'

KIPAHULU VALLEY

Koukulau

Gulch

Stream

Oheo

Waimoku Falls

Waimoku
Falls

PALIKEA
El. 2224'

Pipiwai
Trail

Falls at
Makahiku

KIPAHULU
AREA

TO HANA

El. 349'

Hawaiian
Planting
Area

31

DIRT ROAD

PACIFIC OCEAN

Although clouds often shroud the lower slopes of Haleakala and sometimes fill the crater, the summit is usually in sunshine. The impression everywhere is of dazzling light, which is partly what made this a sacred place for early Hawaiians; the Hawaiian words *Hale a ka la* mean "House of the Sun."

Hawaiian Legend

Stories tell of an early time when days were only three or four hours long because the sun was so lazy and full of sleep that he would hurry through the sky to get back to bed. The whimsical demigod Maui lived in Hana with his mother, a maker of fine tapa cloth. The shortness of the days made it difficult for her to sun-dry her tapa, so the mischievous Maui thought of a plan to lengthen the day. He noticed that the sun rose over the rim of Haleakala by thrusting first one long sunbeam and then another over the rim, much as a spider climbs over a rock. One night Maui took sixteen rope snares and hid in a cave near the summit; when the first of the sun's legs snaked over the edge, Maui threw a rope around it and made it fast. This he did with each leg in turn, and then he tied the ropes to a wiliwili tree. The sun was in no position to bargain, and had to agree to Maui's demand that he walk slowly and steadily across the sky, as he has done to this day.

Early Hawaiians

The first Polynesian settlers arrived in Hawaii about A.D. 350, and over the next several hundred years a flourishing, if sometimes war-like, society evolved. Most Hawaiian villages were in coastal areas where there were fertile lands, abundant water, and an ocean full of fish. There is no evidence that Hawaiians ever made their homes in the hostile environment of Haleakala Crater, but it was central to their unique land-division system. The ancient land sections, or *ahupuaa*, radiated like spokes of a wheel from a point on the northeastern rim of Haleakala Crater; thus each district had a pie-shaped piece of land, giving all people access to the ocean, the coast, and the uplands for sustenance. A particularly dense type of lava rock from the crater was quarried for adzes. There can still be seen in a few places the remains of a cross-island trail, which was used by ancient travelers in preference to routes through dense rain forests and deep valleys.

Most archeological evidence, though, shows that early Hawaiians visited Haleakala Crater only occasionally, and viewed it as a sacred place. Archeological remains have been found inside the park.

An old-time pack outfit meanders across Haleakala Crater.

Early Explorers

One characteristic of Westerners seems to be their inability to resist climbing to the highest point in sight. Missionaries from New England had hardly arrived in Hawaii when three of them went on record in August 1828 as the first non-Hawaiians to reach the summit of Haleakala. They brought back and published a vivid description of the terrors and beauties of "Pele's dreadful reign."

The next recorded exploration of Haleakala Crater was by naval Lieutenant Charles Wilkes and his United States Exploring Expedition of 1841. They did a detailed study of the crater and published a map of the area. To their credit, they recorded the mountain's name as Haleakala—the name that was used locally—even though the custom of the time was to name important landmarks after dignitaries and patrons.

Marauding Animals

By 1900, the "visitors" that were having the biggest impact on Haleakala Cr..er were animals. Cattle ranchers on Maui were in need of upland pasture, and for a while large herds of cattle were driven up to spend the summer in Haleakala Crater—an enormous natural corral. Wild goats, too, were becoming a problem. Brought to the islands originally by Captain James Cook and George Vancouver to use for food for future voyages, goats multiplied so rapidly, because they had no predators, that they presented a severe threat to native vegetation, especially in such a fragile environment as the crater.

Establishment of the Park

In 1916, thanks partly to the eruption of Lassen Peak in California two years earlier, which awakened the public's interest in volcanoes, President Woodrow Wilson signed into law a bill to create Hawaii National Park. The park included the active volcanoes Kilauea and Mauna Loa on the island of Hawaii, and the summit crater of Haleakala Volcano.

Park status came none too soon; the rare and beautiful silversword plants that grow only on the high slopes and crater of Haleakala were being destroyed by the thousands through the carelessness of hikers and sightseers. Introduced animals—pigs, goats, and cattle—were also taking a heavy toll on native plants and thus destroying the habitat of native birds. Rats had arrived on Maui accidentally from ships, and mongooses had been brought in to combat the rats; as it turned out, both animals preyed on ground-nesting birds and drove several species almost into extinction.

The new national park status not only gave protection to the unique and fragile ecosystems of Haleakala Crater, but also made it possible to preserve and interpret the extraordinary volcanic features of the area.

The park was increased in size in 1951, when 9,000 acres of the upper Kipahulu Valley were added. In 1969, the Nature Conservancy and the state of Hawaii donated 880 acres in the Kipahulu coastal area to the National Park Service; in 1976, the boundary was extended to include an additional 837 acres of coastal lands and water. Since 1961, Haleakala has had full status as a national park, separate from the volcanoes on the island of Hawaii.

GEOLOGY

Early Volcanism

Maui, the second-youngest island of the Hawaiian chain, is made up of Haleakala and the smaller, older West Maui Volcano. These mountains are part of a huge undersea volcanic massif that consists of the islands of Molokai, Lanai, and Kahoolawe as well.

Thousands of years ago during the great ice ages, much of the world's water was locked up in continental ice sheets; sea levels were as much as 300 feet lower than they are now. The now-separate islands were joined above water into one large island that geologists call Maui Nui, which was made up of seven volcanoes and was about one-half the present size of the Big Island of Hawaii. As glaciers melted and sea levels rose, the islands became isolated again; in fact, when seas were higher than they are now, the isthmus between East and West Maui was covered, separating those mountains into two islands.

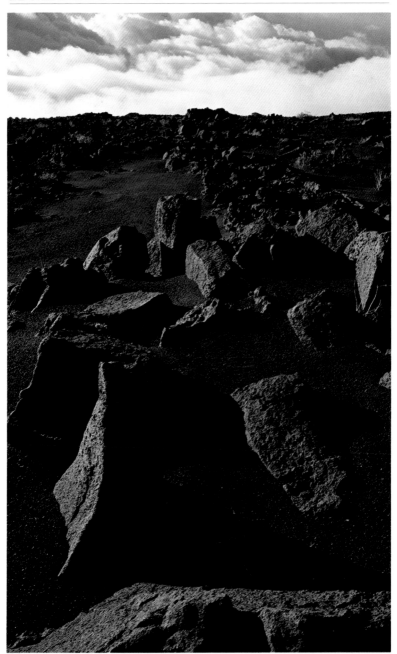

A cinder and rock pattern on the crater's rim, which is 21 miles around and 2.5 miles wide.

Hawaiian volcanoes are born on the deep ocean floor, below as much as 3 miles of water. Quiet outpouring of lava goes on intermittently, and undetected, for thousands of years before the mound reaches the surface. When the growing volcano is a few hundred feet below sea level, gas in lava is able to expand; explosive eruptions start, accompanied by steam blasts and huge ash falls. For a time, it is a contest between the continuing eruptions and the erosive action of the sea, with the sea often the winner. But if the volcano is vigorous and persistent, it can grow; once above water, the growing mountain is armored against wave action by quieter lava flows.

In this way, Haleakala emerged from the sea about 1 million years ago to take its place as the youngest—and last—volcano of the Maui Nui group. It is the only one of the group that is still considered active.

The building stage lasted for tens of thousands of years, with voluminous lava flows piling up an imposing mountain. Haleakala grew strongly and steadily, probably to an elevation of over 13,000 feet. Then for some reason that is not fully understood by geologists, the rate of volcanism slowed. At the same time, world climate became exceptionally wet, and Haleakala was again in a deadly battle with erosion, caused by torrential rains and flooding streams. It was during this period that the spectacular Haleakala Crater was formed.

Lava from the 1790 eruption has been eroded by water into smooth dark pebbles.

Haleakala Crater

This tremendous natural bowl is fondly known locally as "the world's largest extinct volcanic crater," a phrase that makes geologists flinch. In the first place, the volcano is almost surely not extinct, but only dormant. Moreover, the term "volcanic crater," strictly speaking, implies creation by volcanic action—explosion or collapse. Haleakala's crater seems to be largely the result of massive erosion that took place about 100,000 years ago, when rainfall was much greater than it is now and when volcanic activity had lessened. Geologists think that as much as 3,000 feet of the summit was worn away, and that the heads of Kaupo and Keanae valleys were so deeply eroded that they met in the summit area and created the huge craterlike depression. When volcanic activity resumed, this area was filled with the unearthly cinder cones and lava flows that are seen today. Finally, other volcanic craters are larger than Haleakala.

A view from the air shows a line of large cinder cones that runs from Hana at the eastern tip of Maui, westward to the summit, across the summit crater, and down the southwestern flank to the ocean at La Perouse Bay. These late cinder cones—symptoms of old age in a volcano—form the clearly defined rift zones along which several eruptions have taken place in the last 1,000 years.

Late Volcanism

There is no precise historical record of Haleakala's most recent eruption, but a piece of detective work places it at about 1790. When the explorer Jean François Galoup de La Perouse mapped Maui's shoreline in 1786, he showed a broad, shallow bay between two points on the southwest coast. A few years later, Vancouver charted the same area; his map of 1793 shows a prominent peninsula between those points. Because the peninsula lava flow looks very young, and also local legend tells of eruptions at approximately that time, 1790 seems like a reasonable date. The area south of the flow is now known as La Perouse Bay.

Just offshore is Molokini, a crescent-shaped islet formed by an undersea eruption where the rift zone extends into the ocean. Hot lava exploded violently from contact with the sea and built a typical tuff cone, which has been partially destroyed by wave action. If sea levels were to fall, Molokini would be connected to Maui.

The history of Haleakala suggests that because the last eruption occurred about 200 years ago, another could happen within the next 100 years, but no one can predict its precise time or place.

Overleaf: A cinder cone, with the peaks of Mauna Loa and Mauna Kea on the island Hawaii in the distance.

Climate

The Hawaiian Islands in general can claim uniformly mild, subtropical weather, but there are also microclimates with startling extremes of rainfall and temperature. Haleakala National Park could be considered a showcase of those extremes; it extends from the warm, sunny coastal area, through the upland rain forest (where the clouds that ring the mountain almost every day drop copious amounts of rain), to the desert-dry alpine conditions of the crater itself.

Weather near the summit is extremely variable; it can be cold, wet, and windy at any time of the year. In general, though, summit temperatures range from 35° F to 77° F in summer, and from 26° F to 75° F in winter. Severe weather sometimes occurs in winter, when the northeast trade winds weaken and allow subtropical storms to sweep in from the south. Frost is not uncommon at the summit, and some winters see an occasional snowfall.

Hawaii's Island Ecology

The Hawaiian chain is isolated in the North Pacific, 2,500 miles from the nearest continent. All the flora and fauna that colonized the islands before the arrival of humans came by air, on ocean currents, or attached to migratory birds. The odds against any form of life making this journey successfully were immense, but time is always on the side of evolution. Over tens of thousands of years, isolated seeds, spores, insects, and birds found their way to these volcanic islands. Although only a tiny percentage of those that arrived were able to survive the transition, those that did flourished, rapidly evolving and diversifying; climate and topography were ideal for survival, and competitors were scarce.

Hawaii has only two native mammals, a small bat and the Hawaiian monk seal; significantly, one arrived by flying and the other by swimming. Plants and birds, however, had a remarkably successful evolutionary history in Hawaii until humans and their introduced animals reversed the trend and brought many species to the verge of extinction. Haleakala National Park is the last refuge for several endangered species.

Opposite: A view of Haleakala Crater and Maalaea Bay from Papawai Point.

Native Plants

Probably the most famous natural feature in the park is a plant, the Haleakala silversword. A marvel of adaptation, the silversword has evolved to withstand the punishing extremes of climate at these altitudes of 7,000 to 10,000 feet.

Seen at a distance, it is a shimmering sphere the color of moonlight; the Hawaiians used the name *ahinahina*, the word for "gray" repeated twice. Up close, it is a rosette about 2 feet across with fine, sword-shaped leaves that are thickly covered with a lustrous silvery down. The glistening hairs reflect excess sunlight, and the rosette of leaves protects the growing point of the plant. Early explorers described the cinder cones and the crater rim as being covered with so many silverswords that they looked like snowdrifts, but by the 1920s these plants were almost extinct. Humans were the main culprits; souvenir hunters and hikers would uproot the shining globes and roll them downhill to see how far they would go. Wild goats that ate almost everything in sight were a close second. Only the creation of Haleakala National Park saved the silversword; National Park Service protection and the work of dedicated botanists have brought them back from a low of barely 1,000 plants in 1927 to an estimated 50,000 today.

Some other native plants that are found within the crater are the kupaoa, several alpine plants like the Haleakala geranium, and two species of *Coprosma*—one with jet black berries that are a favorite food of the Hawaiian goose.

A common plant along the crater trails is the ohelo (Hawaii's answer to the blueberry), with its shiny clusters of tasty red berries that are welcomed by thirsty hikers. A few mamane trees can be seen also, with bright yellow blossoms that are an important source of food for several native forest birds.

At the eastern end of the crater, the vegetation changes dramatically. Clouds spill over a low spot in the rim, and rainfall is abundant year-round, creating a lush garden of native and introduced plants. Ohia trees with their bright red blossoms, probably the most common native tree of Hawaii, flourish, as do the kolea and the mamane. A native Hawaiian raspberry, the akala, grows profusely and bears large edible berries.

The Kipahulu section of Haleakala National Park, an 8-mile valley that runs from the crater rim down to the sea, is a botanical wonderland; it is probably the largest tract of undisturbed native vegetation in Hawaii.

Botanists and biologists studying the area since 1967 have found 200 species of plants that are indigenous or endemic to Hawaii; 15 of them were previously unknown. The upper part of Kipahulu Valley is a nearly impenetrable jungle of ohia and olapa trees with a rich understory of ferns and flowers. There are at least 75 species of ferns and related plants—all but 1 native—and more than a dozen species of woody lobelias. (This section has been designated a Biological Reserve, and is open only by permit to qualified scientists.)

Native Birds

Hawaii has rightly been called a "museum of evolution," and nowhere is this more evident than in its bird life. It is estimated that the more than eighty kinds of native birds that are known to have evolved before the arrival of humans in Hawaii developed from as few as fifteen original species.

One of the most remarkable Hawaiian birds, and one often seen in Haleakala Crater, is the Hawaiian goose, or nene. Although its ancestry is traced to the Canada goose, it has evolved into a species with distinctly different characteristics. It lives on high, sparsely vegetated lava flows away from water, so its feet have evolved to be only partially webbed and thus better adapted to walking on lava than to swimming. The nene was hunted almost into extinction; in 1951, it was estimated that there were only thirty-three nene in existence, and half of those were in captivity. Since then, through a concerted effort by the state of Hawaii, the National Park Service, and the Wildfowl Trust in England, a breeding and release program seems to be succeeding in reintroducing these handsome birds to their native habitat.

Even more impressive has been the evolution of the Hawaiian honeycreepers. Scientists estimate that there are at least twenty-three species and twenty-four subspecies in Hawaii, probably all evolved from a single ancestral species. Many of these birds make their homes in the protected Kipahulu Valley, where a Nature Conservancy expedition in 1967 found one species that was thought to have been long extinct. The nukupuu and the Maui parrotbill would probably be extinct today if they were not protected here.

The dark-rumped petrel, or uau, which nests on the crater cliffs, is an endangered species of migratory sea bird with a strange call that sounds like the barking of a small dog. It spends March through October at Haleakala, but no one knows where it spends the rest of the year.

Birds that are easier to see at Haleakala include the apapane and the iiwi, bright red birds that are often in the tops of ohia trees, where they resemble the red ohia blooms. Also present are migratory birds, including the golden plover, which migrates to and from

Overleaf: Dense bamboo in Kipahulu, the lush 8-mile valley that extends down to the Pacific Ocean.

Alaska. Still more common along the roads are birds like the ring-necked pheasant and the chukar, both of which have been introduced.

SITES, TRAILS, AND TRIPS

A Drive to the Sun

The drive to the top of Haleakala Volcano is a fitting introduction to the scenery at the summit. This is the only place in the world where one can drive by paved road from sea level to an altitude of 10,023 feet in just 37.5 miles. The drive from Kahului to Haleakala Crater takes at least 1.5 hours, but much more time for sightseeing is recommended.

The first part of the drive up the mountain is apt to be clear, but clouds usually form by mid-day between the altitudes of 4,000 and 8,000 feet. (The little upland town where the clouds usually break is named Pukalani, literally "hole to heaven.") The road zigzags up the slopes of Haleakala, and reaches the national park boundary at 6,740 feet.

Just inside the park, at about 6,800 feet, a paved side road leads to *Hosmer Grove*, with a unique collection of alien trees planted by the forester for whom it is named. Here flourish sugi pine and cryptomeria from Japan, deodar from India, eucalyptus from Australia, and pine, cedar, juniper, and spruce from North America, as well as some native Hawaiian trees like the ohia and mamane. A short (.25 mile) nature trail winds through the grove, and a brochure points out the different species of trees and the native birds such as apapane, iiwi, and amakihi that are often seen flying among them. This is a good place to see the interplay between native and alien plants and animals, and is a pleasant picnic stop.

At an elevation of 8,000 feet is the trail head for the Halemauu Trail into Haleakala Crater. It is a pleasant 1-mile walk along the first part of this trail to the crater rim for a grand view.

The *Leleiwi Overlook*, at 8,800 feet, provides a breath-taking view of the huge bowl of Haleakala Crater, dotted with cinder cones that range in color from gray to orange to red. There is nothing to provide scale until you catch sight of a tiny dot in the distance that proves to be a hiker on one of the trails that wind among the cones. The rim is broken on the north and south by the gaps leading to Keanae and Kaupo valleys.

If the crater is filled with clouds but there is afternoon sunshine, the eerie "Specter of Brocken" phenomenon can sometimes be seen from the crater rim. It is the viewer's shadow projected on the clouds and encircled by a rainbow. (It is so named because it was first observed at Brocken Mountain in Germany.)

The 10,023-foot-high Puu Ulaula Overlook at Red Hill, the highest point on the island.

At *Kalahaku Overlook*, at 9,324 feet, which can be seen on the way down from the Haleakala Visitor Center, are more grand crater views, and also some fine examples of the rare Haleakala silversword. Between May and November, it is sometimes possible to see one or more of these dramatic plants in bloom. The silversword grows for five to sometimes more than thirty years without blooming, and then sends out a stalk that can reach 5 to 6 feet in height with several hundred yellow and purplish flower heads. The plant blooms only once and then dies, but each individual flower produces hundreds of seeds that are scattered by the wind.

The Haleakala Visitor Center is on the crater rim at 9,745 feet, 11 miles from the park entrance. Again the magnificent views are the main attraction; but there is also a wealth of information, including exhibits on the geology, archeology, and ecology of the park as well as the wilderness-protection program. Park interpretive staff give talks.

From the Visitor Center, a .25-mile trail goes to the top of White Hill, past ruins of old Hawaiian sleeping enclosures.

The *Puu Ulaula Overlook* is at Red Hill, the 10,023-foot summit. The view is a breath-taking 360° panorama of the crater and, if the day is clear, of West Maui and other islands in the distance—Hawaii, Kahoolawe, Lanai, Molokai, and Oahu.

Puu Ulaula is the traditional place to view the grand spectacle of a Haleakala sunrise. It is an unforgettable sight as the first rays of the sun creep into the crater; the dark recesses of the walls come alive

Trails of Haleakala National Park

Short Summit Trails

Hosmer Grove Trail: Starts at park road, just inside park boundary, at 7,000-foot level; .25 mile; .5 hour; leads through a unique experimental planting of alien and native Hawaiian trees; trail brochure available.

Halemauu Overlook Trail: Starts at park road at 8,000-foot level; ends at crater rim for panoramic view of Haleakala Crater with its colorful cinder cones and lava flows; 2 miles round trip; 1.5 hours.

White Hill Trail: Starts at Haleakala Visitor Center at 9,745-foot level; .5 mile round trip; .5 hour; short trail to the summit of White Hill, past stone platforms and sleeping shelters used by early Hawaiians.

Crater Trails

Halemauu Trail: Starts at park road at 8,000-foot level; ends at Paliku; 20 miles round trip; 12 hours; makes a steep 2-mile, 1,400-foot descent to the crater floor at Holua; crosses crater past Silversword Loop Trail and winds among colorful cinder cones and other volcanic features.

Red cinders from the volcano color many of Maui's beaches.   *Fields of taro on the Keanae*

SLIDING SANDS TRAIL: Starts from just below Haleakala's summit cone at 10,000-foot level; ends at Halemauu Trail at cinder cone named Oili Puu; 8 miles one way; about 5 hours; descends steeply to 7,300 feet in 4 miles; loose cinder trail; passes jagged cinder cones, lava blisters, and caves; hiking out of crater by Sliding Sands Trail not recommended, because easier exit is by Halemauu Trail.

KAUPO TRAIL: Starts at Paliku in eastern end of Haleakala Crater at 6,400-foot level; ends at Kaupo Road; 8 miles one way; about 4 hours going down; descends Kaupo Valley to park boundary at 3,800 feet; continues 5 more miles over private ranch lands.

KIPAHULU AREA

Waimoku Falls via Pipiwai Trail: Starts at Ranger Station parking area; ends at Waimoku Falls; 4 miles round trip; 3 hours; leads up left side of Pipiwai stream for .5 mile to point overlooking 184-foot falls at Makahiku; trail continues 1.5 miles through lush forest.

KOLUA POINT TRAIL: Starts at Ranger Station; ends at ocean; 1 mile round trip; 1 hour; good swimming and picnicking.

See map on pages 96–97.

Peninsula can be seen on Hana Road, which leads into the park.

with a variety of changing colors, and huge multicolored cinder cones appear on the dark floor as the crater is swiftly flooded with sunshine.

Crater Day Hikes

Hikers will find 32 miles of well-marked trails winding through the moonscape terrain of Haleakala Crater. Three main trails lead into the crater: *Halemauu Trail*, which begins at the 8,000-foot elevation of the summit road; *Sliding Sands* (or *Keoneheehee*) *Trail*, which begins near the summit at the 10,000-foot level; and *Kaupo Trail*, which is usually used as a way out of the crater down a valley to the sea.

Because all crater hiking involves a steep descent into the crater—and a stiff climb out—most day hikes are arduous. These day hikes, of varying degrees of difficulty, are suggested.

Sliding Sands Trail. Hike a short way down the Sliding Sands Trail to get a feeling of this eerie volcanic scenery. The "sands" are really volcanic cinders and ash that were expelled from cones and vents in the crater during many past eruptions. Because of the "sliding" effect, walking downhill is easy but walking uphill is very difficult, especially at this high altitude, so only a short hike is suggested. Use of this trail as an exit from the crater floor is not recommended.

Halemauu Trail, to Holua. This is not a long hike (8 miles), but it gains 1,400 feet in elevation. The Halemauu Trail descends by steep switchbacks to the crater floor, with excellent views of the multicolored cinder cones and across the crater to Koolau Gap. Along the way are native ferns (amaumaus) and pukiawe, with its tiny, evergreenlike leaves and red (inedible) berries. Holua Cabin, at the base of the cliff, is usable by reservation only, but water is usually available there.

Sliding Sands Trail and Halemauu Trail. This difficult, 12-mile hike is recommended for experienced hikers only, but it is immensely rewarding in scenery.

Crater Circle Hike

Sliding Sands Trail and Halemauu Trail. By far the best crater trip if time, physical condition, and reservations permit is a 2- or 3-day circle trip. Hikers enter the crater by Sliding Sands Trail and leave it by Halemauu Trail, while seeing most of the crater's features by way of the short side trails that crisscross the floor. (Obtain reservations for one or two cabins or campgrounds along the route, and arrange for transportation from the Halemauu trail head.)

The starting point for this trip is, appropriately, near Haleakala's summit. The Sliding Sands Trail leaves from just below the summit cone, Red Hill. It descends into the crater over loose reddish-brown ash and cinder, with jagged rocks, spires, and pit craters in the distance.

Near the crater floor the trail passes *Puu o Pele*, a colorful cinder cone that legend says was the former home of Pele, Hawaiian goddess of fire who now lives at Kilauea Volcano on the Big Island. The grass along the trail is mountain pili, a native bunch grass.

On the crater floor, at 7,400 feet, is a trail junction; the trail to the left goes north, reaching Holua, an overnight cabin or campground stop, in 3.9 miles.

Sliding Sands Trail leads across a grassy meadow to Kapalaoa Cabin. Nene (Hawaiian geese) are frequently seen here, and the dark-rumped petrel nests on the high cliffs above.

Leaving Kapalaoa, the trail crosses a flow of the rough, blocky lava called aa. The light-colored lichen on the rock, one of the first plants to appear on new lava flows, is often called Hawaiian snow.

As the trail (now called the Halemauu Trail) rounds the cinder cone called *Oili Puu*, the lava is of the smooth, ropy type known as pahoehoe. The weather here is apt to be foggy and misty, with wetter weather ahead.

At Paliku, 9.8 miles from the start of the trail, annual rainfall averages 250 to 300 inches a year, making this the only lush spot in Haleakala Crater. Native trees and shrubs compete with introduced species of grasses. Paliku is another possible overnight stop, at either the cabin or the campground.

From Paliku, the trail doubles back to the Oili Puu junction. It crosses another aa flow and skirts a lava-rock wall that was built in the days when cattle were driven into the crater to graze on the lush grasses at Paliku. The small dark cinder cone to the left of the trail is named *Puu Nole*, or "Grumbling Hill," which suggests that it was still active after the Hawaiians arrived on Maui.

The trail skirts an old spatter vent called Kawilinau (65 feet deep). Old Hawaiian custom called for throwing the umbilical cord of a newborn child into this pit to ensure that the child would not grow up to be a thief.

Past Kawilinau, the trail winds through *Pele's Paint Pot*, a dazzling display of multicolored cinder cones. Differing mineral composition of the lavas and varying degrees of weathering account for the wide variety of colors.

The *Silversword Trail* leaves the main trail in a .4-mile loop, for a close look at these unique plants. At one time observers spoke of silverswords dotting all the cinder cones, but they are presently found only in isolated spots. Protected now, and with the wild goats being fenced out, the silversword eventually may return to its early abundance. (Please do not leave the trail to view the plants, because trampling around their bases damages the root systems and may kill native insects that are needed to pollinate the silverswords.)

Just ahead are Holua and a return to the summit road 1,400 feet above by the Halemauu Trail.

Kaupo Trail. An alternative—and equally dramatic—hike begins at Paliku Campground and Cabin and leads out of the crater. This trail goes through Kaupo Gap and descends 6,000 feet to the sea in 8 miles, through gradually thickening vegetation. Passing the park boundary at 3,880 feet, the trail continues through private ranch lands to Hawaii 31. Private arrangements must be made for transportation from the trail head back to Hana or Kahului.

Kipahulu

The Kipahulu section of Haleakala National Park is not directly connected by road to the main part of the park, but can be reached in 3 to 4 hours from Kahului by the famous (or infamous) Hana road. This narrow, winding, magnificently scenic road is difficult to drive.

Kipahulu's lush tropical vegetation and cascading waterfalls are a dramatic contrast to the stark, austere views of Haleakala Crater.

Just past Hana, the road enters the national park at Kipahulu, where streams cascade through pools and waterfalls of varying sizes. This is an idyllic setting—heavy, green tropical foliage, black lava, clear blue pools, and the ocean in the distance.

The road crosses a bridge between pools 4 and 5; the *Kuloa Trail* leads along the lower pools to the ocean. The pools are a delightful place for a cool fresh-water swim, but because of the danger of sudden floods from the high-rainfall area in the upper valley, it is important to leave the pools if the water level seems to be rising.

Along the Kuloa Trail, the Park Service is building a replica *Kahuale* site, a group of homes consisting of men's eating house, women's eating house, sleeping house, cookhouse, canoe house, etc.

The *Pipiwai Trail* starts from the Kipahulu parking area and goes up the left side of a stream for .5 mile to an overlook where *Makahiku Falls* drops 184 feet into the gorge below. From the overlook, the trail continues for 1.5 miles across pastures and through a dense forest of exotic bamboo to lovely *Waimoku Falls*.

Cultural demonstrations, talks, and hikes are offered regularly in the Kipahulu District. Check bulletin boards for schedule.

Opposite: Amaumau ferns near Upper Palikea Falls.

HAWAII
VOLCANOES
NATIONAL PARK

Smoking Halemaumau, the inner crater of Kilauea Volcano.

HAWAII VOLCANOES NATIONAL PARK
HAWAII 96718
TEL.: (808) 967-7311

HIGHLIGHTS: Mauna Loa • Kilauea • Lae Apuki • Kalapana Coast • Chain of Craters Road • Heiaus • Holei Sea Arch • Na Ulu Arches • Puuloa petroglyph field • Holei Pali Overlook • Hilina Pali • Sulphur Bank • Steaming Bluff • Thurston Lava Tube • Tree Molds • Kipuka Puaulu

ACCESS: From Hilo or Konda; car rentals available.

HOURS: Year-round.

FEES: None.

PARKING: Throughout park.

GAS: Available at Volcano Village.

FOOD: At Volcano House and Volcano Village.

LODGING: Limited spaces available at Volcano House at park headquarters. Some cabins also available.

VISITOR CENTERS: Kilauea Visitor Center near main park entrance on east rim of Kilauea Summit Caldera; Wahaula Visitor Center at Kalapana Park Entrance.

MUSEUM: In Kilauea Visitor Center; cultural exhibits in Wahaula Heiau Visitor Center.

PETS: Permitted on leash in front country.

PICNICKING: At designated sites throughout park.

HIKING: Permitted. Carry water. Topographical map advisable outside developed area.

BACKPACKING: Permitted with permit. Water available at each designated campground. Register at park headquarters.

CAMPGROUNDS: Limited sites available. Fires only in designated pits. Permits needed for backcountry use.

TOURS: By tour companies. In English and Japanese.

FACILITIES FOR DISABLED: All major facilities are accessible: Visitor Centers, overlooks, restrooms, campgrounds.

For additional information, see also Sites, Trails, and Trips on pages 140–152 and the maps on pages 124–125 and 145.

VOLCANOES SHOCK THE SENSES, PRESENTING awesome beauty to the eye, roars and hisses to the ear, and brimstone to nose and tongue. Watching fountains of incandescent lava on a cold night can warm the body as well as the soul, bringing a subconscious awareness of power and mystery that humans can ponder, but that only nature can possess. Is it any wonder that people once conceived, and many still believe, that the Hawaiian volcanoes are homes of the beautiful and tempestuous fire goddess, Pele?

Hawaii Volcanoes National Park is 30 miles from Hilo on the island of Hawaii, known informally as the Big Island. The park includes two of the world's most active volcanoes, Kilauea and Mauna Loa; both are spectacular yet reasonably safe to watch during eruptions, and still interesting and beautiful when not erupting. The trade winds that blow from the northeast over the park, and the elevation change from sea level to over 13,000 feet, conspire to make rapid climate variations from tropical rain forests through hot deserts to often snow-covered, barren, rocky terrain well above timberline. Added to this are unusual flora and fauna that evolved in isolation and rapidly adapted to the many climatic zones. In this park of great contrasts, geologic changes occur on a human time scale. Hawaii Volcanoes National Park is an outdoor museum for everyone interested in geology, meterology, ecology, scenery, and solitude. Visitors fortunate enough to experience an eruption will remember it for life; those not so lucky will still not be disappointed.

HISTORY

Voyage Across the Pacific

Polynesians had always been a sea-faring people, but the 2,400-mile trip across the Pacific to Hawaii was an epic voyage even for them. Historians think that the first explorers sailed from the Marquesas, probably about A.D. 300 to 400, in large double-hulled canoes. They were explorers intent on settling; they brought with them coconuts and other seeds and plants, as well as fowl, dogs, and pigs to start a food supply in an unknown land.

The Hawaiian Islands as they found them were completely untouched by humans, with a unique ecology that had evolved from the immigration of relatively few species of plants, birds, and insects.

It is believed that for a time, trips were made to the Marquesas for more supplies and more colonists, but then travel between the islands seems to have stopped for several hundred years.

In about A.D. 1200, another wave of immigration took place, this

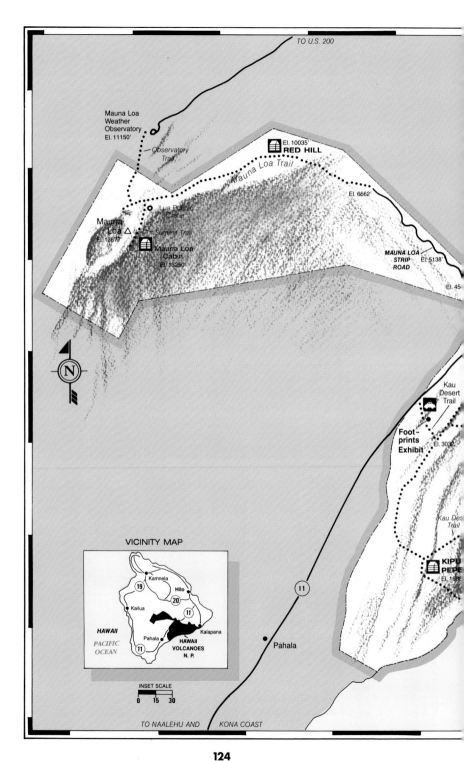

TO U.S. 200

Mauna Loa
Weather
Observatory
El. 11150'

Observatory
Trail

El. 10035'
RED HILL

Mauna Loa Trail

El. 6662'

Mauna
Loa △
El. 13677'

Lua Poholo
Crater

Summit Trail

Mauna Loa
Cabin
El. 13250'

MAUNA LOA
STRIP
ROAD

El. 5138'

El. 45

N

Kau
Desert
Trail

Foot-
prints
Exhibit

El. 3032

Kau Des
Trail

KIPU
PEPE
El. 168

VICINITY MAP

Kamnela

19
Hilo

20

Kailua

11

HAWAII
PACIFIC
OCEAN

Pahala

HAWAII
VOLCANOES
N. P.

Kalapana

11

11

Pahala

INSET SCALE
0   15   30

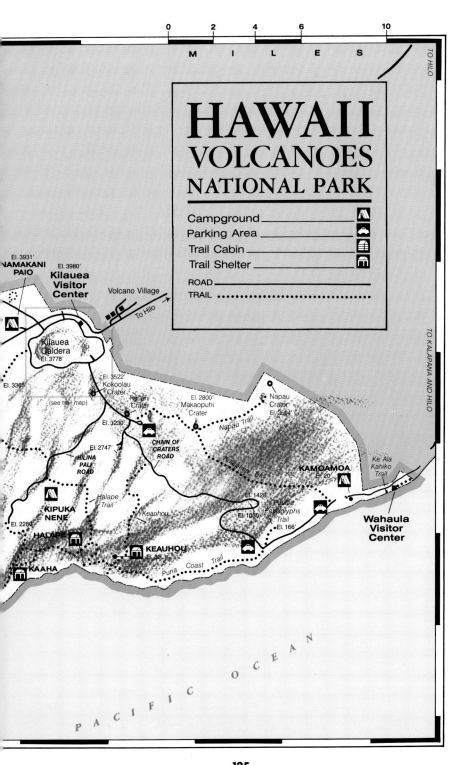

HAWAII
VOLCANOES
NATIONAL PARK

Campground
Parking Area
Trail Cabin
Trail Shelter

ROAD
TRAIL

time probably from Tahiti. These stronger, more aggressive people brought new gods, new customs, and new taboos (*kapu*) and imposed them on the more passive earlier settlers.

Most Hawaiian villages were in the coastal and lowland areas up to about 1,500 feet in elevation. One of the earliest, most sacred Hawaiian temples (*heiau*) was built in the thirteenth century at Wahaula near Kalapana; its ruins are preserved today in the coastal section of Hawaii Volcanoes National Park. Nearby at Puuloa, one of the most extensive petroglyph fields in the Hawaiian Islands, Hawaiians over many hundreds of years left their record in rock carvings of images and symbols.

Early Hawaiians seldom ventured up to Kilauea Volcano, home of the fire goddess, Pele, although ruins of what may have been two *heiau* have been found on the crater rim.

One example of Pele's power can still be seen. In 1790, some of the warriors of Chief Keoua were crossing the island to confront the army of the chief's rival, Kamehameha. They had just passed Kilauea and were several miles into the Kau Desert when they were caught by a giant eruption of steam and ash and were wiped out. Footprints of the few warriors who survived were preserved in the hot ash as it dried and hardened, and they remain along the Kau Desert Trail in the park.

Explorers and Missionaries

The arrival of Captain James Cook in 1778 began an era of incredible change, both for the Hawaiians and for the land itself. The explorers, missionaries, and merchants who followed Cook brought a world of new objects, ideas, religions, and customs—not to mention new diseases—and Hawaiians found their lives reshaped.

The different plants and animals that came with each new group made tremendous inroads on the native species, causing many extinctions and near-extinctions, particularly among the birds.

The first non-Hawaiians to see Kilauea Volcano and provide a written account were missionaries William Ellis and Asa Thurston, who, with Hawaiian guides, made a circuit of the island on foot in 1823. At that time there was an active lava lake in the caldera, and Ellis in his journal gives this unforgettable description:

> Astonishment and awe for some moments rendered us mute, and, like statues, we stood . . . with our eyes riveted on the abyss below . . . .
>
> The bottom was covered with lava, and the southwest and northern parts of it were one vast flood of burning matter, in a state of terrific ebullition, rolling to and fro its "fiery surge" and flaming billows.

Modern travelers can still take the Tree Fern Forest Trail to Thurston Lava Tube, a popular attraction

All dressed up for another eruption.

Establishment of the Park

The accounts by Ellis and subsequent explorers spread around the world, making Kilauea a prime destination for adventurous travelers. It was a long, difficult trip to Kilauea Crater on foot or horseback, but the number of visitors increased every year as the volcano's fame spread.

The proposal to preserve Kilauea as a public park first surfaced in 1906, but Congress was not impressed with the idea. In 1912, the Hawaiian Volcano Observatory was established to study the two frequently active volcanoes, Kilauea and Mauna Loa; Thomas Jaggar, the observatory's dynamic director, joined forces with Honolulu newspaper publisher Lorrin Thurston to press Congress to preserve this unique area as a national park. As luck would have it, in 1914 Lassen Peak in California unexpectedly erupted, and volcanoes suddenly became objects of fascination for both the public and Congress. In 1916, Congress passed only two of sixteen bills proposing new national parks; these two created Lassen Volcanic National Park in California and Hawaii National Park, which included the calderas of Kilauea and Mauna Loa as well as the Haleakala volcano on Maui. (In 1961, Haleakala became a separate national park.)

Hawaii Volcanoes National Park has been expanded five times since 1916 to include rain forest, desert, and the Kalapana area of the coast.

Hawaii's Hot-Spot Volcanoes

Most volcanoes occur near the edges of the earth's great tectonic plates; typical volcanic areas are the "Ring of Fire," where the plates are converging around the rim of the Pacific Ocean, and along the mid-ocean ridges, where the plates are separating. Hawaiian volcanoes are different; they have formed near the middle of the vast Pacific plate. They have another peculiarity as well; instead of the entire Hawaiian Ridge being active, only those volcanoes that are near the Big Island at the southeastern end of the archipelago have erupted in the past few centuries. The nearly extinct volcanic islands and seamounts to the northwest become progressively older with distance from the Big Island. Loihi, a seamount whose summit is 3,000 feet below sea level, lies about 20 miles southeast of the Big Island and appears to be the youngest of Hawaii's volcanoes. The progressive aging of the Hawaiian Islands is about 1 million years for every 60-mile distance northwest of the Big Island; thus, Maui's volcanoes are 1 to 2 million years old,

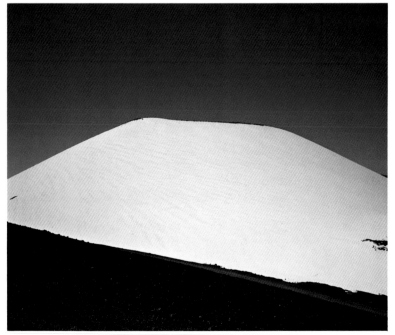

Snow-covered cinder cone.

Oahu's about 3 million, and Kauai's about 5 million.

Geologists offer the hot-spot theory as a possible explanation for these peculiarities of Hawaiian volcanoes. According to this hypothesis, certain locations in the earth's hot upper mantle, at depths of about 50 miles, produce abnormal amounts of molten rock (magma). This magma, being lighter than the overlying rocks, can force its way upward to the surface to form volcanoes. One of these mantle hot spots seems to be located under the southern end of the Hawaiian chain. As the Pacific plate slowly drifts over the Hawaiian hot spot, new volcanoes form at the point above the hot spot, while the older volcanoes, riding on the plate, move past the hot spot, become extinct, and slowly drift northwest in the direction of plate motion. This process of island volcanoes forming and gradually moving away has been likened to smoke signals drifting downwind from their source. This island drift is very slow, only 4 inches a year, and has not yet been directly measured. Whatever its cause, the progressive aging of the Hawaiian Islands to the northwest was recognized by the ancient Hawaiians; legend has it that Pele moved from her early home on Kauai to Oahu, then to Maui, and finally settled into Kilauea Volcano on the Big Island.

Kilauea and Mauna Loa

Most first-time visitors to a volcano expect to see a steep, cone-shaped peak, instead of a gently sloping, flat-topped mountain whose summit is a vast hole in the ground. Hawaiian volcanoes, called shield volcanoes by geologists, owe their gently sloping flanks to the relatively fluid lava that build up these volcanoes like giant piles of candle drippings; viscous, more explosive lavas form the cone-shaped volcanoes.

Magma that builds Kilauea comes from 50 miles below the earth's surface and rises more or less continuously through conduits to a magma storage chamber 2 to 5 miles beneath the volcano's summit. This magma chamber slowly enlarges, causing the summit region to inflate like a giant blister about 6 miles across and only a few feet high. When the pressure in the magma chamber exceeds the strength of the surrounding rocks, the rocks fracture, and magma moves toward the surface to form an eruption. Sometimes the overlying rocks fracture, and a summit eruption occurs; sometimes the rocks on the flank of the volcano are the first to fracture, and the eruption breaks out on a rift zone that is miles from the summit crater. It is even possible for the magma to move underground along a fracture but not break the surface; these shal-

Opposite: Lava cascade at Kaena Point.

low magma injections without eruptions are called intrusions.

When molten rock moves out of the summit magma chamber into the rift zones of Kilauea, the rate at which it is drawn off often exceeds the rate at which it is being resupplied from the deeper sources. This causes the ground surface in the summit region to subside. When the magma pressure has dropped enough, the eruption or intrusion will stop. Long-lasting summit eruptions, such as the almost permanent boiling lava lakes in Kilauea's summit caldera during much of the nineteenth century, are attributed to a near-balance between the slow eruption rates and the resupply to the magma chamber from greater depths.

Both Kilauea and Mauna Loa have great oval summit basins called calderas that are 2 by 3 miles across and several hundred feet deep. The calderas apparently have formed by collapse when an unusually large flank eruption on a rift zone below sea level drained a major portion of the magma chamber beneath the summit. The last time this occurred in a significant way at Kilauea was in 1790, and at Mauna Loa even earlier. Since their last major collapses, both Kilauea's and Mauna Loa's calderas have been refilling with ponded lava flows from summit eruptions. In the long life span of Hawaiian volcanoes, this cycle of caldera collapse and refill probably has occurred many times.

When William Ellis visited Kilauea in 1823, the summit caldera was more than twice as deep as it is now. The slow but nearly continuous eruptions of the summit lava lake until 1924, and the more rapid but intermittent summit eruptions since then, have half-filled the caldera with .5 cubic mile of lava. (Recent flows, which generally appear gray or black, occurred in 1974 and 1982.) Kilauea's east rift zone erupted fairly regularly during the 1980s and early 1990s. The eruptions built up a major new cone called Puu Oo.

Mauna Loa erupts less often than Kilauea, but the individual eruptions are often more voluminous. The eruption of Mauna Loa in 1950 added 600 million cubic yards to its slopes. The entire bulk of Mauna Loa, one of the world's largest mountains, is about 10,000 cubic miles. The 1975 eruption amounted to only eleven-millionths of this bulk. Mauna Loa has been formed by literally hundreds of thousands of eruptions during its 500,000-year lifetime. In the spring of 1984, the northeast flank eruption of Mauna Loa added yet another 240 million cubic yards of lava to the mountain.

Glowing Fountains and Thick Syrup

When magma reaches the surface, the dissolved gases—mostly steam, carbon dioxide, and sulfur dioxide—boil away; the remaining rock is called lava. The first vents in a new Hawaiian eruption

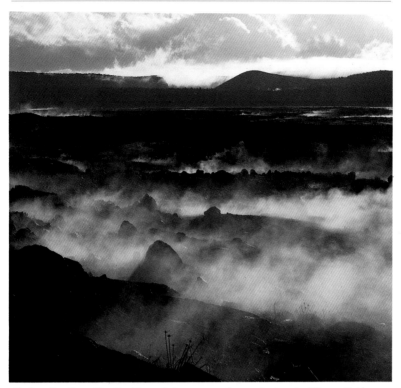

Carbon dioxide, sulfur dioxide, and steam escape from a fracture in Kilauea Caldera.

are generally fractures that are several hundreds to thousands of feet long, out of which spray curtains of incandescent lava. These linear vents soon concentrate to one or more points along the fracture system to become the principal vents. If the magma is rich in dissolved gases, these individual vents erupt huge fountains of glowing lava, sometimes spraying to heights of over 1,500 feet. Mounds of lava fragments and spatter pile up around the vent, and pumice and Pele's hair blow downwind to form volcanic-ash deposits. Pumice consists of fragments of frothy lava glass filled with tiny gas-bubble holes, and Pele's hair is fibers of lava glass; both form by the cooling and solidifying of the drops of molten rock in the lava fountains.

Lava flows form from the fallback of lava fountains, or well out of gas-poor vents, and move slowly downslope like thick syrup. If the flows are hot and thin, often only a few feet thick, they cool to form pahoehoe (pa HOY HOY), lavas with smooth to ropy surfaces. If a flow cools and becomes more viscous while it is still moving, the

Overleaf: Flower petals on the lava.

surface crust of the lava breaks up into millions of jagged, blocky fragments that are rafted along on the still-moving flow. Hawaiians named these foot-slashing lava flows aa (AH AH), a descriptive word that has become the standard geologic name for these rough, clinker-covered flows.

A distinctive feature of lava flows are lava caves, or lava tubes. These form where a thick flow crusts over to form a solid roof while the center of the flow beneath is still moving. If the source of the flow stops, the core may continue to move downslope; the tube in which it was flowing is eventually emptied. Lava caves can be miles in length, and some have stalactites of sulfate minerals or of once-molten volcanic glass.

Hawaiian Volcano Observatory

The Hawaiian Volcano Observatory of the U.S. Geological Survey was established on the rim of Kilauea Caldera (sometimes called Kilauea Crater) in 1912 to investigate the phenomena and basic principles of volcanic activity. The observatory staff monitors changes in volcanic gases, earthquake patterns, surface uplifts or subsidences, electrical and magnetic properties, and the eruptive habits of Kilauea and Mauna Loa. Much of the current knowledge about the deep structure and volcanic processes of Hawaiian volcanoes stems from research done at this observatory.

One of the goals of the observatory is forecasting volcanic activity. By measuring the amount and rate of inflation of the summit areas of Kilauea and Mauna Loa, as well as the increase in number of microearthquakes beneath their summits—earthquakes that are too small to be felt, but still detectable by seismographs—the observatory can now estimate the probability of future eruptions. Although far from precise, these forecasts are more accurate than random guesses based on the statistics of past eruptions.

NATURAL HISTORY

Climate and Precipitation

Hawaii Volcanoes National Park encompasses an incredible range of climate—from the warm, sunny Kalapana coast where temperatures on the glistening black lava flows average 75° F, through the upland rain forests with rainfall approaching 200 inches a year and temperatures averaging 65° F, to the severe alpine conditions at the top of 13,677-foot Mauna Loa with temperatures ranging from 11° F to 66° F.

Even at Kilauea's 4,000-foot elevation, the weather varies dramatically within a few miles. Rain clouds riding on the northeast trade winds drop as much as 100 inches of rain a year on the northeastern edge of the caldera. Clouds dissipate as they cross the caldera, and 2 miles away at Halemaumau, annual rainfall is only about 50 inches. Farther to the southwest, in the lee of the winds, it rains only 20 inches or less a year.

Hawaii's Island Ecology

The Hawaiian Islands are entirely volcanic in origin, made up of initially inhospitable lava rock. Because the islands' nearest continental neighbor is 2,400 miles away, life forms had to be highly specialized to arrive in Hawaii and to take hold in strange territory.

All life had to reach the islands by floating or swimming the ocean, by drifting or flying through the air, or by being carried on the feathers or in the digestive tracts of migratory birds. Hawaii has only two native mammals, the Hawaiian monk seal and a small bat; of those, one came by sea and the other by air.

Incredible as it is that any species survived the journey, the truly amazing story is how the few colonizing species evolved and diversified. For example, it is estimated that the more than 7,000 species of present-day native insects evolved from only about 150 colonizing species.

Native Plants

Plants that had the best chance of survival in this island environment were those whose seeds could float, such as the hala (pandanus) and the beach morning glory, both of which are prevalent along the coasts. Also ideal for adaptation were plants with tiny spores and seeds that are carried easily on the wind, so ferns and tree ferns were early arrivals. Many varieties flourish in Hawaii Volcanoes National Park; easiest to see are the handsome hapuu, a tree fern that grows as tall as 20 feet, and the amaumau, a fern whose young fronds are a reddish color for protection from the sun.

The ohia lehua is the most common native tree in Hawaii. Similar to species found elsewhere in Polynesia, it has tiny, easily airborne seeds that not only ensured its early arrival in Hawaii, but also make it one of the first plants to become established on new lava flows. It appears in Hawaii in a remarkable variety of forms, from a scrubby shrub in dry deserts to towering giants in rain forests. All are easily identifiable by their characteristic brilliant red pompon blooms.

The best known—and most handsome—endemic Hawaiian tree is the huge *Acacia koa*. Besides being prized for its natural beauty,

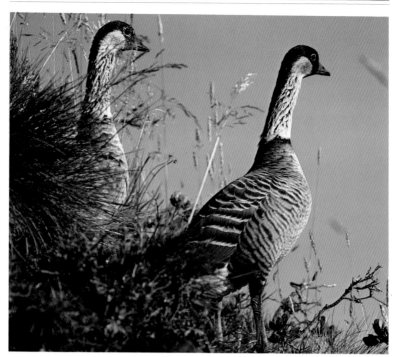

A pair of nene, native Hawaiian geese.

its hard wood was favored by early Hawaiians for canoes and surfboards; it is used today for making furniture and lustrous bowls.

Other native trees to look for are the sandalwood and the mamane, with its clusters of bright yellow flowers.

Common plants along roads and trails are the ti (ubiquitous throughout Polynesia) in the wet forests; the low ohelo bush, with its bright red, edible berries thought to be sacred to Pele, in the drier areas; and the naupaka and beach morning glory near the coast.

Some of the most conspicuous flowers seen in the park are those that have escaped from cultivation, such as the ginger, tritonia, fuchsia, and bamboo orchid.

Regrowth of Plants

Nature seldom provides virgin land for the study of patterns of plant growth, but a new lava flow presents just that opportunity. How fast the renewal of plant life starts on a newly erupted flow depends in large part on the rainfall; some prehistoric lava flows on the dry side of Mauna Loa are so bare that they seem to have erupted only yesterday, while 50-year-old flows in the rain forest of

Kilauea have a lush growth of new plants.

As the lava cools, cracks appear; these cracks are a good place for moisture to collect, and they also provide a bit of shade for germinating plants. In general, algae are first to arrive, with lichens, mosses, and ferns close behind. The sight of a tiny, bright green fern growing in a crack in a glistening black lava flow is a strong reminder of the tenacity of life.

A small colony of these early plants seems to improve moisture retention and makes it easier for other plants to take root. Native woody seed plants like ohia usually appear next, and exotic (nonnative) plants last.

In areas where there is a heavy fall of pumice and ash during an eruption, native plants seem to be able to recover much more quickly than exotic plants. Where the temperatures of the pumice have not been too high, ohia trees have survived pumice falls up to 8 feet thick, and ohelos that have been totally buried have recovered.

Native Birds

Hawaiian birds have an astounding evolutionary history; scientists estimate that the more than seventy kinds of native birds known to have evolved before the arrival of humans in Hawaii developed from as few as fifteen original species. Unfortunately, many of those have been driven into extinction by the predators introduced by humans, by hunting, by avian diseases, and by environmental pressures of exotic plants.

The most famous native bird of Hawaii Volcanoes National Park is the Hawaiian goose, or nene, the state bird of Hawaii. Although descended from the Canada goose, it has evolved to live on high, sparsely vegetated lava flows away from bodies of water, so its feet have lost much of their webbing. A ground-nesting bird, the nene was driven almost into extinction by introduced predators such as rats and mongooses, and by hunters. By 1951, there were only thirty-three known in existence, and half of those were in captivity. A concerted effort by the National Park Service, the state of Hawaii, and the Wildfowl Trust in England to save the nene by a program of breeding and release seeems to be succeeding. Groups of nene can sometimes be seen in the Kilauea area and at the end of the Mauna Loa Strip Road.

Other native birds to look for, especially in forested areas, are the wrenlike elepaio and three members of the large Hawaiian honeycreeper family: the iiwi and the apapane, both bright red birds that resemble the red blossoms of their favorite ohia trees; and the yellowish green amakihi, which prefer mamane blossoms.

Some introduced birds such as the mynah are common in the

park, as are game birds such as the Kalij pheasant and California quail, which live at higher elevations.

SITES, TRAILS, AND TRIPS

A driving tour of Hawaii Volcanoes National Park is best divided into two days. If the volcano is erupting, see that first. If not, do Crater Rim Drive and Jaggar Museum on day one. After a night at Volcano House or the Namakani Paio Campground, a full day can easily be spent exploring the Chain of Craters Road and other fascinating sites in the park.

Crater Rim Drive

The Crater Rim Drive makes an 11-mile circuit around Kilauea Caldera. The trip can begin at any of several places and can be made in either direction, but the following guide starts at park headquarters and goes counterclockwise.

At park headquarters for Hawaii Volcanoes National Park is the Kilauea Visitor Center, which has an up-to-date museum with history, natural history, and geology exhibits. Interpretive talks and movies of volcanic eruptions are presented several times each day.

Next door is the Volcano Art Center, a gallery for local artists and craftspeople, housed in the historic Volcano House, which was built in 1877.

Just beyond park headquarters, a short side road goes to *Sulphur Banks*, an area of volcanic gas seepage along a major fracture that forms an outer ring of Kilauea Caldera. The encrusting minerals include sulfur, gypsum, and hematite, and the lava bedrock has been altered to soft clays by acidic gases. The rotten-egg smell identifies hydrogen sulfide as one of the escaping gases. The ohia trees and ferns in this area have grown since the explosive eruption of Kilauea in 1790, which destroyed the vegetation around the caldera rim.

Steaming Bluff, the next turnout, is a treeless terrace between the inner and outer cliffs of Kilauea Caldera. Steam from ground water that is heated by deep, still-hot volcanic rocks escapes from many cracks. The ground a few feet down is too hot for tree roots to survive, but grasses and bamboo orchids with shallow roots cover the plain.

Ohia and koa trees are common along the stretch of the road past Steaming Bluff; ohia have dark gray-green, round leaves and rough bark; koa have paler green, blade-shaped leaves and

Opposite: Gases escape from fractures in Kilauea Caldera.

smoother, lighter bark. Edible ohelo berries are abundant here, but Hawaiian legend advises throwing a few berries into the caldera for Pele before eating any.

The next stop should be the Jaggar Museum, adjacent to the Hawaiian Volcano Observatory, to learn about how volcanoes work. MIT Professor Thomas Jaggar founded the observatory in 1912, and played a key role in establishing Hawaii Volcanoes National Park in 1916.

The seismographs and tiltmeter inside the museum are real instruments and show what is happening beneath Kilauea as you watch. A careful look at all the exhibits can help greatly in understanding the mysterious ways in which molten rock is formed beneath Hawaii, moves upward, and erupts.

Kilauea Caldera and Halemaumau Crater, seen from the overlook outside the museum, were formed by subsidence as molten rock in an underground chamber was drained away from beneath the summit.

Beyond the museum, the road winds down into the south end of the caldera. Vegetation begins to thin as rainfall rapidly decreases on the lee slopes of Kilauea. The ground is covered by the rocks and cinders explosively erupted in 1790. At 5 miles, the road crosses open fractures that have formed by the widening of the southwest rift as magma underground forced them open.

The desert conditions in this area are caused by low rainfall and the high acidity of the rain that does fall, which picks up the sulfur gases blowing downwind from Halemaumau Crater. When Mark Twain saw Kilauea, he remarked, "The smell of sulphur is strong, but not unpleasant to a sinner."

If the smell of sulfur dioxide is not too disagreeable, take the short trail to the edge of Halemaumau Crater for a glimpse into the inner sanctum of Pele. High lava marks on the sides of Halemaumau show the levels of molten lava lakes in the crater during 1968 and 1974. Partial drainback of these lava lakes into the magma chamber beneath Kilauea is a common ending to Halemaumau eruptions.

Just past Halemaumau, the road was covered by lava flows in 1982, and up the hill at *Keanakakoi Crater*, lava crossed the road in 1974. Rebuilding sections of roads destroyed by eruptions is a routine procedure at Kilauea.

Beyond Keanakakoi, vegetation begins to reappear. The pumice fragments that cover the road shoulders in increasing thickness fell from the great Kilauea Iki lava fountains in 1959, which reached heights of up to 1,900 feet. In another .5 mile, this pumice deposit is nearly 8 feet thick along the sides of the road. The ohia trees here were entirely stripped of their leaves and bark, and their recovery after a few years was totally unexpected.

Closer to the vent of the Kilauea Iki eruption, the thickness and heat of the pumice fall killed even the hardiest ohia trees. The *Devastation Trail* is a .5-mile paved trail through this stark landscape.

Puu Puai Overlook, just off Crater Rim Drive, is at the other end of Devastation Trail. Puu Puai is a large, barren cone of cinders just downwind from the 1959 eruptive vent of Kilauea Iki. Lavas from the same vent ponded in Kilauea Iki Crater to a depth of more than 300 feet. The solid, rocky crust of this lava lake is now nearly 200 feet thick and covers a thin lens-shaped core of near-molten rock. Several drill holes have been made in Kilauea Iki lava lake to study the way lava cools and crystallizes, and to assess the scientific feasibility of extracting energy from molten rock.

One mile farther along the Crater Rim Road, through a rain forest of giant tree ferns and ohia trees, is *Nahuku (Thurston Lava Tube)*. The easy 20-minute walk to and through the lava tube is a delightful contrast of tropical rain forest and mysterious cave, just 4 miles from the barren Kau Desert.

The next turnout is *Kilauea Iki Overlook*, another view of the large cinder cone and lava lake. If hikers are on the trail that leads across the surface of the lava lake below, the grand scale of the crater and other volcanic features becomes much more apparent.

A 2-mile drive through the lush fern and ohia forest completes the circuit back to park headquarters.

Chain of Craters Road

The Chain of Craters Road is about 20 miles long measured from Crater Rim Drive to the point where it has been covered by recent lava flows. Keeping this road open is an ongoing battle with Pele; it has been covered by lava or cracked apart by earthquakes several times. Twelve miles of the road were destroyed in the Mauna Ulu eruption between 1969 and 1974, and 7 miles of the coastal portion have been covered by lava from the Puu Oo eruption from 1986 on.

The Chain of Craters Road follows the axis of Kilauea's east rift zone as far as Mauna Ulu, the site of a major eruption that lasted from 1969 to 1974. The road then zigzags down the south flank of the mountain to the sea, and continues along the coast to where it is blocked by lava flows from the Puu Oo eruption. The first few miles of the road show the marks of the rift zone; cracks, fresh-looking lava flows, and craters with such names as Lua Manu, Kokoolau, Hiiaka, and Pauahi—each worth a stop.

Puhimau, a good example of a pit crater, is about one mile from the start of Chain of Craters Road, on the left. It is about 600 by 400 feet wide and 500 feet deep. This prehistoric crater was formed

TRAILS OF HAWAII VOLCANOES NATIONAL PARK

KILAUEA SUMMIT TRAILS

THURSTON LAVA TUBE TRAIL: Starts and ends at Thurston Lava Tube parking area; .3 mile round trip; .5 hour; leads through a lush fern forest and through a 400-foot lava tube; stair climb to exit tube.

DEVASTATION TRAIL: Starts at Pu'u Puai Overlook parking area; ends at Devastation Trail; 1.2 miles round trip; .5 hour; boardwalk leads through the area devastated by the 1959 Kilauea eruption.

BIRD PARK (KIPUKA PUAULU) TRAIL: Starts and ends at Mauna Loa Strip Road; 1.2 miles round trip; 1 hour; winds through open meadows and native forest along the slopes of Mauna Loa, one of the richest concentrations of native plants in Hawaii.

HALEMAUMAU TRAIL: Starts at the Ka'auea cliff near Kilauea Visitor Center; ends at Halemaumau parking area; 6.4 miles round trip; 5 hours; self-guiding trail across the floor of Kilauea Caldera, through the lava flows of 1982, 1974, 1975, and 1954, and flows dating to before 1900.

KILAUEA IKI TRAIL: Starts and ends at the Thurston Lava Tube parking lot; 5 miles round trip; 4 hours; drops 400 feet down into Kilauea Iki Crater; leads across the crater floor, past main vent, and ascends the Byron Ledge, where it joins the Crater Rim Trail.

BYRON LEDGE ('UWE-ALOHA) TRAIL: Starts and ends along the Halemaumau Trail; 2.5 miles one way; 2 hours; climbs up Byron Ledge and then leads back down into Kilauea Caldera.

CRATER RIM TRAIL: Starts and ends at Kilauea Visitor Center; 11.3 miles; 8 hours; leads around the Kilauea Caldera through dense fern forest and arid wasteland; intersects other trails along the way.

MAUNA IKI (FOOTPRINTS) TRAIL: Starts and ends along Hawaii 11, 9.1 miles southwest of park; 3.6 miles round trip; 2 hours; leads along tracks of early Hawaiians preserved in volcanic ash; a branch leads to the top of Mauna Iki.

COASTAL TRAILS

KE ALA KAHIKO TRAIL: Starts and ends behind the Wahaula Visitor Center in the coastal section of the park; 1.3 miles; 1.5 hours; nature walk passes through lowland forest along sea cliffs and remains of a Hawaiian village.

PUULOA PETROGLYPHS TRAIL: Starts 7.5 miles southwest of Wahaula Visitor Center on the Chain of Craters Road; 2 miles round trip; 2 hours; leads to field of petroglyphs chipped in the lava by early Hawaiians.

MAUNA LOA SUMMIT TRAILS*

OBSERVATORY TRAIL: Starts at Mauna Loa Weather Observatory, at 11,150 feet and 19 miles from Hawaii 20; ends at Summit Trail via North Pit Trail; 6 miles; 8 hours; steep and difficult; do not leave from Mauna Loa Observatory after 10 A.M.; altitude sickness likely.

*Overnight hikers must register at Kilauea Visitor Center; cabins are available on first-come basis; certain equipment required; weather information important.

MAUNA LOA TRAIL: Starts at Mauna Loa Strip Road lookout, 13.5 miles from Hawaii 11; ends at summit of Mauna Loa; 18.3-mile climb from 6,662 feet to summit at 13,250 feet (7.1 miles to Red Hill Cabin, 11.2 miles to Mauna Loa Cabin); 5 is to 7 hours from Mauna Loa Strip Road to Red Hill Cabin; 10 to 12 hours from Red Hill to Mauna Loa Cabin; trail above Red Hill leads past many cinder cones and young lava flows, and into North Pit of the summit caldera; not steep, but footing uneven and sometimes over loose lava; altitude sickness likely above 12,000 feet.

SUMMIT TRAIL: Starts at Mauna Loa Trail at North Pit; ends at the summit cabin, at 13,677 feet; 2.6 miles; 2 hours one way; leads along rim of Mokuaweoweo Caldera.

SEE MAP ON PAGES **124–125.**

by collapse; there are no deposits on the rim to provide evidence that this pit crater was formed by eruption or explosion.

About 3 miles beyond Puhmiau, a short side road turns left into the Mauna Ulu parking area. Walk the few yards to the road's end where it was buried beneath a 1973 pahoehoe lava flow from *Mauna Ulu*, the large shield vent in the background. Beyond the thin pahoehoe flow is a thicker aa flow, erupted from Mauna Ulu in 1974. This is also the trail head for the *Puu Huluhulu* and *Napau* trails.

Three miles beyond Mauna Ulu, at *Mau Loa o Maunu Ulu*, the Chain of Craters Road crosses a glistening sea of pahoehoe that streamed from that vent to the sea. The volume of the 1969/74 lava flows from Maunu Ulu totals about 450 million cubic yards, enough

Halemaumau with Mauna Loa in the background.

to pave a highway around the Earth 45 feet wide and 2 feet thick.

Three miles ahead, the windy open shelter and overlook at the top of a steep escarpment is called *Ke ala Komo*. Hawaiians call these step slopes "pali" (cliffs). Here the pali is part of a fault system along which the coast has moved downward relative to the east rift of Kilauea. The last major movement on these escarpments occurred during a magnitude 7.2 earthquake in 1975, when some of these scarps slipped another 5 feet.

Beyond Ke ala Komo the road switchbacks down the steep slope across many recent aa and pahoehoe flows from Mauna Ulu that spilled down the pali. These cascades of incandescent lava were a spectacular sight to those lucky enough to witness them. Even now

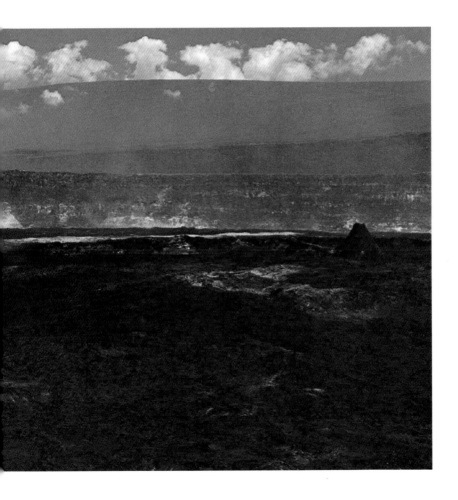

these lava cascades, frozen in place as they cooled, can conjure up an image of primeval fury.

When you reach the flat coastal plain at the foot of the pali, a turnout on the left has a marker describing the *Puu Loa petroglyph field* and the trail leading to it. It is an easy 1-mile walk over the foot-worn pahoehoe of the old Puna-Kau trail to see these remarkable rock carvings, one of the largest concentrations of petroglyphs in Hawaii. Puu Loa means "Hill of Long Life"; for hundreds of years Hawaiians came to this special place to carve figures, images, and symbols, most of which will probably never be deciphered. Vegetation is scarce; a few ohia trees grow, as well as tufts of grass, and occasionally a noni with its strange, many-eyed fruit.

Soon after the road turns left along the seacoast, watch for a pullout on the right labeled *Holei Sea Arch*. Walk the few yards to the edge of the sea cliff to see the power of the ocean waves at work. The arch was formed by the irregular erosive action of waves on cliffs, and is a good example of the constant interaction between the volcanoes (adding to the island) and the ocean (wearing it away). Look for shore birds that nest in these cliffs. In winter, migrating whales often surface and spout along this coast.

Not far beyond the sea arch the road is closed by lava flows from the long-lived Puu Oo eruption. At this writing (1995), active flows were entering the ocean at this site, sending up great clouds of steam from the battle between molten rock and sea water. Lava flows from this eruption have been pouring into the ocean since 1986, but changes in the location and style of the active flows have happened often. Check at park headquarters for the latest information about whether an eruption is occurring, and how you can best see it.

The Puu Oo (Hill of the Oo Bird) eruption began on January 3, 1983, from a broken line of fissures on the east rift of Kilauea. (The vent locations are out of sight behind the crest of the ridge north of where the road is closed by the flows.) Until July 1986, more than 40 episodes of high lava fountains, each lasting about a day, were separated by periods of about a month with no eruptive activity. The principal vent, Puu Oo, built a cone of cinders and lava spatter more than 800 feet high. Aa flows from this phase of the eruption did not reach the sea.

From July 1986 to February 1992, the eruption shifted to a new vent 2 miles east of Puu Oo and became nearly continuous. Pahoehoe flows, fed mainly through lava tubes, reached the ocean in November 1986, and in 1990/91 buried the village of Kalapana and Kaimu's black sand beach.

After 1992, new fractures near the base of the Puu Oo cone opened, sending new flows of aa and pahoehoe to the sea along this coast.

At this writing, the only choice for a return trip is to retrace your path back up the Chain of Craters Road. At some time in the future when this long-lasting Puu Oo eruption has stopped, the road will probably be rebuilt, making it possible to return to Hilo through the towns of Pohoa and Keaau.

Mauna Loa Strip Road

This 11.5-mile road begins about 2 miles west of park headquarters on Hawaii 11, and goes to the 6,662-foot elevation of Mauna Loa. The road is paved but narrow, and is sometimes closed during times of drought when fire danger is high.

Just after the road turns off the main highway, a short (.7 mile) loop road leads to the *Tree Molds*, formed when liquid lava cooled around tree trunks, crusting on the outside but burning on the inside. Some hollow molds are 5 feet across.

A mile and a half farther up the road is *Kipuka Puaulu (Bird Park)*, with picnic shelters and a delightful 1-mile, self-guiding nature trail through one of the richest concentrations of native plants in Hawaii. Kipuka Puaulu is a lush, 100-acre island of vegetation surrounded by younger lava flows, with an astonishing variety of native trees, shrubs, vines, and ferns. Plants along the trail are well marked, and a pamphlet with explanations keyed to the markers is available.

Here are majestic specimens of ohia and koa trees, as well as kukui, soapberry, and the rare holei tree. The forest floor is thick with ground-hugging plants such as native peperomia and wild white strawberries.

As the name of the area suggests, the treetops are alive with birds: imported birds such as the cardinal and the Chinese thrush, and several native species such as the elepaio, iiwi, and apapane.

In another 1.5 miles, the Mauna Loa Strip Road passes through *Kipuka Ki*, another oasis of mature forest with magnificent old koa trees arching over the road.

The Mauna Loa Strip Road ends at the trail head for the 18-mile climb to the summit of Mauna Loa. There is a fine panoramic view of Kilauea with the ocean in the distance.

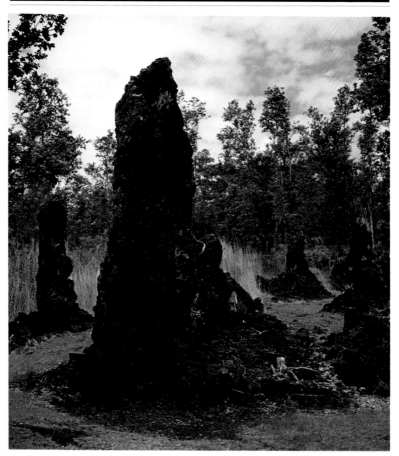

Tree molds formed when lava cooled around trees, burning them but leaving a cast.

Trails

Mauna Loa Trail. The climb to the summit of Mauna Loa is a grand adventure for well-equipped and hardy backpackers with 3 or 4 days to spend. Registration and cabin permits from park headquarters are required.

The Mauna Loa Trail begins at an elevation of 6,662 feet at the end of the Mauna Loa Strip Road, and climbs a steep 7 miles, gaining almost 3,400 feet to Red Hill Cabin, at 10,035 feet. This section of the trail leads through timberline on ancient flows of pahoehoe and aa; the silversword, native geranium, and hinahina (which has been celebrated in Hawaiian song) grow here. Climb slowly to become adjusted to the altitude, because it is still 12 miles from

Red Hill to the summit.

Red Hill is a large cone of red cinders on the northeast rift zone of Mauna Loa. From here, the trail follows along the rift-zone ridge of Mauna Loa and is a garden of geologic delights—young flows of pahoehoe and aa, cinder cones, spatter cones, lava tubes, and fissure vents. The trail is not so steep as it is below Red Hill, but the 3,600-foot elevation gain reaches altitudes above 13,000 feet. The scenery is moonscape, not alpine. The rugged terrain and cold, thin air require caution and good sense.

The summit of Mauna Loa is a vast caldera like that of Kilauea, totally barren and seemingly isolated from the rest of the world. The sight of the primitive summit cabin is a welcome reminder that you are still on earth. Water—often only ice—can be found in deep cracks in the lava about 200 yards beyond the summit cabin.

Only those who have climbed Mauna Loa can truly appreciate its size, and only those who have carefully prepared for this arduous trek will completely enjoy the magnificent experience.

Halemaumau Trail. Probably the most exciting short hike in the park is the 3.2-mile Halemaumau Trail across the floor of Kilauea Caldera and past Halemaumau firepit. The trail starts from Volcano House, with a fairly steep descent through a lovely fern and ohia forest, past recent major rock slides from the 6.8 magnitude earthquake of November 16, 1983 to the caldera floor. The contrast when the trail suddenly leaves the forest and starts across the glistening black lava is astonishing; the caldera floor is an eerie wasteland of lava flows.

The floor is covered with overlapping flows of different ages. Some are pre-1900; but the most voluminous flows are from 1919 and 1974, and the most recent is from September 1982. The trail passes 3,000-foot-wide Halemaumau Crater, legendary home of Pele. This firepit once contained an active lava lake, and could again in the future. The trail ends at the Halemaumau parking area; it is necessary to arrange private transportation from the parking area or retrace the trail.

Kilauea Iki Trail. Similar to the Halemaumau Trail, the Kilauea Iki Trail leaves the Crater Rim Trail about 2 miles from park headquarters and descends 400 feet into Kilauea Iki Crater. It crosses the floor of the crater, actually the cooled crust of a lava lake that ponded in the crater during the massive eruption of 1959. The "lake" still has a hot core at a depth of about 200 feet. The trail climbs up the western wall of the crater and ends at the Thurston Lava Tube parking area.

Kau Desert Trail. The trail to Mauna Iki is an easy, 3.5-mile (round trip) hike in the Kau Desert, leaving from Hawaii 11 at 9.1 miles from park headquarters. This well-defined, mostly level trail provides a look at typical Kau Desert vegetation—scrubby ohia trees, ohelo, and occasional pukiawe—growing in what is mostly ash from the 1790 explosive eruption of Kilauea.

Leaving the volcanic ash, the trail climbs the gently sloping lavas of Mauna Iki (little mountain), the vent of the 1920 southwest rift eruption of Kilauea. The view from the top of Mauna Iki provides a panorama of much of the Kau Desert.

Napau Trail. The Napau Trail offers a strenuous but rewarding 1-day hike past recent volcanic vents and lava flows, and through a fern-forest jungle on the east rift of Kilauea. The first few miles are across recent flows from Mauna Ulu. The trail goes between Mauna Ulu and Puu Huluhulu, a small, old cinder cone that has a trail to a viewpoint at the top—a nice side trip.

From Puu Huluhulu, the Napau Trail then passes Makaopuhi, the largest pit crater on the rift, and enters a thick jungle of tree ferns and ohia trees that were not covered by the recent flows. The contrast between the barren lava and the dense jungle is striking. Life in the humid tropics is tenacious and prolific; the jungle here is growing on lavas that are only 300 to 500 years old. Napau is another pit crater that is almost filled with recent flows.

The hike out and back is 14 miles, but the *Naulu Trail* provides an alternative route from Makaopuhi Crater to the Chain of Craters Road, 2 miles away at Ke ala Komo.

Halape Trail. The Halape Trail is a steep 7-mile descent of 3,000 feet from the Kipuka Nene Campground to a small bay and beach along the rugged desert coast of Hawaii (on the south flank of Kilauea). This is a 2-day trip for sturdy backpackers, and registration and a permit from park headquarters are required.

The trail goes down steep escarpments and benches covered with low shrubs and grass, to a shelter near the beach. Young coconut trees are growing to replace an old grove that was drowned when the land subsided 6 feet during a magnitude 7.2 earthquake in 1975.

Allow most of a day and carry plenty of water for the hot climb back to the trail head. There is an alternative 12-mile trail out along the seacoast to the Chain of Craters Road, but that route requires arranging for private transportation back to Kipuka Nene.

Opposite: In 1959, Kilauea Iki erupted, throwing lava a record 1,700 feet into the air.

JOSHUA TREE
TREE
NATIONAL PARK

Mojave mound hedgehog cactus near Barker Dam.

JOSHUA TREE NATIONAL PARK
74485 NATIONAL PARK DRIVE
TWENTYNINE PALMS, CALIFORNIA 92277
TEL.: (619) 367-7511

HIGHLIGHTS: Hidden Valley • Barker Dam • Cottonwood Spring • Oasis of Mara • 49 Palms Canyon • Jumbo Rocks • Keys View • Keys Ranch • Wonderland of Rocks • Cholla Cactus Garden

ACCESS: I-10 parallels the southern boundary, with access about 25 miles east of Indio. California 62 extends north from I-10 near Desert Hot Springs, 120 miles east of Los Angeles. It parallels the northern boundary, with main entrances into the park at the towns of Joshua Tree and Twentynine Palms.

HOURS: Open year-round; some campgrounds partially closed during hotter summer months; and some roads subject to periodic closure because of ice and snow during winter.

FEES: Charged for cars and at some campgrounds.

PARKING: Throughout the park.

GAS, FOOD, LODGING: In communities surrounding the park.

VISITOR CENTER: Twentynine Palms Oasis Visitor Center, Utah Trail and National Park Drive, in Twentynine Palms, offers information, maps, publications, exhibits, orientation slide program, and video program; Cottonwood Spring Visitor Center near the south boundary offers information, maps, and publications. Black Rock Canyon Visitor Center offers information, maps, publications, exhibits, and video programs.

PETS: Permitted on leash in developed areas, but not permitted on trails or in the backcountry.

PICNICKING: At designated sites throughout the park.

HIKING: On trails and cross-country throughout the park. Carry water.

BACKPACKING: Permitted throughout the park either on trails or cross-country with a permit. Backcountry registration sites are scattered throughout the park providing access to most locations. Water must be carried, none is available.

CAMPGROUNDS: Individual sites at Hidden Valley, Ryan, Jumbo Rocks, Belle, White Tank, Indian Cove, Cottonwood, and Black Rock Canyon. Group sites at Cottonwood, Indian Cove, and Sheep Pass. Fees charged at Black Rock Canyon, Cottonwood, and group sites. Reservations required for Black Rock and group sites. Horse camp at Black Rock and Ryan.

TOURS: During the winter season, approximately October through May, interpretive walks and talks are offered.

OTHER ACTIVITIES: Horseback riding on California Riding and Hiking Trail, bicycling on established roads, and rock climbing.

FACILITIES FOR DISABLED: Restrooms at Twentynine Palms and Black Rock visitor centers. Campsites at Cottonwood, Jumbo Rocks, and Black Rock.

For additional information, see also Sites, Trails, and Trips on pages 170–177 and the map on pages 158–159.

O N OCTOBER 31, 1994, JOSHUA TREE National Park became one of the newest national parks. After many years of citizen effort, the California Desert Protection Act passed, converting Joshua Tree National Monument to a national park. Approximately 234,000 acres were added to the monument lands, bringing the total to 793,000 acres, or 1,241 square miles.

With portions of both the Mojave and Colorado deserts within its boundary, Joshua Tree National Park contains a rich diversity of plant and animal life. Scattered occupancy of the region by early prehistoric cultures, later Native American groups, and more recent miners and homesteaders has contributed to an equally diverse cultural history.

Just 150 miles east of Los Angeles in the Southern California desert, the park offers a variety of vistas and activities. Picturesque Joshua trees of the Mojave Desert, widely spreading ocotillos in the Colorado Desert, and colorful fields of spring wild-flowers all are invitations to spend time here. Walk into the 12-square-mile "Wonderland of Rocks," hike up a desert wash, climb to the top of Ryan Mountain, or hike to historic Wall Street Mill. Rock climbers will find 4,000 established climbing routes suitable to skill levels ranging from beginner to expert. Photographers will find desert cacti and wildflowers in bloom from March through June. Coyotes and desert bighorn sheep occasionally put in appearances, as do slithering snakes and basking lizards. Birdwatchers will enjoy seeking out the phainopeplas, LeConte's thrashers, and roadrunners. In addition to abundant biological and cultural resources, the geologic appearance of Joshua Tree should create a sense of wonder about the forces responsible for this unusual landscape.

HISTORY

Early Americans

Perhaps as long as 10,000 years ago the Pinto culture occupied campsites along a slow-moving river in the bottom of the Pinto Basin. Archeologists describe the region of that time as more moist, with a wide river containing backed-up marshes or shallow lakes. Along the outer limits of this water body, campsites stretched for more than 6 miles. That these campsites were essentially all at the same level was evidence of a lake shoreline. Archeologists found evidence of stone tools, points for hunting, and manos and metates for food preparation. Decreased precipita-

JOSHUA TREE
NATIONAL PARK

Ranger Station — US
Campground — 🏕
Picnic Area — 🌄
Drinking Water — 🚰

Road ———
Unpaved Road — — —
4-Wheel Drive — — —
Trail . . . .

N

TO 15

247

Yucca Valley

Joshua Tree

Twentynine Palms

Oasis of Mara Visitor Center

Entrance Station

West Entrance Station

INDIAN COVE

49 PALMS OASIS

Morongo Valley

BLACK ROCK CANYON

Quail Springs Road

HIDDEN VALLEY

Barker Dam

COVINGTON FLATS

Lost Horse

SHEEP PASS

QUEEN VALLEY

BELLE

WHITE TANK

LITTLE SAN BERNARDINO MOUNTAINS

LOST HORSE VALLEY

RYAN

JUMBO ROCKS

62

Desert Hot Springs

KEYS VIEW

LOST HORSE MINE

Geology Tour Road

HEXIE MOUNTAINS

111

TO LOS ANGELES

Palm Springs

Dillon Road

Berdoo Canyon Road

10

111

Indio

Palm Desert

Coachella

Pink

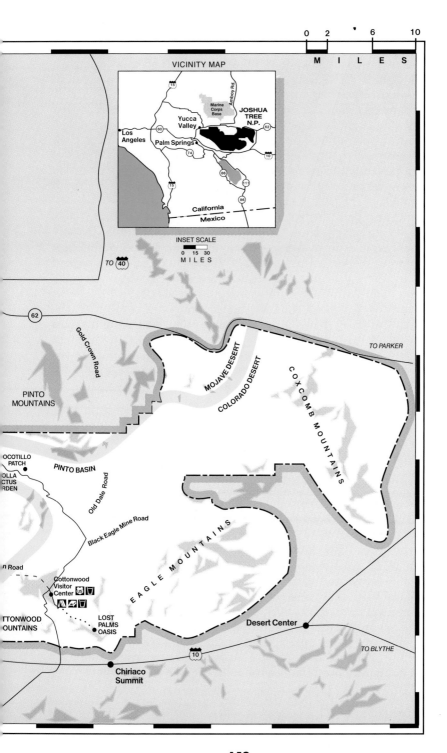

MILES

0   2   6   10

VICINITY MAP

15

Amboy Rd

Marine
Corps
Base

JOSHUA
TREE
N.P.

Yucca
Valley

62

60

Los
Angeles

Palm Springs

74

10

15

86

11

California

Mexico

86

INSET SCALE

0   15   30
MILES

TO 40

62

Gold Crown Road

MOJAVE DESERT

COLORADO DESERT

TO PARKER

C O X C O M B   M O U N T A I N S

PINTO
MOUNTAINS

OCOTILLO
PATCH

OLLA
CTUS
RDEN

PINTO BASIN

Old Dale Road

Black Eagle Mine Road

E A G L E   M O U N T A I N S

n Road

Cottonwood
Visitor
Center

US

TTONWOOD
OUNTAINS

LOST
PALMS
OASIS

Desert Center

10

TO BLYTHE

Chiriaco
Summit

tion since that time brought about environmental changes, undoubtedly influencing the movement of these people away from the area.

Around 2,000 years ago, the ancestors of the Serrano and Cahuilla Indians were present in this region. Pottery, arrow points, and other evidence of the peoples of this more recent period have been identified. Numerous petroglyph (rock engraving) and pictograph (rock painting) sites, as well as food-preparation sites, with bedrock mortars and grinding slicks, are scattered throughout the park, usually near water sources.

Serrano and Chemehuevi Indian groups lived at what is now the Twentynine Palms Oasis. Serrano Indians were primarily mountain dwellers, living in the San Bernardino Mountains. However, as with other groups of their time, their hunting and food-gathering habits took them to the lower desert during the winter and the higher mountains during the summer. Chemehuevi Indians lived, hunted, and traveled from the Colorado River to the oasis. Currently living in the Coachella Valley and Gorgonio Pass are members of the tribal bands of the Cahuilla Indians. Ancestors of the Cahuilla were also hunters and gatherers who visited the area to collect acorns, pinyon nuts, and mesquite beans for food, creosote leaves for medicine, and yucca fibers for baskets.

Explorers, Ranchers, Miners, and Homesteaders

Colonel Henry Washington, in 1855, was the first government surveyor to visit the Twentynine Palms Oasis. Deputy Surveyor Green described the oasis as having many small springs, large palm trees, and Native American peoples living at the site in huts and cultivating the grounds near the springs. Attracted by grass "up to a horse's belly," cattlemen brought herds into the desert. One of the first was Oliver Smith, whose Texas longhorns grazed in the Quail Spring area from 1870 to 1876. In about 1879, Bill and Jim McHaney brought a herd into the Keys Ranch area, and rumors circulated about the legal ownership of their cattle. Legend has it that these rustlers drove cattle into the high desert, rebranded them in the rock-enclosed hidden valleys, then drove them on to the coast to sell.

Tall tales about gold mines are common. One story regarding the Lost Horse Mine suggests that Johnny Lang, while looking for his lost horse, found the rich claim. In another version, Johnny met

Opposite, top: The historic Desert Queen Ranch, owned by Bill Keys.
Below, left: Keys served time for shooting to death a neighbor who had fired at him; he was later pardoned.
Below, right: Stone marks site where Keys' adversary "bit the dust."

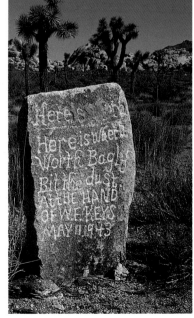

a prospector, who sold his claim to Johnny. Just who discovered the Desert Queen Mine is another question. According to one report, a man named James discovered the claim and staked it out, but his markers were found by some cowboys, who took them down and put up their own. During the argument that followed, James was shot and killed. Charles Martin, who worked for the McHaney Gang, claimed self-defense, stating that James came after him with a knife. As the only witnesses were other McHaney hands, Martin was acquitted, and the McHaneys had a gold mine. Remnants of these mining days are scattered throughout the high desert, testifying to the widespread activity.

Establishment of the Park

On August 10, 1936, President Franklin Roosevelt signed a proclamation establishing Joshua Tree National Monument. Approximately 825,000 acres encompassing parts of the Colorado and Mojave deserts were included within the monument. This took place after ten years of crusading by Minerva Hamilton Hoyt, who was prominent in Los Angeles society, and others who were alarmed at the number of desert plants being removed for cactus gardens in southern California communities.

In 1950, because of a strong appeal for continued mining operations, 265,000 acres were removed from the monument.

On October 31, 1994, President Bill Clinton signed the California Desert Protection Act (see page 58), which established Joshua Tree National Park. Acreage added to the new park included portions of the Coxcomb, Little San Bernardino, and Eagle mountain ranges, essentially completing ecological units by adding areas previously left out of the monument.

GEOLOGY

Light-brown rock piles stand in the middle of the Lost Horse and Queen valleys. These granite mounds are the result of hot molten rock, magma, that rose toward the surface 125 million years ago. Not quite reaching the surface, this molten rock solidified and remained through an extensive period of mountain building and fault shifting. During these years, the east-to-west-trending transverse mountain ranges were lifted up from the southern California coast to the inland desert region. As faults shifted, mountains rose and valleys dropped, creating the "basin and range" topography seen today. Two types of valleys are found in

Opposite: One of many unusual granite formations in the Jumbo Rocks area.

this region: those that have been directly formed by down-dropping along faults and those that have been formed by erosion and are often partially filled by the erosion materials. Pleasant Valley, along the Geology Tour Road, and the Pinto Basin resulted from fault activity. Queen and Lost Horse, on the other hand, are erosion-filled valleys.

The oldest rock formation found in the park today is the Pinto Gneiss, a darker-gray layer on the tops of the mountain ranges. Formerly a combination of sedimentary and igneous (volcanic) rocks, it had become a metamorphic rock, changed by pressure and temperature. As the overlying gneiss formation slowly eroded away, the rock piles that make up the 12 square miles of the Wonderland of Rocks were uncovered. The largest proportion of the granite rock piles is a formation called the White Tank monzogranite.

Cracks between the rock piles were the result of water seeping down into subsurface joints and surface pressure being released. Once surfaces were exposed to the elements, erosion continued to carve at the rock formations. Water in the form of rain and snow is the biggest force. Freezing and thawing on the surface help expand small cracks into larger ones. Where rock surfaces are more shaded or closer to the ground or vegetation, more moisture accumulates, erosion is heightened, and small caves are formed, a process known as cavernous weathering. Ultimately, this erosion produces a pile of rounded rocks. The overall process is called spheroidal weathering and is best seen at Hidden Valley and Jumbo Rocks.

Additional erosion is taking place throughout the park. Along the flanks of the mountain ranges are examples of extensive alluvial fans. As rain occurs in the mountains, flash floods carry large amounts of rock and gravel down the washes. Because of the extreme dry conditions, the water soaks into the ground rapidly and deposits the gravel along the base of the mountains. As one channel fills up, others form and often these deposits fan out across the floor of the basins between the ranges. Where a number of fans flow together a *bajada* is formed.

A major system of earthquake faults occurs in this region. To the south, the famous San Andreas Fault runs through the Coachella Valley. The Blue Cut Fault extends from the Little San Bernardino Mountains, marking the southern flank of the Hexie Mountains, and into the Pinto Basin. On the north side of the Pinto Basin, the Pinto Mountain Fault follows the Pinto Mountains to Twentynine Palms and farther west.

Climate and Precipitation

Three to four inches of precipitation fall annually in the Twentynine Palms area of the park. Less falls in the lower Colorado Desert and more in the higher Mojave Desert. The San Jacinto and San Bernardino mountain ranges toward the south and west prevent the coastal moisture from reaching this inland desert, creating a rain-shadow effect, typical of many deserts. An area of high pressure over the southwest is often pointed to as the influence keeping away any possible cold, wet weather. As long as this high pressure remains, most storms pass north of the region. By October or November, this high weakens, allowing occasional winter storms to pass through. They often bring snow to the high-desert portions of the park.

Summer thunderstorms are common, resulting in widely scattered, often torrential rains that may deposit several inches of rain in very short periods of time. Temperatures can be extreme. During July in the bottom of the Pinto Basin, it is not uncommon to experience a 120° F reading. During January, temperatures as low as —10° F can occur in the Lost Horse Valley. Spring and fall

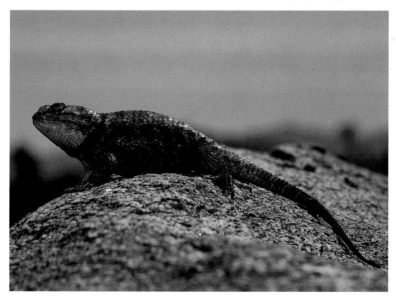

The large (7–12 inch) desert spiny lizard eats insects, flowers, and leaves.
Overleaf: The Joshua tree reminded early Mormon travelers of Joshua, raising his arms to implore the Lord.

are relished by all residents of the desert. With a temperature change of about 35 degrees, a wide range typical of desert areas, days are warm and nights are cool.

Plants of the Mojave Desert

Joshua trees, pinyon pines, California junipers, and scrub oaks are among the plants that have adapted to conditions found in the Mojave Desert. Because of its extreme cold temperatures, only the hardiest plants can tolerate the winters. Lost Horse and Queen valleys receive 6 to 8 inches of precipitation annually, the amount required for good Joshua tree growth. The tallest Joshua trees reach about 30 to 40 feet, and the trunk may be 4 feet in diameter. The oldest may be more than 700 years old. Although the large clusters of creamy white flowers do not bloom every year, they usually begin to appear in late February.

Joshua trees will grow from seeds or they can develop from root or crown sprouts. These sprouts around the base of the trees, or the scattered seedlings, are extremely vulnerable to squirrels and rabbits. Seedlings that can find a protective nurse plant to grow up under have a much greater chance of survival. Interspersed between the Joshua trees are thick occurrences of blackbrush, areas of scattered cheesebush, Mojave yucca, and occasional creosote bushes. Scattered throughout the Queen Valley, Mojave mound cactus, old man cactus, and the dead, or devil, cactus can be found.

Plants of the Colorado Desert

Spreading their wandlike branches 10 or 12 feet from the base, the ocotillos put on a startling display of color when in bloom. Adapted to living in the harsh, dry Colorado Desert, ocotillos are patient survivors. They wait in an almost dormant state most of the year. Then, following a good rain shower, green leaves appear along the stems, and if conditions are right, sprays of brilliant red flowers appear on the end of each stem.

Cactus are well adapted to the low rainfall and high heat of the Colorado Desert. A small garden of teddy-bear cholla can be found in the Pinto Basin. Mixed within this cactus garden are colorful calico cactus and desert senna. Paloverde trees line the washes, and ironwood trees are scattered occupants of the flats in the Colorado Desert. Farther down in the lower desert, where the environment reaches its most inhospitable state, the creosote bush and burrow bush are likely to be the only plants found, often widely spaced in order to get adequate moisture.

Red-tailed hawk chicks enjoy a snake dinner.

Wildflowers

The extent and timing of the spring wildflower blooms in California deserts may vary greatly from year to year. Late-fall or early-winter precipitation and spring temperatures are key environmental factors affecting the spring blooming period. Normally, desert annuals germinate between September and December, usually requiring a good soaking to get started. Spring flowering begins as temperatures rise, usually starting at lower elevations in February with yellow desert dandelions, white pincushions, and desert gold poppies in the Colorado Desert south of Cottonwood. Cactus blooming usually begins with scattered beaver-tail cactus in the lower elevations in March, followed by mound cactus, calico cactus, and others at higher elevations in April and May.

Wildlife

Evidence of wildlife in the desert is seen more often than the animals themselves. Desert bighorn sheep may lie all day on the side of a rock pile, then at dusk make their way down to the water source. Footprints in the sand may be the only clue of their passing. Wash bottoms where there is regular water are good places to see tracks of mule deer, coyotes, gray foxes, and, once in a while, a mountain lion. Black-tailed jack rabbits and cottontails are more abundant and can often be seen darting out from under bushes. Numerous small rodents live in the desert. Kangaroo rats live underground through the heat of the day, coming out at night to feed. They exist without water to drink, converting the food they eat into the water required.

Reptiles—including six species of rattlesnakes, collared lizards, desert iguanas, chuckwallas, and the endangered desert tortoise—slither, slide, and lumber across the desert sand. Joshua Tree is one of the few good remaining places to see the desert tortoise. Lizards bask on top of rock piles or downed Joshua tree logs.

More than 230 species of birds occur in the park. Residents often observed include cactus wrens, Gambel's quail, ravens, black-throated sparrows, and occasionally a roadrunner. Others, such as northern orioles, ash-throated flycatchers, and western kingbirds, migrate into the area, nesting during the summer months. Warblers and flycatchers pass through the park during spring and fall migrations.

SITES, TRAILS, AND TRIPS

Joshua Tree National Park has about 80 miles of paved roads, more than 100 miles of dirt roads, and 70 miles of designated trails. It would be easy to spend a week and not visit all the sites accessed by these roads and trails.

High-Desert Road

From either the town of Joshua Tree or Twentynine Palms, the main park road traverses a 30-mile portion of the Mojave Desert. Five miles from the west entrance, large granite rock piles begin to appear beside the road. These rocks attract climbers from all over the world. Hikers can enjoy them by walking short trails to their bases. This road provides some of the best views of Joshua trees. There are also a number of interpretive pullouts and parking areas for nature trails.

Nine miles from the west entrance, just west of the Hidden Valley Campground, the road south leads to *Hidden Valley Nature Trail* and picnic area. Labels along a 1-mile loop trail describe the historic cattle ranching and mining in the high desert.

From the east side of Hidden Valley campground trails lead to Echo Rock, a popular climbing area, and Barker Dam.

Barker Dam nature trail, featuring a dam built by early cattlemen, is about 2 miles east of Hidden Valley Campground and is reached by the dirt road that leads off to the right or northeast, just inside the campground entrance. At the T intersection, turn right, or east, to Barker Dam. Interpretive signs explain the difference water availability makes to desert organisms.

The left fork at the T intersection leads to the south gate of the historic Desert Queen Ranch. Conducted tours are offered on weekends in the fall and spring.

Keys View Road

Eleven miles from the west entrance, look for Keys View Road. Just beyond the turn, a large parking area on the left provides access to Cap Rock and a wheelchair-accessible nature trail.

Two miles out, this road crosses the *California Riding and Hiking Trail*, with parking for overnight or day hikes to Juniper Flats to the west or Ryan Mountain to the east. One can hike from Black Rock Campground to Twentynine Palms, a distance of 35 miles, on this trail.

Three miles out is the turnoff for a dirt road to the Lost Horse Mine trail head. The parking area is about 2 miles from the Lost Horse Mine and mill. Between 1890 and 1940, this mine operated intermittently and was one of the most productive in the region. More than 9,000 ounces of gold and 16,000 ounces of silver were mined. Remnants of the old ten-stamp mill can be seen at the mine site. Stamp mills used 900-pound stamps to crush the gold ore to a fine powder, releasing the gold from the rock so it could be reclaimed through amalgamation (combination with mercury) or other recovery methods.

At the end of this 5-mile spur road is Keys View, named after Bill Keys, who built the road primarily for access to a gold mine. Visitors can see the Salton Sea, Coachella Valley, and Mount San Jacinto from this overlook. On a clear day, Signal Mountain, 70 miles away in Mexico, is often visible.

Back on the main road, about 1 mile east of Keys View Road, parking is available for a hike up Ryan Mountain. This 3-mile round trip offers excellent views of the Wonderland of Rocks, as well as distant mountain ranges.

Jumbo Rocks Campground offers a loop trail that starts at either the campground or Skull Rock, .5-mile to the east. This trail passes between rock piles and in and out of desert washes, with trail signs that interpret the diversity of plant life in the Mojave Desert.

The Road to Cottonwood

From a junction about 8 miles south of Twentynine Palms, the second main park road extends southward to the Cottonwood Spring area and on to Interstate 10, about 40 miles from the junction. Travelers bound for the Pinto Basin will leave the Mojave Desert, pass through a section of mixed Mojave and Colorado desert plants, and enter the Colorado Desert, a subdivision of the Sonora Desert between the Mojave Desert and the Colorado River.

About 3 miles down this road, the White Tank Campground contains the starting point for the short geology trail to Arch Rock. Interpretive signs explain the main geological processes that have occurred throughout the region.

Ten miles down this road the *Cholla Cactus Garden Nature Trail* leads past the jumping, or teddy-bear, cholla. The very bristly, thick-spined cactus joints are good for shading the plant, but not good for most animals that might come in contact with them. Sharp, barbed spines easily penetrate flesh or get snagged in hair. These segments are thus transported to another location, where they start other plants.

At the Ocotillo Patch, 2 miles farther along the road, an interpretive display helps visitors understand the life history of this plant.

From the Turkey Flats backcountry registration board, a 1-mile cross-country hike brings the explorer to a small area of sand dunes. Here one can see fringe-toed lizards and other dune-dwelling organisms. A hike to the top of Pinto Mountain is also possible from this point.

About 20 miles down Cottonwood Road, look for the junction with the Old Dale and Black Eagle Mine roads. These four-wheel-drive dirt roads offer other opportunities for exploration.

In the Cottonwood Spring area, the campground road also leads to the Cottonwood Oasis. This fan-palm oasis is a good place to look for migratory birds and provides access to several trails leading into remote canyons and other palm oases. The 3.5-mile *Lost Palms Oasis Trail* starts here.

Primitive Roads

Dirt roads in Joshua Tree provide close-up looks at the desert environment at slower speeds. Covington Flats can be reached by turning south on La Contenta Road from California 62 about 2

Prickly pear cactus, Eagle Mountains in background.

miles east of Yucca Valley. Typical high desert, with some of the area's largest Joshua trees, can be seen.

Queen Valley dirt roads can be accessed from either the Hidden Valley Campground, taking the road to the right, or east, or by taking the dirt road north opposite the *Geology Tour Road,* or by another dirt road that leads northwest 1 mile farther west. These are excellent opportunities to view the Joshua tree plant community close up, with possible looks at devil cactus and old-man cactus. These dirt roads also provide a good opportunity for bike riders.

Using an interpretive guidebook available for numbered stops along the Geology Tour Road, one can locate unusual features, including the Blue Cut Fault, the down-dropped Pleasant Valley, or Malapai Hill, a volcanic dome.

Four-wheel-drive roads into the Black Eagle Mine area, the Pinto Basin and Old Dale mining area, the Gold Park mining area, and Berdoo Canyon are available for the more adventuresome. Carry water and let someone know your destination and expected time of return. Rugged backcountry areas can be visited, as well as some of the early mining sites.

Overleaf: The fan palm, rare in the wild, grows on many streets in California, Arizona, and Florida.

Trails of Joshua Tree National Park

BOY SCOUT TRAIL: Starts at either Indian Cove Campground or the Keys West backcountry pullout .5 miles east of Quail Springs picnic area. Scenic trail through western side of Wonderland of Rocks. Strenuous (because of its length) hike, round trip 16 miles.

FORTYNINE PALMS OASIS: Entrance by Canyon Road south from California 62, 4 miles west of Twentynine Palms, about 1 mile to parking area. This trail is 3 miles round trip, offers good look at several stands of fan palms, evidence of past fires, and small pools of water. Moderate.

LOST HORSE MINE: Trail is accessed by dirt road 3 miles out Keys View Road. Four-mile round-trip hike provides close look at the Lost Horse Mine and the ten-stamp mill that was used for processing the ore. Moderately strenuous.

LOST PALMS OASIS: From the Cottonwood Oasis, a 7-mile round-trip hike to Lost Palms Canyon and Munsen Canyon will provide a look at two of the largest fan-palm oases in this area. Excellent opportunities for varieties of spring wildfowers. Strenuous.

MASTODON PEAK: Starting from Cottonwood Spring, a 3-mile round trip will provide a view of the Mastodon Mine and a chance to scale Mastodon Peak. Strenuous.

RYAN MOUNTAIN: Starting point is from Ryan Mountain parking area or Sheep Pass Campground. The hike is 3 miles round trip and offers excellent views of the Lost Horse and Queen valleys and the rock formations. Summit elevation is 5,461 feet.

CALIFORNIA RIDING AND HIKING TRAIL: Thirty-five miles for horses and hikers can be accessed from either end at Black Rock Campground or Twentynine Palms. Other access points include Covington Flats, Keys View Road, Geology Tour Road, or Ryan Campground. Excellent opportunity for longer hikes across the Mojave Desert. Carry water; none is available.

INTERPRETIVE TRAILS:

ARCH ROCK: This short nature trail winds through and around some good examples of the unusual rock formations found in Joshua Tree. Signs interpret the geologic story of the formation, weathering, and erosion of the granite rock piles.

BARKER DAM: With a theme of Water in the Desert, interpretive trail signs illustrate how plants and animals adapt to the amount of water available. Also providing a look at an early water impoundment, the trail passes the dam and loops past a Native American petroglyph (rock art) site. Total distance is 1 mile.

CAP ROCK: This nature trail provides a look at the variety of plants of the

Mojave Desert. The .5-mile loop paved trail is accessible for those who [use] wheelchairs.

CHOLLA CACTUS GARDEN: An interpretive trail provides a close look at the teddy-bear, or jumping, cholla, an extremely spiny and dangerous plant. Some animals, like the wood rat, have learned to live in harmony with the cholla, building their nests around its base, and using the spiny joints to line the entrances, preventing predators from entering.

COTTONWOOD SPRING: Trail signs interpret the plants of this region of the Colorado Desert and how they were used by Native American inhabitants. The trail begins at the Cottonwood Campground and ends at the Cottonwood Oasis, a distance of about 1 mile.

HIGH VIEW: Starting point is just northwest of Black Rock Campground. A trail guide is available at the campground Visitor Center. This 1.3-mile hike provides a good understanding of one of the higher regions of the Mojave Desert and the associated plant life. Summit Peak (elevation 4,500 feet) provides an excellent view of the surrounding desert.

HIDDEN VALLEY: The story of people in the high desert and how they utilized the resources is explained on interpretive signs along this 1-mile loop trail. Starting point is next to the Hidden Valley picnic area.

INDIAN COVE: A .6-mile loop trail from the upper west end of Indian Cove Campground provides interpretation of a typical desert wash ecosystem, including interrelationships of plants and animals inhabiting the area.

OASIS OF MARA: The Pinto Mountain Fault passes beneath the Oasis of Mara and is the reason for its existence. Here, the fault has been shifting over the years, grinding up rock layers, making them less permeable, thus forcing underground water toward the surface. When you walk into this oasis, you walk into a managed ecosystem. The interpretive signs along the trail explain the artificial resource management practiced at the site in order to assure its survival. This is a 1-mile, handicapped-accessible loop trail through a fan-palm oasis.

SKULL ROCK/JUMBO ROCKS: In the Jumbo Rocks Campground, look for the trail head near the Loop E entrance. From here, interpretive signs explain the rich biological diversity of the Mojave Desert. This portion of the trail is about .5 miles. A loop trail with additional plant labels continues from Skull Rock across the road and returns to the campground entrance. The total loop is 1.7 miles.

OTHER OPPORTUNITIES: Whether you are staying at the park or just driving through, there are many additional opportunities for exploration. Canyons and washes provide pathways into the interior; mountain peaks offer extensive views. Walking out at night provides opportunities to view a star-filled sky, unequaled in most areas of the world today. Whether climbing, camping, birdwatching, or photographing spring wildflowers, Joshua Tree National Park offers many opportunities to gain a greater understanding of the cultural and natural resources of the Colorado and Mojave deserts.

KINGS
CANYON
NATIONAL PARK

The South Fork of Kings Canyon.

KINGS CANYON NATIONAL PARK
THREE RIVERS, CALIFORNIA 93271
TEL.: (209) 335-2856

HIGHLIGHTS: Cedar Grove • Frypan Meadow • Roaring River Falls • Mist Falls • Paradise Valley • John Muir Trail • Manzanita Trail • Viola Falls • Ella Falls • General Grant Tree • Rae Lakes • Glen Pass • Fin Dome • Dragon Peak • Painted Lady • Mount Rixford • The Sphinx

ACCESS: From Fresno, 55 miles east on California 180.

HOURS: Grant Grove open year-round. Cedar Grove open from May through October.

FEES: Per car, and per person on bus. Golden Eagle, Golden Age, and Access passes accepted.

PARKING: At Big Stump picnic area, General Grant Tree, and Grant Grove Village.

GAS, FOOD, LODGING: At Grant Grove (year-round) and Cedar Grove (summer only).

VISITOR CENTER: At Grant Grove; open daily, 8 A.M.–5 P.M. At Cedar Grove; open daily, 8 A.M.–5 P.M., May to October.

GIFT SHOP: At Grant Grove Village and Cedar Grove.

PETS: Permitted on leash in campgrounds and on roads, but not in buildings or on trails.

PICNICKING: At designated sites throughout park.

HIKING: Many trails available.

BACKPACKING: Permitted with permit on more than 700 miles of trails.

CAMPGROUND: At Cedar Grove and Grant Grove area, 7 campgrounds with a total of 730 sites. First-come basis. Showers available. No hookups.

TOURS: In summer, free naturalist-guided walks are given daily. In winter, snowshoe walks are given weekends and holiday periods (snoeshoes provided for nominal fee). In English.

OTHER ACTIVITIES: Horseback riding (in summer), cross-country skiing, fishing (license required), and mountain climbing.

FACILITIES FOR DISABLED: Most buildings and marked campsites.

For additional information, see also Sites, Trails, and Trips on pages 193–202 and the maps on pages 182–183 and 197.

W HEN CALIFORNIA 180 IS ABOUT halfway to the bottom of the Kings River Canyon, it comes to a wide viewpoint. Dead ahead, two of the deepest gorges in North America, the South and Middle forks of the Kings River, rush together, carrying between their granite ribs tumults of white water. Thousands of feet higher, rising out of the ice-sculptured ridges bordering the chasms—the one separating the Middle and South forks is aptly named Monarch Divide—are knobby peaks. Because of that dramatically elevated ground, the viewer cannot see the Sierra Crest itself, 35 to 40 miles away, east and northeast. But the whole collapsing shape of the land indicates that such peaks must be there—high, frost-riven, streaked by snow, with quiet sapphire lakes caught in pale granite cups around their flanks. Just as surely as neighboring Sequoia National Park is a celebration of giant trees, Kings Canyon National Park is a celebration of the beauty and irresistible power of water in its various forms.

After reaching the narrow canyon bottom, the road turns up the South Fork toward the park boundary. When snowmelt is pouring out of the mountains during spring and early summer, the swollen

The Sierra Nevada rises sharply on its eastern flank, over 10,000 feet above the valley.

KINGS CANYON NATIONAL PARK

SEQUOIA NATIONAL PARK

Ranger Station
Campground
Picnic Area
ROAD
TRAIL

MILES

0 2 5 10 15

N

SIERRA
NATIONAL
FOREST

McCLURE
MEADOW

Mt. Darwin
El. 13830'

John Muir Trail

Muir Pass
El. 11955'

LECONTE
CANYON

Bishop
Pass

Mather Pass
El. 12100'

Split
Mtn.

Tabloose
Pass

Mt.
Pincipot
El. 13495'

Pinchot
Pass
El. 12050

John Muir Trail

Independence
El. 3923'

KINGS CANYON NATIONAL PARK

Mt. Woodworth
El. 12211'

Granite Pass
El. 10673'

REA LAKES

ONION VALLEY

Glen
Pass El. 11978'

Kennedy
Pass El. 10900'

Copper Creek Trail

Motor Nature Trail

Cedar Grove
Trails

CEDAR
GROVE

Obelisk
El. 9700'

MIDDLE FORK Kings River

Kings River

South Fork Kings River

180

stream at your elbow thunders over boulders into churning holes, then curls back on itself in ragged crests. Reflex waves recoil from the banks to clash with the main current; sunlight glistens on tall, erratic bursts of spray. Then, at the entrance to the park, the scouring action of vanished glaciers becomes evident. The canyon widens. Its bottom is more thickly forested, and the river loses some of its impetuosity. At Cedar Grove, good camping sites open up—a boon that the Native Americans who once occupied the area learned about hundreds of years ago.

HISTORY

Native American Settlers

The first humans who came into these Sierra valleys were Monaches, a Paiute group who had left its homeland on the east side of the Sierra and had migrated to the western foothills. Those who found the South Fork strung their small settlements along the canyon bottom from Cedar Grove eastward to Bubbs Creek, a principal tributary. Excavations have revealed many pestles and grinding holes that were used for pulverizing acorns, hammerstones that enabled their users to crack bones containing marrow, crude stone axes, and arrowheads and knives that had been chipped out of obsidian.

The Monache soon came to rely on acorns as a staple food. After grinding hulled acorns and removing tannic acid from the meal by leaching, the cooks boiled the meal into mush by dropping hot rocks into baskets filled with water. To supplement their diet, the Monache occasionally feasted on small game animals or deer. Deer hunters often disguised themselves under buckskins and antlers in order to be able to creep close to their prey and shoot the animal with arrows whose tips were sometimes poisoned with rotted deer liver impregnated with rattlesnake venom. What they wanted but did not have, they obtained by trading during the summer with Paiutes who were still living in the Owens Valley on the far side of the Sierra. An amazing trail, laid out as nearly due east as the terrain allows, ran up Bubbs Creek to Kearsarge Pass, 11,823 feet above sea level, and then dropped steeply down the eastern side. Large numbers of obsidian flakes found at pleasant sites along the way suggest regular rest stops where the traders whiled away the time by making arrowheads out of the obsidian they had obtained in the east.

Spanish Explorers and American Trespassers

The Spanish who colonized California apparently did not get far enough into the foothills to contact the Monaches. Spain's military

John Muir was a leading advocate of the establishment of national parks in the late nineteenth century. This is his sketch of Kings Canyon.

explorers, however, did find and name the main rivers that debouch into the Central Valley. Some of the names—Sacramento, San Joaquin, Merced—retain their original forms. Others became Anglicized. The river that Gabriel Moraga discovered on January 6, 1806, the anniversary of the day on which, it is said, the Magi first saw the infant Jesus, was named *El Rio de los Santos Reyes.* The River of the Holy Kings has since been shortened to Kings River.

During California's Mexican period, two groups of Americans who had entered the province without permission tried unsuccessfully to find ways out by crossing the Sierra in the vicinity of the

Kings River country. Jedediah Smith's trappers failed in the spring of 1827 because of huge snowdrifts. John Charles Frémont had no better luck in December 1844. Although he reached an elevation of 11,000 feet somewhere along the North Fork, Frémont was finally turned back by rugged terrain and a gathering storm. After the American occupation, militiamen, pursuing Indians in 1851, saw parts of the present-day park before being halted by what they declared was the roughest country they ever had encountered. In 1858, a Paiute guided five residents of Tulare County, probably prospectors, along the Indian trail up Bubbs Creek and over Kearsarge Pass. But no really sound idea of the uplifted country emerged until after a five-man detachment of the California State Geological Survey issued a report of a sweeping reconnaissance that it had made in 1864.

Early Exploration

That was the year of California's worst drought. After riding across the Central Valley through smothering June heat, the explorers, led by William H. Brewer, climbed gratefully into the shade of the forest belt south of the South Fork of the Kings River. On hearing of a fallen sequoia tree whose hollow trunk was big enough to admit a horse and rider, they set out on foot up an almost unscalable 2,000-foot slope, dragging along one unhappy saddle animal so that they could test the assertion. True enough. Brewer rode 76 feet into the log. When he stood up in the saddle, his head still did not reach the top. Probably it was the prostrate log in the Grant Grove that is known today as Fallen Monarch.

From the tree, the small party worked out a difficult route eastward into the canyon of the Roaring River, turned up a tributary creek, and confronted a broad, pyramidal 13,570-foot peak, set with its flanking pinnacles at the northern end of the Great Western Divide. Brewer's companions named it for him. The next day, eager to solve the geographic puzzle of the interlocking headwaters of the Kings, Kaweah, and Kern rivers, Brewer and Charles Hoffman, the party's topographer, spent eight laborious hours reaching its summit. They felt well repaid. "A hundred peaks over thirteen thousand feet," Brewer wrote in his journal, "many very sharp—deep canyons, cliffs in every direction, sharp ridges almost inaccessible to man on which human foot has never trod."

Excited by speculations that there were higher peaks than Mount Brewer in that granite jungle, Clarence King and Dick Cotter set out on a six-day hiking expedition to examine them.

After picking a way through snowy basins and past lakes still half clogged with ice, King and Cotter, using lariat ropes for support, clawed their way up 14,025-foot Mount Tyndall. A partial victory only, for to the south they saw two higher peaks, Mount Williamson (14,384 feet) and Mount Whitney (14,494 feet)—names they bestowed to honor prominent contemporary surveyors.

Brewer's own concern lay farther north with massive Mount Goddard (13,568 feet), for "from it," he wrote, "we could get the topography of a large region." So north the party went. When they reached Granite Pass, they discovered that they could not get their eleven saddle horses and five pack animals down the other side into the Middle Fork, near whose headwaters dark Goddard loomed. After climbing such peaks as were close at hand, they went back to the South Fork, turned up Bubbs Creek, and followed the Indian trail into the Owens Valley. They rode north for several miles, recrossed the crest, and tried to reach Goddard's summit from that direction—only to fail by 300 feet. No matter. By that time their field maps contained enough information about the lay of the land that the central Sierra could no longer be considered one of the major unexplored regions in the United States.

Another energetic explorer of the region was the naturalist John Muir, who zigzagged through parts of it in 1873 and again in 1875. Sometimes he traveled on horseback, with two or three companions. At other times he went entirely alone, walking and leading a disconsolate mule named Brownie, which found some of Muir's impulsive forays into trackless country more arduous than any pack animal should be expected to endure.

Muir claimed that he had named Giant Forest in Sequoia National Park, and he showed his approval of certain sections of the Kings River Canyon—especially Cedar Grove and Paradise Valley on the South Fork and Tehipite Valley on the Middle Fork—by calling each a "yosemite," for what could be more flattering, in his mind, than a comparison with the valley farther north that he loved beyond all else?

The real significance of the trips lay in the moral fervor that they awakened in him. Muir watched lumbermen at work—lumbermen who by then knew that the wood of sequoia trees is extremely brittle. The impact of a tree's falling badly shattered all but the lowest part of the huge bole, and even the clean lumber near the base was not strong enough for heavy construction. But because sequoia wood decays slowly, it had some value for shingles, fence posts, and grape stakes. So for the quick gleaning of small profits, down the trees went, along with the more commercially valuable ponderosa and sugar pines among which they grew.

Another distressing greed was that of sheepherders, who crowded their animals onto every available grassy site, until hills and meadows could no longer function as natural reservoirs. And although Muir knew that occasional natural fires are necessary for clearing the ground so that seeds and sunlight can reach it, he deplored the wanton setting of more conflagrations than the forest could absorb merely to stimulate the growth of more grass the following year. With like-minded conservationists of the Central Valley, Muir campaigned vigorously against the despoliation, not only because preservation of trees and ground cover would conserve water that was needed by farmers, but also because respect for nature was morally right.

Establishment of the Park

The effort bore small fruit. In 1890, the General Grant Grove of big trees and another grove a little farther north were set aside in a 2,560-acre reserve called General Grant National Park. At about the same time, Yosemite and Sequoia national parks came into being. But no official nod was made toward the Kings River country.

Park or no, growing numbers of visitors began trickling into the South Fork by trail. (A hike from Cedar Grove up Sheep Creek will give today's tourist some notion of what the experience was like.) During the mid-1930s, a decade after Sequoia National Park had been extended eastward to the crest of the Sierra, a dazzling automobile highway was finally hewn into the South Fork from General Grant National Park. Almost simultaneously, the construction of the famed 212-mile Muir horse and hiking trail, from Yosemite National Park to the top of Mount Whitney, was completed. Popularity was immediate and led to more demands that the Middle and South Fork river systems, from mountaintops to lower canyons, be protected. (The North Fork, already littered with man-made "lakes," was not seriously considered.) In 1940, Congress obliged by creating Kings Canyon National Park, extending its northern boundary far enough along the headwaters of the South Fork of the San Joaquin River to include the magnificent ring of colorful peaks that surrounds Evolution Valley. The General Grant Grove section and adjoining groves in Redwood Canyon, although attached geographically to Sequoia National Park, were included in the new Kings Canyon unit. Exuberant expansion—roughly 450,000 acres—yet ironically, the "yosemites" of Cedar Grove and Tehipite Valley remained outside because irrigationists and hydro-electric-power interests thought that the sites might someday be needed for reservoirs. Not until 1965 were the park boundaries redrawn to include them.

Quartz crystal is commonly found in the High Sierra.

GEOLOGY

Continental Drift and Uplift

The light-colored granite that is so prominent a feature of the Kings Canyon scene—and of all the Sierra—is, in a sense, the result of geological trespass. The original materials of the range were indurated (hardened) sediments that some 250 million years ago were bent, buckled, and thrust upward from their seabeds when the North American continental plate, drifting slowly westward across the earth's viscous mantle, collided with the much heavier, eastward-drifting plate that underlies part of the Pacific Ocean. In time, the uplifting ceased, and the hills eroded away, only to suffer the effects of another collision some 100 million years later. This time, the heavy Pacific plate was forced to slide underneath the lighter North American one. Intense frictional heat pro-

Overleaf: Sixty Lake Basin, in the northern section of the park, is a popular destination for backcountry hikers.

duced magma that pulsed upward and metamorphosed the overlying sedimentary strata: siltstone into shale, sandstone into quartzite, limestone into marble, volcanic material into schist. As the intrusive magma cooled, it crystallized into various forms of granite. Again the uplifting paused, and erosion, ever active, stripped away most—but by no means all—of the colorful, overlying metamorphic blanket.

About 60 million years ago, renewed tectonic pressures broke the eastern edge of the granite block loose from the surrounding land. But as the eastern edge lifted, the western stayed in place, like the hinged part of a trap door. As a result of the tilt, meandering streams quickened their pace and began transforming their valleys into deep, V-shaped canyons. On three more occasions the fault block was pushed higher, steepening the tilt and revitalizing the streams.

Glaciation and Erosion

The fourth and largest of these uplifts began something more than 1 million years ago and raised the Sierra crest to approximately its present elevation.

Thereafter, the Northern Hemisphere grew cold and wet. Throughout the High Sierra, except where wind swept some peaktops clean, snow accumulated to great depths. As drifts compacted into ice and weight increased, gravity tugged the masses down into the narrow canyons. Records of three such advances, each interrupted by warming trends, have been discovered by geologists. The last was halted and melted away between 10,000 and 20,000 years ago.

During the forward thrusts, each glacier picked up quantities of loose rock that studded its sides and bottom with an infinite variety of cutting points. With these "knives," and helped by glacial water that seeped into cracks, refroze, and split more fragments loose, the ice reshaped the land. It quarried huge amphitheaters called cirques into the sides of the peaks, created knife-edged ridges between them, and shaved certain exposed high points into steeples called horns. It straightened canyons by removing the ends of promontories and rounded their V-shaped bottoms into broad U's. Because the last glaciers were enormous—the one in the South Fork was 1,600 feet deep—they were able to dig farther into the main canyons than could the smaller tongues in the tributaries. The differential resulted in hanging valleys whose mouths end high above the bottom of the main gorges. Today, streams plunge down the drops in leaping cataracts that are punctuated by occasional waterfalls.

Cataracts in the high country often form the descending sections of glacial staircases. One theory that has been advanced to explain the phenomenon goes like this: if granite is fractured by many joints (vertical cracks), a glacier easily quarries out the rock between the joints, producing the precipitous slopes that form the risers of the steps. But massive granite, whose joints are widely spaced, is more resistant. The ice slides across it with little more effect than to polish the stone to almost mirror smoothness and, sometimes, to scoop out hollows that are later filled by gleaming lakes. These relatively level stretches are the treads of the stairway.

Not all erosion is glacial. Frost shatters wide stretches of closely jointed rock, creating rugged flutings in tall cliffs and repetitious ledges on gentler slopes. Colorful lichens, aided at times by weak vegetal acids in percolating water, slowly disintegrate rock into soil. More amazing are domes composed of massive granite whose surfaces, exfoliating bit by bit, finally produce huge, rounded knobs that generally rise out of the upper reaches of deep, steep-walled canyons. The most impressive one in the Kings Canyon region, and one of the most impressive in the entire Sierra, is Tehipite Dome, towering 3,000 feet above Tehipite Valley in the Middle Fork, reachable only by trail.*

SITES, TRAILS, AND TRIPS

More than most national parks, Kings Canyon has been designed to offer its visitors a true wilderness experience. The only highway, other than those in the General Grant section, reaches 8.5 miles from the park boundary past Cedar Grove to Road's End, a dead end near the junction of Copper Creek and the South Fork. All other travel must be on horses rented from the pack station at Cedar Grove, or on foot with the wayfarers' food and equipment loaded on their own backs or on the backs of burros they lead with them. Day hikes and rides range from easy jaunts along the canyon floor to more strenuous climbs beside nearby tributary creeks—Sheep, Hotel, Lewis—all of them offering, here and there along the way, wonderful relief-map views of the torn and tumbled country. Longer forays into the lake-spangled headwater basins of the watershed can occupy as much time as the participants wish—or as they can carry food for.

Cedar Grove

The trails in Cedar Grove vary from short, easy walks to strenuous hikes that require careful planning. In any case, hikers should take care no matter how long they are out or how far they travel. The

*For a discussion of the natural history of Kings Canyon, see Sequoia National Park, pages 267–274.

best estimate of physical exertion is to allow 1 hour for every 2 miles on level ground and for every 1,000 feet gained in elevation.

Lewis Creek Trail. This steep former sheep trail climbs through an area still recovering from the Lewis Creek fire of October 1980. Along the first 1.3 miles to the junction with the Hotel Creek Trail, dry chaparral vegetation is returning. The next 1.6 miles leads through a charred forest of yellow pine to Comb Creek and then on to the Lewis Creek crossing. Frypan Meadow is 1.6 miles beyond; the wildflowers that bloom in July and August make this 7,800-foot-high meadow a photographer's delight.

Hotel Creek Trail. The Hotel Creek Trail passes through an experimental forest-restoration area where burning was started in 1969; the cascade on Hotel Creek is a short distance beyond. The trail then climbs rather steeply by way of switchbacks to the top wall of the canyon, a total of 5.5 miles from the trail head. It is an 80-foot climb to the cascade, and a 1,200-foot ascent to the valley view.

Don Cecil Trail. The Don Cecil Trail to Sheep Creek and Lookout Peak passes through a forest of ponderosa pine, incense-cedar, white fir, and black oak. Before arriving at Sheep Creek (1 mile), which was named by early sheepherders, look back (north) at the 11,000-foot Monarch Divide. This ridge separates the drainage areas for the Middle and South forks of the Kings River. Lookout Peak is 5 miles ahead. Just beyond the peak is Summit Meadow (outside the park boundary), which presents a fine display of wildflowers in the summer.

River Trail. The short, easy River Trail is one of the most attractive hikes in the park; it leads both to Roaring River Falls (.5 mile) and to Zumwalt Meadow (1.6 miles). During years of heavy runoff, the river races through the gorge and over the falls with a tremendous roar; but the falls are impressive at any time. From the falls viewpoint only about 80 feet, or one-third, of the falls is visible; people who climb for a better view are too frequently swept over the falls when they slip and fall into the water. The river trail to Zumwalt Meadow leads off to the left just before the falls viewpoint.

Zumwalt Meadow Trail. Zumwalt Meadow was named for D. K. Zumwalt, an attorney for the Southern Pacific Railway Company, who was responsible for having this land set aside as a forest reserve in the early 1900s. It is .75 mile from the Zumwalt Meadow

Opposite: The General Grant Tree, 267 feet tall and 107.6 feet in circumference, is a major attraction of the park.

Trails of Kings Canyon National Park

Cedar Grove Area

Lewis Creek Trail: Starts on main road, 2 miles down canyon from Sentinel Campground entrance; 11 miles; 6 to 8 hours; 3,200-foot ascent; passes through charred remains of 1980 fire; Frypan Meadow, at 7,800 feet, is filled with wildflowers in July and August; carry water.

Hotel Creek Trail: Starts .25 mile down canyon from pack station; .25 mile round trip to the cascade (80-foot ascent); 5.5 miles (4 to 6 hours) round trip to valley view (1,200-foot ascent); passes through an experimental forest-restoration area begun in 1969.

Don Cecil Trail: Starts on main road, .25 mile up canyon from Sentinel Campground entrance; 2 miles round trip to Sheep Creek (600-foot ascent); 12.2 miles round trip to Lookout Peak (3,900-foot ascent); passes through ponderosa pine forest; magnificent views of 11,000-foot Monarch Divide; wildflowers abundant; strenuous climb beyond Sheep Creek; carry water.

River Trail: Starts at Roaring River Falls parking area; easy 1 mile round trip (.5 hour) to the falls; 3.2 miles round trip (2 to 3 hours) to Zumwalt Meadow; wide variety of trees and shrubs.

Zumwalt Meadow Trail: Starts at Zumwalt Meadow parking area; 1.5 miles round trip (1 to 2 hours) to meadow; 2.2 miles round trip (2 to 3 hours) to Roads End; easy walk along river, across a suspension bridge, through a forest, and on to the meadow.

Copper Creek Trail: Starts and ends at Roads End long-term parking area; 7 miles round trip; 6 to 8 hours; 2,800-foot ascent; one of the more strenuous trails in Cedar Grove area; switchbacks and steep climbing lead to the northern portions of the Kings Canyon backcountry; carry water.

Paradise Valley Trail: Starts at Roads End short-term parking area; 8 miles round trip (6 to 8 hours) to Mist Falls; 14 miles round trip (14 to 16 hours) to Paradise Valley (1,500-foot ascent); hot and dry first 2 miles to Bubbs Creek bridge, where right-hand branch leads off to Sphinx Creek and the backcountry; links with John Muir Trail at Upper Woods Creek.

Grant Grove Area

Manzanita Trail: Starts at far end of Visitor Center parking area; ends at Park Ridge; 3.3 miles round trip; 2 hours; 800-foot ascent; climbs up Manzanita Hill and back along the Azalea Trail; first section in forest; steep in places.

Park Ridge Trail: Starts at the Panoramic Point parking area; ends at fire lookout tower (manned May to October); 4.7 miles round trip; 3 hours; 200-foot ascent; easy trail that provides magnificent view of Hume Lake in Sequoia National Forest and the San Joaquin Valley.

Dead Giant Loop Trail: Starts and ends at extreme end of General Grant Tree parking area; 2.2 miles round trip; 1.5 hours; 400-foot ascent; easy trail that first goes downhill along an old road through forest of sequoia, fir, and pines, to the Dead Giant and the Sequoia Lake Overlook; 6-mile loop trail at end affords a view of the lower Kings Canyon and remnants of the 1955 fire, which destroyed 13,000 acres of forest.

SUNSET TRAIL: Starts across the main highway from the Visitor Center (take trail going to left below highway, skirting Sunset Campground); 6 miles round trip; 3 to 4 hours; 1,400-foot ascent; leads to Viola and Ella Falls, and to Sequoia Lake; return by same trail or follow old road to General Grant Tree parking area.

GENERAL GRANT TREE TRAIL: Starts and ends at Visitor Center or at the General Grant Tree parking area; 2.3 miles round trip; 1.5 hours; easy walk to the famous tree named after the Civil War general and president; passes the Michigan Tree, which fell in 1931.

NORTH GROVE LOOP TRAIL: Starts and ends at extreme end of the lower General Grant Tree parking area; 1.5 miles round trip; 1 to 1.5 hours; easy walk that follows old one-way road through grove of giant sequoias and sugar pines.

SEE MAP ON PAGES 182–183.

parking area to the meadow, and 1.1 miles to Road's End. After an easy walk along the river, hikers will reach a suspension bridge across the South Fork and should turn left after crossing the river. The trail climbs onto the talus slope above the meadow for some magnificent views. A return loop trail goes around the meadow.

Copper Creek Trail. The Copper Creek Trail is one of the most strenuous in the Cedar Grove area. By a series of switchbacks, it climbs steeply into the Kings Canyon backcountry. After 1 mile, hikers will have excellent views of the glaciated Kings Canyon, Bubbs Creek Canyon, and Zumwalt Meadow. This is superb backpacking country.

Mist Falls and Paradise Valley Trail. The Mist Falls and Paradise Valley Trail is one of the most popular trails in the park. Thousands of backpackers travel this route to the high country in the summer. The trail is hot and dry for the first 2 miles to Bubbs Creek Bridge, where the trail splits. The right branch goes off 2 miles to Sphinx Creek and on into the backcountry. The main trail continues straight ahead for 2 miles to Mist Falls and for another 3 miles to Paradise Valley. Look for the many small cascades and waterfalls on Glacier and Gardiner creeks across the canyon. Once at Paradise Valley, the trail is on an easier grade than the 1,500 feet climbed thus far; it meanders through the valley, linking up with the John Muir Trail at Upper Woods Creek.

Grant Grove

The Grant Grove trails do not lead to the backcountry; instead, they are just a few minutes' walk from the road and turnoffs and take visitors into an area of solitude and beauty. There are many trails; just a few of them are described here.

Manzanita Trail. The Manzanita Trail is a 3.3-mile, 2-hour round trip that leads from the Visitor Center parking area up Manzanita Hill to Park Ridge and back by the Azalea Trail. Azaleas abound along the trail, as does manzanita, a shrub identified by its smooth red bark, roundish thick leaves, and small applelike berries. The Azalea Trail meets a tributary of Sequoia Creek a short way downhill, and from there leads to a connector trail to the South Boundary. The hiker then crosses the Wilsonia Road and heads back to the Visitor Center.

Opposite: Muir Hut was built in the early 1930s by the Sierra Club to provide refuge to hikers on the John Muir Trail.

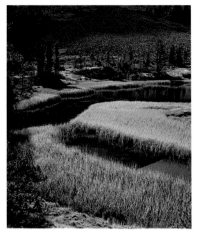

Bullfrog Lake.   *Rae Lakes Basin.*

Park Ridge Trail. The 4.7-mile Park Ridge Trail begins at the Panoramic Point parking area and leads first to the point, .25 mile from the trail head, for an excellent view of the valleys and mountains to the east; in the foreground is Hume Lake in Sequoia National Forest. A little farther along the trail there is a view of the San Joaquin Valley and, if the sky is clear, the Coast Range 100 miles to the west; the elevation at this point is about 7,540 feet. The fire tower at the end of the trail is operated from May to October; permission must be obtained to ascend. Hikers must retrace their route from the tower.

Dead Giant Loop Trail. The Dead Giant Loop Trail is an easy, 2.2-mile, 1.5-hour round trip that begins at the extreme end of the General Grant Tree parking area and proceeds downhill along an old road to a meadow, off of which a short trail leads to the Dead Giant, a large sequoia felled some years ago. The trail continues to the left to Sequoia Lake Overlook, from where there is an excellent view of the lake. The lake, now the location of YMCA camps, was constructed around 1890 as a millpond to supply water for the flume to carry lumber to the San Joaquin Valley. A short distance back up the ridge, the return trail turns to the right. Off to the left of this ridge can be seen the lower Kings Canyon. From here the trail leads back to the road and the parking area.

Sunset Trail. The Sunset Trail is 6 miles round trip, takes about 3 to 4 hours, and is strenuous; but the rewards are many. It leads through an open and varied forest of firs, pines, and oaks to Viola

Falls, Ella Falls, and Sequoia Lake. The trail begins across the main highway from the Visitor Center, skirts the Sunset Campground, branches to the right .25 mile later, and then winds downhill. After about 1.25 miles, it intersects with the South Boundary Trail. Hikers follow the South Boundary Trail for .25 mile to Viola Falls, sometimes called Laughing Waters Cascades. In the spring and early summer the falls are spectacular with water from snowmelt. Ella Falls is about 1 mile farther along the trail toward Sequoia Lake. The old park road leads from the lake to the General Grant Tree parking area, where another trail returns to the Visitor Center.

General Grant Tree Trail. The General Grant Tree, one of the most popular and famous landmarks in the park, is only a short distance from the Visitor Center. The round-trip walk is a little over 2 miles, and it takes only 1.5 hours. The trail begins at the Visitor Center, passes through Azalea Campground and Columbine picnic area, and leads to the self-guiding loop trail around the General Grant Tree. Or, start at the Grant Tree parking area for a loop of only one-third mile.

North Grove Loop Trail. The pleasant 1.5-mile North Grove Loop Trail begins at the end of the lower General Grant Tree parking area and follows an old one-way road through a beautiful grove of giant sequoias, sugar pines, white firs, and dogwoods. Just to the right of the first junction, an unpaved road leads downhill to a meadow where many giant sequoias grow. The trail follows the road to the left up the paved road to the parking area.

High Country

The 43-mile hike to the Rae Lakes—considered by some to be as beautiful a spot as any in the High Sierra—and back begins at Road's End. Although the walk can be completed in 5 days, it is well to allow 2 or 3 more for loitering—fishing, sketching, or just sitting still. Obtain permits at the ranger station. This is one of the most popular hikes in the High Sierra; for the sake of the land and the enjoyment of the campers, the National Park Service has placed limits on the number of visitors who can start the hike each day and has restricted camping at most lakes to a single night.

From the parking area, walk 2 miles—hot, dry miles late in the summer—to the bridges that lead across the South Fork to the steep, deep trench of Bubbs Creek. The trail climbs along the north side of the impetuous creek, sometimes high on the wall above it. The character of the forest changes: soft-needled firs now, slender lodgepoles and Jeffrey pines, and occasional aspens, their white trunks gleaming against the darker background. Past avalanche chutes carved into granite and sudden meadows spangled with wildflowers. Reaching the Muir Trail is always exciting—there is no more famous pathway in the West. You swing left along it, still climbing. The forest thins out; the foxtail and white-bark pines grow gnarled. Fat, golden-hued marmots interrupt their sun baths long enough to whistle as you approach; pikas scurry with their harvests of grass among the talus boulders; gray and black Clark's nutcrackers scold like the raucous jays they resemble. And still the switchbacks climb and climb, leveling out only occasionally to skirt small tarns and gentle meadows. Thin sheets of water slide like moving glass over low granite ledges, beside white marsh-marigolds and maroon shooting stars.

Glen Pass, nearly 12,000 feet high, opens the way to the Rae Lakes and a stupendous view. From there, knee-jarring switchbacks lead down to the scooped-out hollows, rimmed with thin strands of trees, that hold the lakes. On still mornings they are shining mirrors for the striking thumb of granite called Fin Dome and for Dragon Peak, Painted Lady, and Mount Rixford, whose colored bands of metamorphic rock, called roof pendants, somehow escaped the erosive forces that elsewhere stripped bare the intrusive granite.

From the lakes the return to the South Fork is by way of the tilted trench of Woods Creek, as profound as the one that encases Bubbs Creek. The descent of the South Fork brings you to the magnificent, 3-mile-long "yosemite" of Paradise Valley. Then the trail begins to pitch downward again; toward Mist Falls, the glacier-sharpened point of the Sphinx comes into view, its huge flanks smoothed and grooved by rock-studded masses of ice that may return eons hence to finish their work.

Here is another of those spots where it is good to sit still for a moment and contemplate the riddle of an older sphinx, though more recently named, than the one beside the Nile. Earth cycles: new roots finding energy in decay; the ceaseless circulation of water from sea to land and back again; mountains raised up and worn down to provide materials for more uplifts. These are old mysteries that are often forgotten during the day's distractions, but they grow fresh again when you ponder as monumental a carving as the Sphinx or as tiny a thing as a drop of dew. Part of the Park Service's task is to maintain that freshness amid increasing hordes of people. It is not an easy dilemma to resolve, but perhaps it can be done if the land receives from all its visitors the one boon it needs most—respect.

Opposite: Cascading streams are a characteristic sight in Kings Canyon.

LASSEN
VOLCANIC
NATIONAL PARK

Lava formations from the 1914 eruption of Lassen Peak frame Mount Shasta.

Lassen Volcanic National Park
Mineral, California 96063
Tel.: (916) 595-4444

Highlights: Emerald Lake • Hot Rock • Lake Helen • Chaos Jumbles • Horseshoe Lake • Juniper Lake • Hot Creek Valley • Badger Flat • Summit Lake • Hat Lake • Nobles Pass

Access: From Red Bluff, 40 miles east via California 36. From Redding, 40 miles east via California 44. From Susanville, 65 miles west via California 36.

Hours: Open year-round; park roads and trails open June through September. Park road closes during winter.

Fees: At entrance, per car.

Parking: Throughout park.

Gas: At Manzanita Lake Camper Service Store.

Food, Lodging: In park, Drakesbad Guest Ranch.

Visitor Center: At Loomis Museum, Manzanita Lake.

Gift Shop: At Manzanita Lake and southwest entrance.

Pets: Permitted on leash in front country, but not permitted on trails.

Picnicking: At designated sites throughout park.

Hiking: More than 150 miles of trails. Boil water.

Backpacking: Permitted with permit. Boil water.

Campgrounds: Tents permitted from May to October. Fires only in designated areas.

Tours: In English. Full schedule of interpretive programs.

Other Activities: Skiing, swimming, boating, and fishing.

Facilities for Disabled: Restrooms and Visitor Center.

For additional information, see also Sites, Trails, and Trips on pages 219–227 and the map on pages 208–209.

WITHOUT ANY WARNING . . . A HUGE COLumn of black smoke shot upward with a roar . . . and in an instant the air was filled with smoke, ashes, and flying rocks from the crater. They all ran for their lives." This eruption of Lassen Peak, described by B. F. Loomis, happened on June 14, 1914, surprising a party of local lumbermen who were standing at the crater's very edge. One hid behind an overhanging ledge; another slid down a steep snowbank; and a third had the misfortune of being hit by a block that gashed his shoulder and broke his collarbone—the only known injury during the entire seven years of Lassen's activity.

Small explosive eruptions of Lassen Peak began on May 30, 1914, and continued with varying intensity until 1921. The activity climaxed on May 22, 1915, with a major explosive blast that leveled 3 square miles of forest, and held the attention of the fascinated American public for the next few years while the eruptions waned in intensity. Until the eruption of Mount St. Helens in 1980, Lassen Peak had been the only volcano in the forty-eight contiguous United States to erupt in the twentieth century. Although Lassen's eruption was a significant one, the remote location and low population density forestalled disaster, and the final result was a fortunate one: the inclusion of this wild and beautiful area on the honor roll of U.S. national parks.

Lassen Volcanic National Park is 200 miles north-northeast of San Francisco. Its 106,000 acres of volcanic terrain lie east of the northern end of the Central Valley of California and comprise the southern end of the Cascade Range, which stretches from northern California through Oregon and Washington into southern British Columbia. With elevations in the park ranging from 5,300 feet to the 10,457-foot summit of Lassen Peak, the winters are cold with deep snowfalls, and the summers are cool and dry. Besides its volcanic and thermal-spring attractions, Lassen is a lovely wilderness of coniferous forests and mountain meadows, worthy of a visit for a day or for a full summer. Destruction and creation, two of the many faces of nature, can both be witnessed here.

HISTORY

Native Americans

Several tribes of Native Americans lived in the Lassen area, hunting in the higher country in the summer and migrating to lower surrounding lands in the winter.

The Yana tribes lived southwest of Lassen Peak along the streams that lead into California's great Central Valley, subsisting

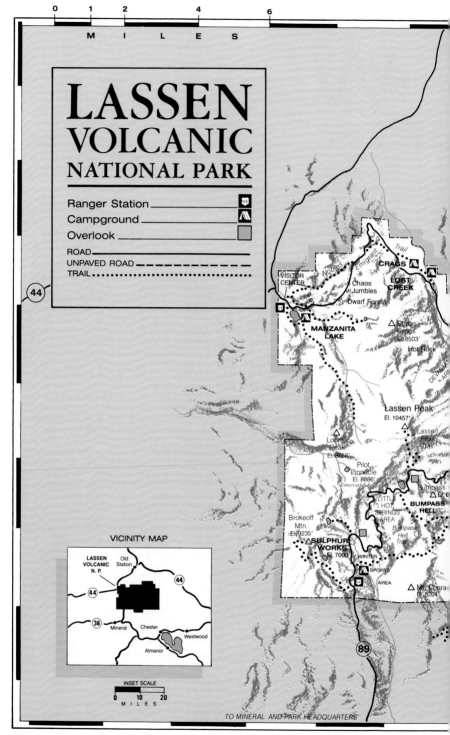

LASSEN
VOLCANIC
NATIONAL PARK

Ranger Station ———————— 🏢
Campground ———————— 🏕️
Overlook ———————— 🔲
ROAD ————
UNPAVED ROAD — — — — — —
TRAIL ••••••••••••••••••••••••••••

⑷

M I L E S

0   1   2   4   6

CRAGS

LOST CREEK

VISITOR CENTER

Chaos Jumbles
Dwarf Forest

MANZANITA LAKE

Chaos Crags
El 8503'

Hot Rock

Noble's   Emigrant   Trail

Lassen Peak
El. 10457'

Lassen Peak Trail

Loomis Peak
El 8658'

Pilot Pinnacle
El. 8886'

Emerald

Bumpass
△ El. 8

BUMPASS HELL

LITTLE HOT SPRINGS AREA

Brokeoff Mtn.
El. 9235'

Bumpass Hell Trail

SULPHUR WORKS
El. 7000'

WINTER

SPORTS AREA

Mt. Conard
El. 8204'

89

TO MINERAL AND PARK HEADQUARTERS

VICINITY MAP

LASSEN VOLCANIC N. P.

Old Station

⑷

⑷

�36

Mineral   Chester

Westwood

Almanor

INSET SCALE
0   10   20
M I L E S

LASSEN
NATIONAL
FOREST

Prospect Peak
El. 8338'

El. 6100'
BUTTE
LAKE

BADGER FLAT
El. 6290'

Nobles Emigrant Trail

Cinder Cone
El. 6907'

Fantastic
Lava
Beds

Painted Dunes

Fairfield
Peak
El. 7272'

Cinder
Cone
Trail

Snag
Lake

Hat Mtn.
El. 7635'

SUMMIT
LAKE

Red
Cinder
Cone
El. 8008'

Summit Lake
El. 6700'

Pacific
Crest
Trail

Crater
Butte
El. 7267'

Grassy
Lake

CAMERON
MEADOW

Reading
Peak
El. 8701'

Horseshoe
Lake

HORSESHOE
LAKE

CLOSED IN WINTER

Kings Creek

JUNIPER
LAKE
El. 6792'

Juniper
Lake

GS
EEK
ADOWS
00'

Devil's
Kitchen

FLATIRON RIDGE

Drakesbad

WARNER VALLEY

Boiling
Springs
Lake Trail

Boiling Springs
Lake

Mt.
Harkness
El. 8045'

Sifford
Mtn.
El. 7608'

TO CHESTER

mainly on the abundant acorns from the foothill oak trees. By about 1900, the settlers and ranchers who were moving into the area had dispersed or killed most of the Yana, and the survivors had been driven into hiding in remote mountain valleys. In 1911, years after the last Yana had been seen, a young Indian who was almost dead from starvation was found wandering in the outskirts of the town of Oroville. He spoke a dialect that none of the local Indians could understand, and gradually an incredible story began to unfold. This Indian, whom anthropologists named Ishi, was the last survivor of the Yahi tribe of the Yana, and probably the last American Indian to live by purely Indian ways. His appearance in "civilization" was an act of desperation when he could no longer survive alone.

Anthropologists found a gold mine of information preserved in Ishi, and were able to piece together much that had been either unknown or misunderstood about the American Indian culture. Ishi came to believe that the whites were "smart but not wise, knowing many things including much that is false." Nature remained for him the ultimate truth.

Indian tribes other than the Yana made more gradual transitions to coexistence with settlers, and some of their stories have been assimilated into local folklore. The Atsugewi, some of whom still live north of the park, have a legend about a warrior chief who

Tourists visit Hot Rock, not long after it was deposited by mudflows following the 1915 eruption. The boulder, now cool, is still there.

Eruptions of Lassen Peak were common from 1914 through 1917.

dug his way into Lassen Peak to recover his abducted lover. Impressed by his power, the mountain spirits invited him to marry his beloved and live with them inside the peak. The storm clouds that sometimes are seen above the volcano are said to be smoke from the warrior chief's peace pipe.

The Maidu tribes, who lived south of Lassen in the area that is now covered in part by impounded Lake Almanor, had an explanation for the earthquakes that often are felt in this volcanic region; they believed that the world was anchored in a great sea by five ropes, and that earthquakes occurred when the gods were angry and tugged on the ropes. The Atsugewi also have an earthquake legend: one time the shaking of the ground was so bad that people who lived on flat land became sick, and people who lived in the canyons were buried by rocks falling from the cliffs. It is possible that this legend had its origin in the great avalanche that formed Chaos Jumbles about 300 years ago.

The Indians knew Lassen Peak by several names, including Water Mountain, Little Shasta, Broken Mountain, Mountain-ripped-apart, and Fire Mountain. This last and most forthright has a good ring to it in its original—*Amblu Kai.*

Early Explorers

The Spanish and the Americans conferred their own names on this "unnamed" mountain. Don Luis Arguello, one of the early governors of Spanish California, called the mountain San José; explorer Jedediah Smith called the landmark St. Joseph; and Charles Wilkes on his 1841 map altered this name to Mount St. Joseph.

About this time the man for whom the peak was eventually named appeared on the scene. Peter Lassen, a Danish blacksmith, was lured to California by immigrant fever in the years just before the gold rush. He was given a large tract of land east of the Sacramento River by the Mexican government, established a ranch there, and set himself up to guide parties to California by way of his "Lassen's Cutoff."

Unfortunately, Peter Lassen was something less than a natural woodsman, and the route he chose was circuitous and extraordinarily difficult. He used the now-Lassen Peak as a landmark, but occasionally mistook Mount Shasta for Lassen, making the trip even more hair-raising than usual. Some of his emigrant parties almost starved, and others were aroused to fury when they realized that their guide was frequently lost. Local legend has it that one outraged party forced Lassen at gunpoint to climb the peak that now bears his name to get his bearings. When the groups eventually reached Peter Lassen's ranch, however, his kindness and hospitality generally won back their admiration.

Establishment of the Park

As more and more settlers moved into the region, the need for lumber increased. By 1907, lumbering was threatening the magnificent forests of the Lassen area; to protect it, Lassen Peak and Cinder Cone were set aside as national monuments. Lassen Peak was assumed to be extinct, but the eruptions of 1914 and 1915 created so much nationwide interest that in 1916 the area was given full national park status.

Ancient Volcanism

The geological story that is still evident in the surface rocks began about 2 to 3 million years ago with the growth of the first of three ancient volcanic centers in the Lassen area. Geological mapping by Michael Clynne identified these three ancient centers as Dittmar Volcano in the southeastern part of the park, Tehama Volcano in the southwestern corner of the park, and Maidu Volcano to the southwest of the park (near the town of Mineral). None of these once-massive volcanic peaks is still visible as an obvious volcanic cone; explosion and collapse, and the ravages of more than 1 million years of waxing and waning glacial erosion, have torn these volcanoes into rugged mountains and valleys. Only by careful mapping of the remaining volcanic rocks can their majesty be reconstructed in the mind's eye of geologists.

The youngest of the three ancient volcanoes was Mount Tehama. Its main cone-building stage, from a vent in the vicinity of the present Sulphur Works thermal-spring area, lasted from about 600,000 to 350,000 years ago. Mount Tehama was a strato-volcano, so called because its cone was built up of layers of lava and volcanic ash. Mount Fuji in Japan is the archetypal strato-volcano, but there is no way of knowing if the cone of Mount Tehama, probably 11,000

Manzanita Lake, which was formed by an avalanche that blocked Manzanita Creek, reflects 10,457-foot Lassen Peak.

feet high, was as strikingly symmetrical as that of Mount Fuji.

Following its long buildup, Mount Tehama exploded and collapsed into a 3-mile-wide basin called a caldera. Glacial erosion has destroyed much of the shape of this caldera, but the remnant peaks—seen today as Brokeoff Mountain, Mount Diller, Pilot Pinnacle, and Mount Conard—mark its rim.

Thick flows and domes of viscous lava then poured from the northern and western flanks of collapsed Mount Tehama; they now form the high western peaks of Lassen Volcanic National Park. These silica-rich volcanic rocks, infamous for their explosive behavior, erupted during the last 250,000 years. They issued from many vents, the youngest and most prominent of which are Lassen Peak (25,000 years old) and Chaos Crags (only 1,100 years old).

Lassen Peak and Chaos Crags are interesting volcanic features called lava domes, great upwellings of viscous lava that is so sticky that instead of flowing away from the vents, it forms huge mounds at the surface over the conduits that delivered it from below.

Modern Eruption

The 1914 eruption of Lassen Peak was just one of thousands of volcanic eruptions that have occurred in the Lassen area in the last million years. But it was unique in having been witnessed by many observers and carefully documented by the pictures of B.F. Loomis and other photographers.

Bert McKenzie, a resident of Chester, California, reported the first explosion of steam and volcanic ash that rose several hundred feet over the peak on the late afternoon of May 30, 1914. The next day a forest ranger climbed to the summit and found that a small new crater, about 30 feet across, had been blown open on the inside wall of Lassen's 1,000-foot-wide and 360-foot-deep summit crater. More than 170 steam explosions during the next year blasted out old volcanic debris, enlarging the active crater until it encompassed the entire former crater.

Almost a year after the steam explosions had begun, molten rock reached the surface and overflowed the crater, tumbling in a deep-red sheet down the western side of Lassen Peak. Some of this same lava apparently also flowed or avalanched down the eastern side of the peak, rapidly melting the snow. The melt water mixed with loose volcanic ash from previous eruptions to form large mudflows that moved as far as 30 miles down the valleys of Lost Creek and Hat Creek. Mudflows are floods of water that is so laden with sediment that it has the consistency of wet cement; they are dense

Opposite: Bumpass Hell is the most active thermal area in the park.

enough to transport huge boulders and knock down trees. Mudflows are much more destructive than are floods of clearer water, for when the crest recedes, the mud and rocks remain, filling homes, fields, and entire valleys. Miraculously, the few inhabitants along Lost Creek and Hat Creek, warned by barking dogs and upstream neighbors, escaped the Lassen mudflows, and no one was hurt.

The largest explosive eruption occurred on May 22, 1915. A huge mushroom cloud, 7 miles high and seen as far away as Sacramento, formed over Lassen Peak. The cloud was accompanied by a lateral blast of hot gas and lava fragments that blew down a swath of forest 1 mile wide and 3 miles long on the eastern side of Lassen Peak. The devastated area is still visible, but a young forest is now growing there and will eventually heal the scar. Smaller explosive eruptions continued through 1916 and ended in 1917; steam "puffs" were occasionally seen until 1921, but since then Lassen Peak has remained dormant.

Thermal Springs and Future Eruptions

Ground water that is heated by hot rocks in the volcanic conduits keep several thermal-spring areas warm to boiling: Sulphur Works, Devil's Kitchen, Hot Springs Creek, Boiling Springs Lake, Terminal Geyser, and Bumpass Hell—an area named for an old-timer who had the misfortune to break through the crust of a hot spring and badly burn his leg. Although these thermal features at Lassen are not as large and spectacular as those in Yellowstone National Park, they indicate that much of the southern part of the park and the area beyond it may be a large geothermal system with underground steam contained in the pores and cracks of subsurface rocks. The thermal-spring areas, with some steam jets as hot as 318° F, are simply surface leakages of this vast underground steam reservoir. If geothermal power were to be developed south of the park, it could affect the thermal features within the park. The dilemma of economic development versus preservation of nature will probably soon raise its horns.

The central and eastern areas of Lassen Volcanic National Park are a rolling tableland of older lava flows with a few well-preserved volcanic forms like Hat Mountain, Crater Butte, and Fairfield Peak. Cinder Cone, a 700-foot young volcano in the northeastern corner of the park, has erupted basaltic lava and ash several times over the past 400 years. Geologic evidence indicates that Cinder Cone dates back to approximately 1750 to 1800. Several of the small, beautiful lakes that decorate the Lassen landscape, especially in the eastern part of the park, were formed by lava flows and glacial deposits that damned the stream drainages.

What is next in volcanic activity in the Lassen area? Probably a long wait followed by renewed eruptions at or near Cinder Cone. Eruption of a new lava dome near Chaos Crags is another reasonable possibility. Only one thing is certain: nature will continue to create violence, majesty, and beauty in this volcanic wonderland.

NATURAL HISTORY

Climate and Precipitation

Lassen Volcanic National Park is located at the junction of the Sierra Nevada Range to the south and the Cascade Range to the north. Both ranges are noted for their heavy winter snowfalls—up to 30 feet or more from the moisture-laden Pacific storms. In the summer, the Pacific storms are often blocked by a high-pressure area off the coast of California, and summer weather is generally dry except for occasional thunderstorms. The temperature is strongly affected by altitude, which ranges from 5,300 to 10,457 feet. The highest elevations are cold in summer and severely cold in winter; the lower areas are warm on sunny summer days, cool on summer nights, and cold in winter.

Flowers and Trees

Volcanic rocks slowly disintegrate into rich soils that support lush vegetation, and Lassen is a showcase of the results. Some of the higher elevations are above timberline, but the rolling tableland of the central and eastern areas of the park is covered by majestic coniferous forests and lovely mountain meadows with as elegant a display of wildflowers as can be found anywhere in the Cascade Range.

From May to October, flower watchers can follow the melting snowpack up the mountainsides as nature progressively uncovers its gardens. Brilliant red snow plants push through the edges of the retreating snow, followed by fawn lilies (dogtooth violets), alpine shooting stars, Columbia monkshood, and a profusion of other early flowers. The lavish display of blooms along the roads and trails changes as the seasons progress, and the moisture-loving corn lilies and monkey flowers give way to lupine, pussy paws, and the ubiquitous mountain mule-ears in drier locations. Lassen has several hundred species of wildflowers, and some can be seen until the snow falls again.

Lassen's forests are made up of trees that are native to the Sierra and Cascade ranges. Fine stands of Douglas-fir, incense cedar, and

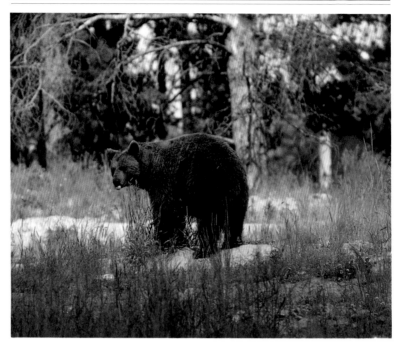

Although bears live in the park, they are shy and restrict themselves to the backcountry.

ponderosa pine grow at lower elevations, while red fir and lodgepole pine flourish in the higher forests. Nearer to timberline are beautiful groves of mountain hemlock—a tree much admired by John Muir—and gnarled specimens of the white-bark pine.

Perhaps the most unusual and least-recognized plants at Lassen are the algae that grow in the hot-spring waters between 125° F and 196° F. Millions of these microscopic organisms provide a spectrum of colors that can be seen in the thermal-spring areas.

Wildlife

Fishing is allowed in the backcountry lakes; most of the lakes are accessible only by trail or an occasional dirt road. Most fishermen, however, are disappointed; no stocking is going on, and natural reproduction is low. The lakes are havens for migratory birds; in the fall, it is not unusual to see large numbers of waterfowl, including Canada geese and wood ducks, on their way to wintering grounds. These and all other animals are protected in the park, of course, and some have become quite tame. Black-tailed and mule deer, fox, marten, marmot, chickaree, and black bear are often seen, and begging chipmunks can hardly be avoided.

Lassen Park Road

The summer visitor to Lassen Volcanic National Park can see many of the main features in one day, although that is just an appetizer for a longer stay. A 34-mile highway (closed in winter) climbs and winds around the southern, eastern, and northern sides of Lassen Peak.

From the south, at the junction of California 36 and California 89, the Lassen Park Road (California 89) climbs 4.9 miles to the entrance station at 6,650 feet. The road is kept open only this far in winter.

At 6 miles and 7,000 feet, the road passes *Sulphur Works* thermal-spring area, near the center of the eroded volcano Mount Tehama. Prowling off the boardwalks or well-trodden trails around the steaming cracks, hot springs, and mud pots can lead to painful and sometimes crippling burns. The thin crust of apparently firm ground may give way into scalding mud beneath. With a little caution and common sense these hazards can be avoided, and the sights to be found far outweigh the risks. The rotten-egg smell is caused by hydrogen sulfide gas, and the yellow, pink, and white clays are formed by the breakdown of volcanic rocks in the hot, acidic springs.

At 6.8 miles, there is a fine view of 9,235-foot Brokeoff Mountain across the valley to the west.

At 7.8 miles, a striking view of Lassen Peak appears to the north.

Emerald Lake, at 10.7 miles and 8,000 feet, fills a small glacially eroded basin.

The start of Bumpass Hell Trail is at 11.1 miles. Bumpass Hell is Lassen's most interesting thermal-spring area and well worth the 3-mile round-trip hike.

Lake Helen, at 11.3 miles and 8,164 feet, is a beautiful glacial lake that is often still partly frozen in early summer. The trail that zigzags up Lassen Peak can be seen across the lake to the northwest.

The Lassen Peak Trail parking area, at 12.4 miles, is the start of a strenuous but worthwhile climb of 2,000 feet along a 2.5 mile (one way) rocky trail.

The highest point on the highway is 12.4 miles from the junction of California 36 and California 89. Snowbanks may last all summer at this 8,512-foot elevation. The highway next winds down the southeastern slopes of Lassen and Reading peaks.

At 14.5 miles and 8,000 feet, Prospect Peak, a shield volcano (so named for its gently sloping sides) can be seen to the far northwest.

Passing through Kings Creek Campground, at 16.8 miles and 7,400 feet, the road leads through fine stands of red fir and some mountain hemlock. By *Summit Lake*, at 21.3 miles and 6,700 feet, red fir is still

Trails of Lassen Volcanic National Park

Forest Lake and Brokeoff Mountain Trail: Starts at road marker 2; ends at Brokeoff Mountain; 7.4 miles round trip; 5 hours; 2,600-foot ascent; steady uphill climb for 2 miles; rugged mountain scenery; wildflowers are abundant every season; excellent views of other peaks, including Mount Shasta.

Mill Creek Falls Trail: Starts at Southwest Campground; ends at the highest waterfall in park; 4.6 miles round trip; 2.5 hours; 600-foot ascent, but first descends about 300 feet; rather steep climb for 1,000 feet; wildflowers and birds in abundance.

Ridge Lakes Trail: Starts at Sulphur Works parking area; ends at several small lakes in a cirque below the rim of Mount Tehama Caldera; 2.2 miles round trip; 2 hours; 1,000-foot ascent; passes through red fir and white pine forests; the striking leopard lily is found on this trail.

Sulphur Works Trail: Starts and ends at east end of parking area; .3 mile; .5 hour; one of the easier trails in park to the thermal area; a few steep places but no substantial ascent; mineral deposits stain the formations yellow, red, green, and orange; one of the largest fumaroles in the park is found at Sulphur Works.

Bumpass Hell Trail: Starts at Bumpass Hell parking area, road marker 17; ends at Bumpass Hell; 3 miles round trip; 3 hours; 500-foot ascent; spectacular mudpots, fumaroles, and boiling springs in most active thermal area in park; outstanding views of other peaks and high mountain meadow flowers; trail guide available.

Lassen Peak Trail: Starts at Lassen Peak parking area; ends at summit of Lassen Peak; 5 miles round trip; 4.5 hours; 2,000-foot ascent; the view from the summit is worth the arduous climb up a 15 percent grade, from 8,500 feet to 10,400 feet; recent volcanic activity; mountain hemlock and white-bark pine mark the timberline; trail guides available.

Kings Creek Falls Trail: Starts at road marker 32; ends at Kings Creek Falls; 3 miles round trip; 2.5 hours; 700-foot ascent; flowers in bloom all summer; this is one of the few places in the park where mountain ash is found.

Summit Lake to Echo and Twin Lakes: Starts at Summit Lake; ends at Lower Twin Lake; 8 miles round trip; 6 hours; uphill 500 feet in first mile, then descends 500 feet to lake; excellent trail for viewing wildflowers, trees, and birds; deer commonly seen along trail.

Summit Lake to Horseshoe Lake via Upper Twin Lake: Starts at east side of Summit Lake; ends at Horseshoe Lake; 14 miles round trip; 12 hours; 700-foot ascent; a major trail to the eastern section of the park; crosses two bridges; several lakes along the way; typical of park flora and fauna; a good day hike through pine and fir forests and meadows.

Summit Lake to Cluster Lakes: Starts and ends at east side of Summit Lake; 10.5 miles; 7 hours; leads to Bear Lakes, Cluster Lakes, and Upper and Lower Twin Lakes.

Paradise Meadow Trail: Starts at road marker 42; ends at Paradise Meadow; 3 miles round trip; 3 hours; .5 mile steep ascent of 600 feet; best area in park for mid-summer wildflowers; lush meadow with many birds and deer.

Cinder Cone, in the northeast near Butte Lake, was last active in 1853.

PACIFIC CREST TRAIL: Starts at Little Willow Lake; ends at Badger Flat; 19 miles round trip; 16 hours; 1,000-foot ascent; trail crosses park north to south.

CINDER CONE TRAIL: Starts and ends at Butte Lake Campground; 5 miles; 3 hours; 800-foot ascent; loop trail around one of the most perfectly formed cinder cones in the United States; excellent view of other nearby peaks; trail guide available.

BUTTE LAKE TO SNAG LAKE: Starts and ends at Butte Lake parking area; 3.5 miles; 5 hours; 100-foot ascent; example of recent volcanic activity; hike can be extended an additional 3 miles and 3 hours to the south end of Snag Lake; portion of trail winds along the base of a large basalt lava flow.

HORSESHOE LAKE TO SNAG LAKE: Starts and ends at Horseshoe Lake ranger station; 6 miles; 3.5 hours; 600-foot ascent; trail touches south end of Snag Lake; remains of a drowned forest can be seen along edge of lake.

JUNIPER LAKE TO SNAG LAKE: Starts and ends at Juniper Lake ranger station; 6 miles; 4.5 hours; 1,000-foot ascent; trail passes through ponderosa pine forest most of way; wide variety of wildflowers in July and August; remains of an early settler's cabin in Cameron Meadows.

BOILING SPRINGS LAKE TRAIL: Starts and ends at Warner Valley picnic area; 3 miles; 2 hours; 200-foot ascent; trail crosses a meadow and passes through a mixed coniferous forest and steam vents and mud pots along the lake's shoreline; trail guide available.

DEVIL'S KITCHEN TRAIL: Starts and ends at Warner Valley picnic area; 3 miles; 2.5 hours; 300-foot ascent; an excellent trail for those interested in biology and geology; very active thermal area, one of the more important in the park.

SEE MAP ON PAGES 208–209.

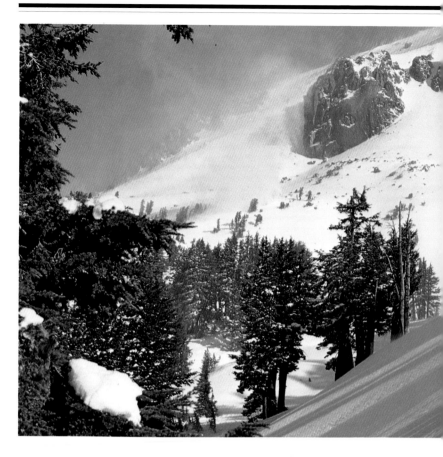

prominent, and lodgepole pine and western white pine begin to appear.

Dersch Meadows, north of the road at 22 to 24 miles and about 6,500 feet, is a good area to see deer and many varieties of wildflowers.

Hat Lake, at 24.2 miles and 6,450 feet, was formed by the mudflow eruption of May 19, 1915, and is now rapidly filling with sediments and becoming a new meadow. At 24.7 miles, the devastated area on the eastern and northeastern flanks of Lassen Peak becomes clearly visible. Now an area of young forest and brush, this was a 3-square mile stand of mature forest that was destroyed by the mudflows of May 19 and the steam blast of May 22, 1915. Some of the downed trees can still be found, all pointing away from the blast, which originated high on the eastern summit of Lassen Peak.

Hot Rock (long since cooled), one of many boulders seen at 26.7 miles along Lost Creek, was carried there by the 1915 mudflows.

From 28 to 30 miles, the road passes through white fir, Jeffrey

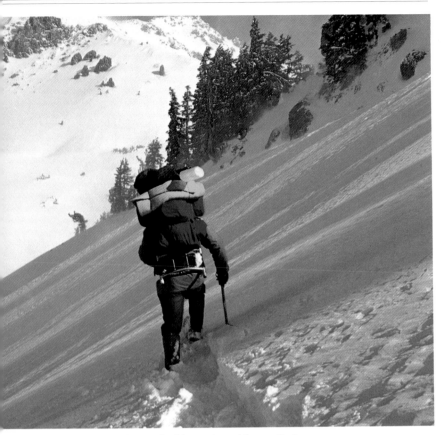

A solitary snowshoer makes his way toward Lassen Peak.

pine, sugar pine, ponderosa pine, and incense cedar. *Nobles Pass*, at 31.5 miles and 6,000 feet, was an important way through the mountains for an old emigrant trail between the Black Rock Desert in Nevada and Shasta City, California, a cutoff from the Humboldt Trail across Nevada to northern California.

From 32 to 33 miles, the road crosses *Chaos Jumbles*, a large rock avalanche that fell about 300 years ago from a group of lava domes called Chaos Crags, which formed only 1,100 years ago.

Just as volcanism has created much of the fascinating scenery of the Lassen area, it also poses future hazards to the park. Although the risks are vanishingly small to any one person at any one moment, they do concern the National Park Service in its interest for the collective safety of all visitors over many years. Geologists Dwight Crandell and Donal Mullineaux, who warned accurately in 1975 that Mount St. Helens might erupt violently before the end of the century, have evaluated the volcanic hazards at Lassen Volcanic National Park. Their principal concern is the Chaos Jumbles area. This avalanche covered a tract of about 2 square miles and reached downhill for 3 miles. It dammed Manzanita Creek to form *Manzanita Lake*. It is not known if the rockslide was triggered by a steam explosion, a major earthquake, or some other cause.

Because of the possibility of another avalanche, which could occur without any warning, the Manzanita Lake Visitor Center was closed in 1975. Subsequently, volcanic investigations utilizing the technology of computer modeling indicated that the Loomis Museum and Lily Pond areas were safe for visitor use. In 1993, the Loomis Museum was re-opened to the public and dedicated to telling the story of B. F. Loomis, his family's contributions, and the geologic history of the park. The National Park Service planned to operate the museum between June and September, funding permitting.

The chance of renewed explosive eruptions in the Chaos Crags area is also a potential hazard. They probably would not occur without some premonitory signs such as earthquake swarms or ground-surface displacements. Such symptoms in the Lassen area are now being monitored by seismographs and tiltmeters by the U.S. Geological Survey. These instruments can detect the microearthquakes and slight bulging of the ground surface that often precede volcanic eruptions. The combination of volcanic monitoring and awareness of the hazards should help to ensure the safety of visitors to this magnificent park.

At 34.3 miles, the Lassen Park Road ends at the junction of California 89 and California 44.

Other Roads

Four dead-end dirt roads lead to various backcountry areas in the park. The road to Drakesbad, a starting point for pack trips, begins from Chester, California, 19 miles southeast.

Horseshoe Lake and *Juniper Lake* in the southeastern portion of the park can also be reached by dirt road from Chester. (Between Horseshoe and Juniper lakes, the road is closed to motorized vehicles.)

Hat Creek Valley and *Badger Flat* in the north central portion of the park are accessible by a dirt road (also closed to vehicles) that turns north from the Lassen Park Road near Hat Lake.

The dirt road to Butte Lake Campground and the trail head to Cinder Cone in the northeastern corner of the park is reached by 29 miles of paved road (California 44) that circles north of the park from its junction with California 89.

Opposite: Kings Creek meanders through Kings Creek Meadows in the south of the park.

Clusters of arrow-leaf balsam root, with 9,235-foot Brokeoff Mountain in the distance.

Trails

Bumpass Hell Trail. Bumpass Hell Trail leads through stands of mountain hemlock and white-bark pine to the largest thermal-spring area in the park. The 3-mile (round trip) trail climbs and descends several hundred feet, and is usually open by July 1. The hot and boiling springs, steam vents, and mud pots are leaks from a major underground reservoir of steam that is heated by the molten roots of the volcanoes. Colors in the thermal springs come from both living algae and chemical decomposition of volcanic rock.

Cinder Cone Trail. Cinder Cone Trail begins at Butte Lake ranger station, and the 5-mile round trip takes 3 to 4 hours. The last eruption of Cinder Cone was probably between 1750 and 1800, and the deposits are still vividly fresh. The climb up the loose cinders gains an altitude of about 800 feet. All cinder cones look like giant anthills. The larger fragments thrown out by the exploding volcanic vents fall nearby and create steep cones of loose debris that surround the summit craters. Rugged lava beds near the base of Cinder Cone are partly covered by volcanic ash, forming a colorful area called the Painted Dunes. Butte Lake and Snag Lake were formed by the lava flows from Cinder Cone, which damned the natural stream drainages. The summit of Cinder Cone provides fine views of a variety of nearby volcanic peaks.

Lassen Peak Trail. Lassen Peak Trail begins from the Lassen Park Road at 8,500 feet and climbs a steep but steady grade to the summit of Lassen Peak at 10,457 feet, the highest point in the park. The trail is usually open by July 1, but snowbanks often persist all summer. Four hours round trip (5 miles) is about the average time needed to hike this rocky trail. Mountain hemlock and white-bark pine are common near the trail head, but much of the trail is above timberline. The gray to tan rock that forms Lassen Peak is called dacite. It erupted about 25,000 years ago, forming a steep dome of lava that was too viscous to flow away from its vent. Much of the broken lava lies in talus piles that tumbled down the steep dome as it pushed upward. The darker rock at the summit and high on the western slope of the peak is the dacite that erupted in 1915. The panorama from the summit on a clear day is superb (if there is any indication of a thunderstorm, it is best to retreat from the lightning-scarred mountaintop): looking north to Chaos Crags and turning clockwise, you can see Prospect Peak, Cinder Cone, the distant ranges in Nevada, Dyer Peak and Lake Almanor, the distant Sierras near Lake Tahoe, Brokeoff Mountain, Loomis Peak, the Trinity Alps in the distance, and, 75 miles to the northwest, 14,161-foot Mount Shasta—the next major Cascade volcano.

Boiling Springs Lake Trail. Boiling Springs Lake Trail begins just west of the campground on the dirt road to Drakesbad Lodge. It is an easy 2-hour (3-mile) round trip that ascends only 200 feet, yet travels through backcountry forest and meadow to a most interesting thermal-spring area. Boiling Springs Lake is small, and is heated to a fairly steady 125° F by underwater hot springs and steam vents. There is also an extensive area of mud pots along the shore. En route to and from the lake are stands of incense cedar, Douglas-fir, white fir, ponderosa pine, and sugar pine. This trail is generally open by June 15, and wildflowers are abundant as melting snow waters the meadows.

Other Trails. Other trails in Lassen Volcanic National Park add up to well over 100 miles in length. A few, such as the short trails at *Manzanita Lake* and *Sulphur Works*, are often open by May 15. One or two, such as the steep trail to *Brokeoff Mountain*, may not be open until July 15. However, most of the thirty-five other trails—some with such intriguing names as *Devil's Kitchen*, *Bathtub Lake*, *Paradise Meadow*, *Widow Lake*, and *Crystal Lake*—are generally open by June 15 or July 1.

REDWOOD
NATIONAL PARK

Redwoods, rhododendron, and salal grow near Redwood Creek.

REDWOOD NATIONAL PARK
1111 SECOND STREET
CRESCENT CITY, CALIFORNIA 95531
TEL.: (707) 464-6101

HIGHLIGHTS: National Tribute Grove • Stout Grove • Jedediah Smith Redwoods State Park • Del Norte Coast Redwoods State Park • Prairie Creek Redwoods State Park • Saddler Skyline Trail • Fern Canyon Trail • Tall Trees Grove • Enderts Beach • False Klamath Cove • Lady Bird Johnson Grove

ACCESS: U.S. 101 runs through the park, north and south. From Grants Pass, Oregon, U.S. 199 to north boundary of park.

HOURS: Daily, 24 hours, year-round.

FEES: None.

PARKING: At Crescent City Visitor Center, Hiouchi ranger station, and Redwood Information Center (Orick).

GAS, FOOD, LODGING: In Crescent City, Klamath, and Orick.

VISITOR CENTER: Crescent City Visitor Center, Hiouchi ranger station, and Redwood Information Center (Orick) offer exhibits, talks, and audio-visual programs.

PETS: Permitted, except on trails and in backcountry.

PICNICKING: At designated sites throughout park.

HIKING: On designated trails throughout park. Treat water before drinking.

CAMPGROUND: At Jedediah Smith (Hiouchi) and Del Norte Coast (Mill Creek) redwoods state parks, Prairie Creek, and Gold Bluffs Beach; primitive sites elsewhere.

TRAIL GUIDES: Tall Trees Grove, Lady Bird Johnson Grove, Yurok Loop.

OTHER ACTIVITIES: Horseback riding, swimming, and fishing (license required).

FACILITIES FOR DISABLED: Booklet entitled *Access National Park* available.

For additional information, see also Sites, Trails, and Trips on pages 244–251 and the maps on pages 232–233 and 249.

THROUGHOUT REDWOOD NATIONAL PARK AND the state park system within it, wilderness prevails: dense, moist forest; three major streams; and abundant wildlife. More than 1,000 species of plants and animals are found within the park's 110,000 acres in coastal northern California. The coast redwood, *Sequoia sempervirens*, dominates, but its cathedral-like forests support and are in turn supported by dozens of other trees, shrubs, flowers, and associated understory.

Wildlife that can be seen along the park's 100-mile trail system includes such majestic creatures as the Roosevelt elk, black bear, and deer. Beaver and porcupine are here, too, and offshore is the domain of whales, porpoises, seals, and sea lions. Myriad animals, large and small, inhabit the park's tidepools.

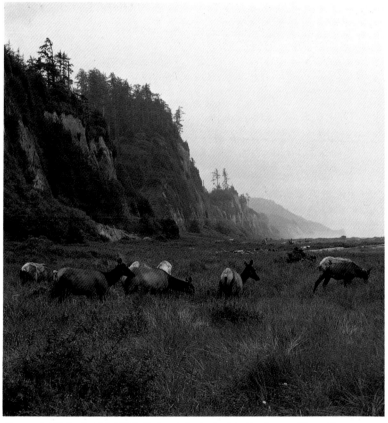

Roosevelt Elk herd off Gold Bluffs Beach in the Prairie Creek area. These elk now survive only in some areas of northern California, Oregon, and Washington.

REDWOOD
NATIONAL PARK
NORTH AREA

Ranger Station
Campground
Picnic Area

ROAD
UNPAVED ROAD
TRAIL

N

MILES
0   1   2   3

SIX RIVERS NATIONAL FOREST

TO GRANTS PASS

199

Smith River

South Fork Smith River

SOUTH FORK ROAD

DOUGLAS PARK ROAD

Little Bald Hills Trail
El. 1958'

Hiouchi Information Center El. 163'

Stout Grove Trail

Simpson and Peterson Trails

El. 160'

Hiouchi Trail

Stout Grove

JEDEDIAH SMITH REDWOODS STATE PARK El. 845'

Mill Creek Trail

Hatton Trail

El. 145'

Leiffer Trail
Ellsworth Trail

Boy Scout Tree Trail

Nickerson Trail

HILLS ROAD

Equestrian Trail

Mill Creek

MILL CREEK El. 370'

Saddler Skyline Trail

El. 675'

El. 1006'

Hobbs

HAMILTON ROAD

TO OREGON COAST

WALKER ROAD

101

El. 462'

HOWLAND HILLS ROAD

HUMBOLDT ROAD

ENDERTS BEACH ROAD

Demonstration Forest

El. 226'
Enderts Beach

Crescent Beach

ELK VALLEY ROAD

Mill Creek

El. 44'
Crescent City

Hiouchi Area

LAKE EARL

Crescent City Area

232
REDWOOD

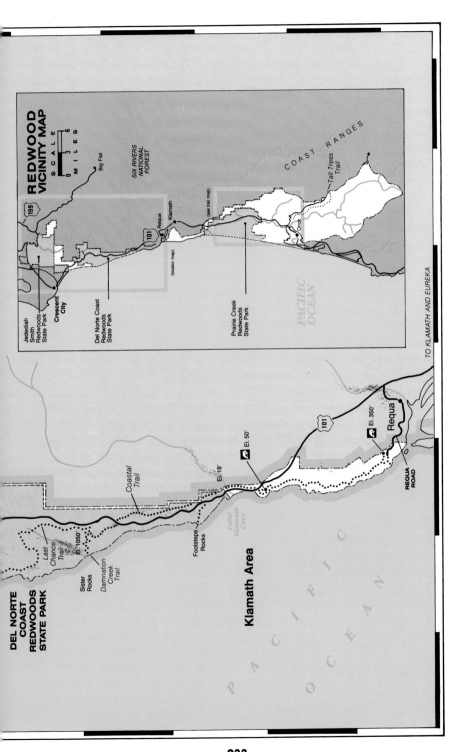

REDWOOD
VICINITY MAP

SCALE
MILES
0   3   6

199

COAST RANGES

SIX RIVERS
NATIONAL
FOREST

Big Flat

Jedediah
Smith
Redwoods
State Park

Crescent
City

101

Requa

Klamath

(locator map)

(see trail map)

Del Norte Coast
Redwoods
State Park

Prairie Creek
Redwoods
State Park

Tall Trees
Trail

Orick

PACIFIC
OCEAN

TO KLAMATH AND EUREKA

DEL NORTE
COAST
REDWOODS
STATE PARK

Coastal
Trail

Last
Chance
Trail

El. 1050'

Sister
Rocks

Damnation
Creek
Trail

El. 18'

Footsteps
Rocks

False
Klamath
Cove

El. 50'

101

El. 350'

Requa

REQUA
ROAD

Klamath Area

PACIFIC OCEAN

Native Americans

The earliest inhabitants of Redwood National Park were three groups of Indians: the Yurok, the Tolowa, and the Chilula. They maintained several dozen villages and a well-ordered society along streambanks and on the seacoast of the region. For these original residents, the environment easily fulfilled most needs. The forests provided timber for frame houses, canoes, and implements. Their canoes, usually hollowed-out redwood logs, were quite efficient and could be paddled safely offshore as well as on local streams and rivers.

Fish, mostly salmon, supplemented the Indians' main diet of acorns, and there was an abundant supply of shellfish and deer. Seaweed satisfied salt requirements, and mussels were taken from tidepools. For additional meat, hunters imitated the barking of seals in order to entice their prey. And when a whale was occasionally beached, it was time for a special feast.

The Yuroks maintained numerous villages along the Klamath River, which, then as now, was an excellent source of fish. The Tolowa territory was the Smith River, in present-day Jedediah Smith Redwoods State Park, while the Chilula built their settlements in the Redwood Creek Basin farther south. Although the three groups spoke different languages and their cultures differed, they frequently joined together for social activities. Wars among the groups were not unknown, however, nor were the Indians always at peace with later white explorers and settlers.

Early Explorers

Beginning with the party of Joao Rodrigues Cabrilho, a Portuguese navigator commissioned by Spain for New World exploration, a succession of Spanish and English maritime explorers sailed past the Humboldt coast beginning in the mid-1500s. Because of the rugged coastline, however, they could view redwood country only from afar. The first white to actually walk through the present-day park probably was Bruno de Heceta, a Spaniard, who arrived in 1775. Heceta was impressed with the fertility of the soil, and remained in the area for nine days. Credit for the coast redwoods' actual discovery, however, generally goes to the Franciscan missionary Fray Juan Crespi, who saw these trees six years before Heceta, but much farther south. Crespi recorded that the redwood was "the highest, largest and straightest" tree he had ever seen, and that "although the wood resembles cedar somewhat in color, it is very different." He named the tree *palo colorado*, or "red tree" in Spanish. It was not until the 1800s that white explorers came again, occasionally trading for food and furs with the local Indians. There were no permanent settlements on the north coast, and, after its original discovery of California, Spain virtually ignored its holdings in the western part of the New World.

Overland Explorers and Settlers

In April 1828, the famed explorer and mountain man Jedediah Smith led a party of twenty men westward from California's north Central Valley. He was determined to reach the Pacific. It was an arduous journey; for days the men beat through thick underbrush and tangled forest in driving rain. But Smith succeeded in reaching the redwood region, crossing the Smith River on June 20, 1828. The

A traveler in earlier times takes the Howland Hill Road from Crescent City to Gasquet, California, through what is now the park.

next white figure of note was Dr. Josiah Gregg, who passed through the area in 1849; members of his party later built the first tiny settlements in the Humboldt coast area.

The discovery of gold at Gold Bluffs Beach in 1850 touched off an immigration boom that still has not subsided. Copper and silver also were found in the region, but their mining was a short-lived enterprise. In later years, the area now within Redwood National Park was host to a succession of humanity with divergent goals: settlers, farmers, dairymen, fishermen, trappers, military servicemen of two world wars. Traces of their tenure are preserved and marked within the park.

The Loggers

Logging began in what is now Redwood National Park in 1850, and had reached an annual cut measured in millions of board feet by 1900. As developing technology replaced hand equipment with power tools for cutting, hauling, and processing the huge redwood logs, the rate of decline of these magnificent trees accelerated. Not only were the trees disappearing, but as the tempo of logging increased through the housing boom that followed World War II, road after road was slashed through the virgin wilderness, coastal roads were built, and settlers supporting the timber industry began to clear other forests for their communities. From 1947 through 1958, logging rose to a peak of more than 1 million board feet per year throughout the entire redwood region. Clear-cutting removed thousands of old-growth, virgin trees. Indeed, by 1960 so many trees had been cut that some mills were forced to shut down because of the shortage of easily available timber.

Establishment of the Park

The establishment of Redwood National Park in 1968 was the culmination of several efforts over many years to preserve and protect some of the remaining stands of magnificent coast redwoods, the world's tallest trees, which occur naturally only in coastal northern California. In 1902, Big Basin Redwoods State Park was created south of San Francisco, formally bringing the state of California into the effort for the first time. In 1908, Congressman and philanthropist William Kent donated Muir Woods, north of San Francisco, to the federal government; the grove of virgin redwoods, named for naturalist John Muir at Kent's request, is a national monument.

For half a century, various conservation groups, notably the Save-the-Redwoods League, campaigned for protection of old-growth forests, and more state parks were added to the system. Aided by a grant of $64,000 from the National Geographic Society, and at the instigation of the Sierra Club, the National Park Service conducted

The Dobeer Donkey steam engine. Logging was a prime activity in the region, which is now the park, for a century preceding its establishment in 1968.

an inventory of remaining California coast redwoods in the early 1960s. The report, released in 1963, galvanized public action: from an original 2 million acres of primeval redwoods in the state, only about 300,000 acres remained, and only 50,000 of these acres were protected within the state park system. In 1968, President Lyndon B. Johnson signed the act that established Redwood National Park.

The Sierra Club, led by Dr. Edgar Wayburn, a Club president, and his wife, Peggy, had been in the forefront of the effort to establish the park. They, and others, now contended that the original boundary did not ensure adequate watershed protection for Redwood Creek or Mill Creek, areas threatened with damage as a result of logging and other activities. Ten years of lobbying paid off when President Jimmy Carter signed the park expansion act in 1978. It added 48,000 acres to the park, and, after further aquisitions, the acreage totaled 110,232. The expansion helped to ensure that logging and other activities outside the original boundaries would not further endanger the lofty trees. It also provided for a massive rehabilitation program for cutover lands already damaged. By the 1990s, the immense job of restoration accomplished there had surpassed any similar effort in the National Park System.

The geology of Redwood National Park is complex, and only recently have scientists begun to fully understand what they term its "scrambled" nature. The major geologic feature is the Franciscan Formation, which consists of the muddy sandstones, igneous rocks, and metamorphic rocks that underlie most of coastal northern California. Very few fossils are contained in this formation. The origin of the rocks dates to 100 million years ago, when a gigantic collision began to occur between the sea floor of the eastern Pacific and the edge of the North American continent. The accumulation of sediments was greatly deformed and reshaped during this collision.

As "the squeeze" slowly pushed sediments upward, it formed the present Coast Range, which bisects Redwood National Park

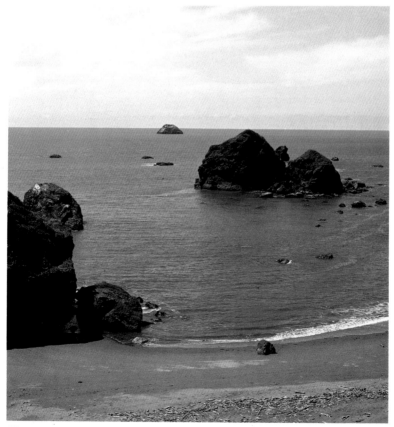

"Sea stacks," small rock islets, are a common sight off the coast of Redwood.

from north to south. The range rises from sea level to a maximum altitude of 3,097 feet. Gently rounded summits are found in some parts of the range; in others, steep-sided drainages have been created by uplift and erosion of less-resistant rocks. The uplift continues even today.

The oldest rocks in the park are those in the Kerr Ranch Schist. The schist forms the base for most of the southern portion of the park, and outcrops may be seen along Redwood Creek Trail and stream. Geologists are uncertain about the age of these rocks, but it is believed that they are older than rocks formed during the Coast Range Orogeny (episode of deformation that leads to the formation of a mountain range), and possibly older than 135 million years. Soils developed from rocks of the Kerr Ranch Schist appear reddish because they contain oxidized iron. Such soil is seen frequently along U.S. 101 just west of the Orick gateway.

River flood plains are evident in the park, and may extend upstream for several miles. They are formed during periods of heavy rainfall, which causes rivers to overflow and spill silt, sand, and gravel. River waters erode downward through underlying rock to carve canyons and river terraces from the remnants. Tall Trees Grove on Redwood Creek in the southern area of the national park is one of the best places to view both terraces and flood plains. Ancient river terraces may rise as high as 100 feet above the present stream level upstream from the grove. Another good example of a flood plain is where the Klamath River empties into the Pacific Ocean near Requa.

The growth and melting of glacial ice less than 2 million years ago also has affected the landscape of Redwood National Park. The glaciers did not reach the park itself, but wave-cut benches, or terraces, common in the park's 35-mile-long seacoast, are evidence of glacial action. They were formed during periods of wave erosion, and in some respects they are similar to terraces that are now developing below off-shore waters of northern California.

The shoreline includes rock sections and sandy beaches. In some places, small rock islets—called sea stacks—rise beyond the surf. Seaside lagoons, such as Freshwater Lagoon, can be seen in the southern section of the park. Several thousand years ago, the sea level rose and drowned stream valleys. Wave action then built sand bars across small outlet streams and formed the present-day lagoons.

Cliffs along some beaches are composed of river sediments that were deposited as an ancestral delta of the Klamath River about 2 million years ago. Older Franciscan rocks form a rocky shoreline in other places. Sand is delivered to the beaches from the erosion of waves and from inland sources.

Climate and Precipitation

Cool summers with frequent coastal fog, and mild but wet winters: that best describes the annual weather cycle in Redwood National Park. The climate is ideal for the coast redwood; in fact, without the summer fog and winter rains, the species probably could not survive because these trees consume great quantities of moisture daily.

The park rarely experiences extreme heat or cold. The January mean temperature is 47° F near the coast, while in August it is 57° F. There is a more pronounced temperature variation inland.

The climates of both southwestern Oregon and northwestern California are determined largely by a weather system that originates in the North Pacific. In spring and summer, a massive semipermanent system called the Pacific high dominates atmospheric circulation; in autumn, the high weakens and is pushed about by low-pressure fronts moving in from the Gulf of Alaska. Rainfall, fog, ocean winds, and wave patterns are controlled by the pressure systems and by the effect of the southward-flowing California Current, which parallels the seacoast.

Trees and Other Plants

Redwoods such as those found in Redwood National Park, which are living links to the Age of Dinosaurs, once were distributed over vast regions of the earth. Together with the longer-living sequoia of mountainous eastern California and a smaller cousin found only in China, they and their ancestors grew as far north as the Bering Sea, and in Europe and Asia. But even the hardiest of these trees could not withstand the influence of sheets of ice that moved south in the ice age, and the coast redwood's retreat drove it to its present last stand in a 450-mile-long strip of coastal California.

There are more than 1,000 species of plants and animals in Redwood National Park, but this single species literally towers over them all. It is the awe-inspiring, reddish-barked, long-living giant that John Muir called "the king of its race."

The coast redwood is the world's tallest tree. Average mature trees reach a height of 200 to 250 feet, a diameter of 10 to 15 feet, and an age of between 400 and 800 years (individual trees can live up to 2,000 years). The world's tallest tree grows on the banks of Redwood Creek: when it was measured in 1964, it was 367.8 feet tall.

Coast redwoods grow both from cone seeds and from sprouts

Opposite: Redwoods are the world's tallest trees, commonly reaching between 200 and 250 feet, with many individuals much taller.

Sea otter.

generated on injured or fallen trees. (Sprouting is a rare characteristic among conifers.) The mature tree produces seeds almost every year; compared with the height of the full-grown tree, the seeds are almost infinitesimal; 120,000 seeds weigh 1 pound. The redwood is a tree that resists fire, fungus diseases, and insect damage. Its surprising durability and resistance to rot is a major reason why it is a lumberman's dream; few other trees combine so many commercial advantages.

The root system of the redwood is broad and shallow; despite the tree's great height, the species has no taproot but manages to remain upright during its long life with only a shallow support.

The redwood shares its forest domain with a variety of other trees, shrubs, and flowers. The trees include Douglas-fir (the redwood's closest rival in size), tanoak, the distinctively reddish-barked madrone, and western hemlock. Where redwoods grow close to the coast, they are usually protected from wind and salt spray by the Sitka spruce.

Bleeding hearts, several species of ferns, and myriad herbs carpet the forest floor. Perhaps the most distinctive flower is the redwood sorrel, or oxalis, with its cloverlike leaves; the leaves fold up like tiny umbrellas when exposed to sunlight. Salal (with its leathery green leaves and purple summer fruit), salmonberry, and huckleberry also are found in profusion. In May and June, rhododendrons and azaleas burst forth in glorious color.

Grasses are the predominant plant of the prairie-meadows,

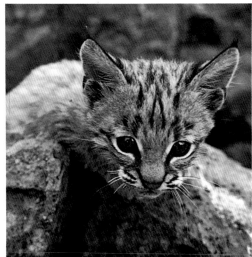

Douglas iris.   *Young bobcat.*

which are bordered by trees such as the Douglas-fir. On the prairie, too, is the hazel (a favored basket material of the Indians), exquisite irises, native blackberries, thistle, and lupine.

Wildlife

The most imposing land mammal in Redwood National Park is the Roosevelt elk, which was once widely distributed from Mount Shasta to California's Central Valley. The elk shares its forest and prairie habitat with many other mammals, including deer, bobcat, beaver, otter, raccoon, porcupine, fox, and mountain lion. Shrews may be seen scampering through the forest in search of prey; the Douglas squirrel, or chickaree, feeds on the cones of both the redwood and the Douglas-fir. The park's three major rivers are prime suppliers of trout and several species of salmon, for which the region is famous. Smelt, silverside perch, herring, and flounder tempt anglers in seaside lagoons.

The largest mammal of all is the California gray whale. It is not a resident, however, but only a seasonal visitor en route from the Arctic to Mexico during winter. Offshore, too, on a more regular basis, are porpoises, seals, sea lions, and, on rare occasions, sea otters.

Redwood National Park is a bird lover's paradise. More than 350 species of birds have been recorded in the region. Many are migrants that follow the Pacific Flyway during spring and fall, and more than half are associated with water: gulls, cormorants, and brown pelicans are examples. Inland birds include jays, crows, hawks, owls, bald eagles, falcons, and myriad songbirds.

Sites, Trails, and Trips

Three California state redwoods parks, each with its special features and visitor attractions, lie within the boundary of Redwood National Park. There are more than sixty trails within the combined park systems, facilitating access to the various ecosystems of forest, meadow, stream, and seacoast.

Where to begin? One of the park's three Visitor Centers—in Crescent City, Hiouchi, and Orick—is best; each is a good place to gather information and advice for a venture through redwood country.

Unlike trails in some national parks, which may require days to traverse, those in Redwood National Park are generally short, and the effort required is minimal. Some longer loops are formed by joining shorter trails.

Jedediah Smith Redwoods State Park

Located along the scenic Smith River off U.S. 199 north of Crescent City, this 9,200-acre park is indeed tall-timber country, home of some of the finest preserved stands of coast redwoods. Howland Hill Road, a historically important gravel artery, meanders through the hushed groves, which include the 5,000-acre National Tribute Grove dedicated to men and women who served in the two world wars. The park's largest measured redwood—16 feet in diameter, 340 feet high—is in Stout Grove. Thick stands of other Pacific Northwest trees, as well as flowers and shrubs, can best be seen by hiking this park's fine system of trails.

Two of them, *Lieffer* and *Ellsworth*, combine for an excellent 1.3-mile, 1-hour sampling of Jedediah Smith. Together they form a moss-laden path through big maple and old-growth forest with plenty of benches for resting. The trail head is on the left side of Walker Road, .4 mile from U.S. 199.

Chinese gold mines are thought to have been operating in the 1800s along *Boy Scout Tree Trail*, which extends 3.7 miles from a trail head on Howland Hill Road and forks after 3 miles. Enclosed in a mature redwood forest, the right fork leads to the Boy Scout Tree, while the left leads to Fern Falls, where the chattering of wrens pleases the ear.

Huckleberries, trillium, and rhododendrons brighten *Hiouchi Trail* in summer; this 2-mile, 1.5-hour walk starts at the Jedediah Smith Campground or at the U.S. 199 turnout south of Hiouchi Bridge. The murmur of Smith River is always within earshot.

Little Bald Hills Trail, 4.5 miles long, is an old road that takes the visitor through several open meadows that once were the site of a ranch. Hugged by pines and firs, the trail is excellent for bird-watching, and begins just east of Stout Grove.

The *Stout Grove Trail* is an easy 30-minute walk that leads to its namesake, Stout Grove, where fishing and swimming in summer provide a restful change from a day of exploring old-growth forests. It is accessible from Howland Hill Road.

Another popular loop in Jedediah Smith is the combination of *Simpson* and *Peterson* trails. Each is less than 1 mile long and leads the visitor through stands of virgin redwoods featuring large burls. There are many fern species along the trail, and skunk cabbage is abundant in the creek drainage.

Del Norte Coast Redwoods State Park

Covering 6,400 acres south of Jedediah Smith, Del Norte Coast Redwoods State Park borders the Pacific Ocean and is noted for both its wide variety of foliage and wildlife and its scenic marine vistas. It is thickly forested in old-growth redwoods, and its western boundary slopes to the sea with easy access to beachcombing and tidepool exploring. Here the visitor can well appreciate the dramatic variety of northern California's seacoast: rocky offshore islets, wave-eroded cliffs, long stretches of lonely beaches sprinkled with driftwood. In the spring, Del Norte sports a dazzling display of rhododendrons, some growing 30 feet high, as seasonal precipitation creates a rain-forest effect.

One of the most popular trails in this park, *Damnation Creek Trail*, leads northward along the coast for 2.5 miles from U.S. 101 near False Klamath Cove. Heavily forested in old-growth redwoods, it descends steeply to a small rocky beach that is ideal for studying marine life. The trail winds through a spruce forest on its way to the sea. Near the trail head, hikers cross a paved road that once was U.S. 101.

A longer trail, 6-mile *Last Chance Trail*, offers exceptional bird-watching opportunities and photographic vistas of the redwood seacoast. It begins at the end of Endert's Beach Road in the Crescent City area of the national park. Spruce is prominent here, as are redwood and alder that extend to coastal bluffs.

Named after Hobbs Wall Company, a major logging firm of the late 1800s, *Hobbs Wall Trail* provides evidence of timbering in its heyday in the form of logging cables and machine parts. The redwoods seen here are of the second-growth variety—trees that have grown up

Overleaf: Coast redwoods, such as these in Del Norte State Park, grow both from cone seeds and from sprouts.

Trails of Redwood National Park

There are more than sixty hiking trails in the Redwood National Park complex, many of which are in the state-park areas. Highlighted here are those within the boundaries of the national park.

Enderts Beach Trail: Starts at Crescent Beach Overlook, end of Enderts Beach Road in north area of Redwood National Park; ends at beach; .6 mile; .33 hour; features tidepools, primitive camping, and picnic areas.

False Klamath Cove Trail: Starts at Wilson Creek picnic areas, Lagoon Creek picnic area, or False Klamath Cove turnout in north area of Redwood National Park and Del Norte Coast Redwoods State Park; ends at Klamath Cove; .5 hour; tidepools, surf fishing, driftwood collecting, and birdwatching.

Coastal Trail (DeMartin Prairie section): Starts at Wilson Creek picnic area or Damnation Creek trail head; ends at bluffs overlooking ocean; 5.5 miles; 4 hours one way; runs through Del Norte Coast Redwoods State Park.

Coastal Trail (Hidden Beach section): Starts at Lagoon Creek picnic area or Klamath Overlook (Requa), in north area of Redwood National Park; ends at Requa Hill; 4 miles; 2 hours; whale watching, berry collecting, birdwatching, and listening to sea lions offshore; not level, but not difficult walk above the sea.

Coastal Trail (Flint Ridge section): Starts at Flint Rock Head Overlook or Douglas Memorial Bridge; 4.5 miles; 3 hours one way; old-growth redwoods; connects loop of Coastal Drive.

Lost Man Creek Trail: Starts at Lost Man Creek picnic area; ends at Bald Hills Road, in south area of Redwood National Park; 10 miles; 8 hours one way; near trail head is site of National Park dedication as a World Heritage site.

Redwood Creek Trail: Starts at Redwood Creek trail-head parking area, off Bald Hills Road (take Bald Hills Road off U.S. 101 and drive 2 miles north of Orick); ends at Tall Trees Grove; 8.2 miles; 5 hours; wildlife photography, swimming, backcountry camping allowed on stream bars; foot bridges are removed from September 30 to May 30; suggested loop starts with morning shuttle-bus pickup at trail head (summer only), then to Tall Trees Grove via bus and hike to parking area; do not drink this water or any other creek water without purifying or boiling.

Lady Bird Johnson Grove Nature Loop Trail: Starts and ends at Lady Bird Johnson parking area, 2 miles up on Bald Hills Road, south area of Redwood National Park; 1 mile; .5 hour; leads through old-growth redwoods along an old logging road; steep drive to parking area not recommended for trailers or large recreational vehicles; site of national park dedication.

Tall Trees Trail: Accessible only in summer months by shuttle-bus system; shuttle starts at Redwood Information Center and drops off passengers at Tall Trees trail head, where they can hike to Tall Trees Grove and back; option to return to vehicles via Redwood Creek Trail; 1.2 miles; round-trip time from information center via bus is 3 to 4 hours; total time, including hike back to vehicle, is 8 hours; bus fee charged; mature redwood forest including the Tall Trees Grove on alluvial flat formed by Redwood Creek; buses tour through extensively logged area where forest rehabilitation can be seen; steep grades.

See map on pages 232–233.

TO CRESCENT CITY

Butler Creek Trail

Little Creek Trail

West Ridge Trail

El. 957'

Boat Creek Trail

Prairie Creek

Fern Canyon
El. 420'
El. 78'

PRAIRIE CREEK REDWOODS STATE PARK

Brown Creek Trail

Fern Canyon Trail

Clintonia Trail

James Irvine Trail

West Ridge Trail

South Fork Trail

Miners Ridge Trail

El. 403'

El. 550'

Rhododendron Trail

Prairie Creek Visitor Center

Gold Bluffs Beach

Elk Prairie

El. 154'

Elk Prairie Trail

El. 475'

DAVISON ROAD

El. 443'

Lost Man Creek Picnic Area
El. 64'

Little Lost Man Creek

Lost Man Creek

Lost Man Creek Trail
El. 1972'

Lady Bird Johnson Nature Loop Trail

El. 1000'

Lady Bird Johnson Grove

El. 1079'

BALD HILLS ROAD

El. 1610'

Redwood Creek

Redwood Creek Trail

Orick El. 34'

SOUTH AREA
TRAIL MAP

Ranger Station _____

Campground _____

Picnic Area _____

Shuttle Bus _____

ROAD _____

UNPAVED ROAD _ _ _ _ _ _

TRAIL • • • • • • • • • •

N

M I L E S

0   1   2

249

REDWOOD

since their virgin predecessors were felled for industry. The 3.7-mile trail begins at one of three trail heads and takes about 3 hours to hike.

The Mill Creek Campground entrance station is the trail head for the 20-minute, 1-mile *Nature Loop Trail*, which provides a hurry-up, short glimpse of a redwood forest if one is indeed in a hurry. Madrone trees—with bright red bark that recalls that of manzanita—are scattered throughout Redwood National Park, and some of the best examples are along this trail.

Douglas-fir and a young redwood forest, plus huckleberries and bird life, make *Saddler Skyline Trail* an enjoyable walk. The 1.5-mile trail begins either between campsites 7 and 8 at Mill Creek Campground or on the Nature Loop Trail, and can be walked in 1 hour.

Prairie Creek Redwoods State Park

Covering 12,500 acres, Prairie Creek Redwoods State Park is composed mostly of old-growth coast redwoods and is the southernmost of the state parks within the boundaries of Redwood National Park. Many of its redwoods exceed 300 feet in height. They are hardy survivors of logging activities that doomed many of their centuries-old relatives in the past century. Two herds of Roosevelt elk roam in Prairie Creek. It was near this park, at Lady Bird Johnson Grove, that Redwood National Park was dedicated in 1968 to culminate a half-century of conservationists' efforts. Prairie Creek has 75 miles of trails, including the *Revelation Trail* for the blind. These visitors may "see" the park's features both on signs and in a Braille handbook that is available at park headquarters.

Fern Canyon Trail is a .7-mile streamside loop through Fern Canyon, where delicate five-fingered ferns cling to 50-foot-high canyon walls. In summer, the trail requires only about 1 hour of easy walking; in winter, the creek is often impassable, but the canyon is still visible by looking down from the rim. The trail runs up to a prairie that once was a mining settlement.

Redwood National Park

Redwood Creek Trail is one of the major trails in Redwood National Park. Extending 8.2 miles, it is not a trail for the visitor in a hurry, because at least 5 hours are necessary to fully appreciate what it offers. The walk can begin just off Bald Hills Road north of Orick or, less strenuously, from a trail head to the Tall Trees Grove, reached by permitted vehicle access via the Bald Hills Road, or in summer by shuttle bus. Wildlife viewing, photography, and swimming are popular activities. A highlight is the Tall Trees Grove, where the world's tallest living thing was discovered in 1963.

Agate Beach at Patrick's Point State Park is on the coast highway south of Redwood.

Backcountry camping is allowed on stream bars, but permits, available at the trail head, are required.

Coastal Trail extends from Enderts Beach, in the Crescent City area, to Skunk Cabbage Trail trail head, at the southern end of Prairie Creek Redwoods State Park. (Eventually, it will be a link in a series of trails along the coast between Canada and Mexico.) It wanders high above the sea through spruce and alder forests that entice the berry collector, bird-watcher, and wildflower lover. From this elevated vantage point, the hiker often can hear the barking of sea lions offshore and, in winter, see the telltale spouts of migrating California gray whales.

Boat Creek Trail, 2 miles long, follows a creek through a steep canyon that was logged during World War II to provide spruce wood for airplane building. Vistas of the coast are seen by hikers as they walk through old-growth redwood groves.

Beach Trips

Those with an affinity for the ocean will find many sites in Redwood National Park to their liking. Enderts Beach, for instance, is one of the finest for tidepool exploring on the northern California coast. Depending on the condition and height of the tide, thousands of marine organisms can be seen, each within its special "niche," or zone. Just north is 3.5-mile Crescent Beach, which is noted for its excellent opportunities for surf fishing, driftwood collecting, clamming, sandcastle building, and birdwatching. There are fine tidepools, too, at False Klamath Cove, while at Gold Bluffs Beach can be found some of the largest numbers of elk in the park.

SEQUOIA
NATIONAL PARK

These huge sequoia trees grow within the 5 square miles of Giant Forest.

SEQUOIA NATIONAL PARK
ASH MOUNTAIN, THREE RIVERS, CALIFORNIA 93271
TEL.: (209) 565-3341

HIGHLIGHTS: General Sherman Tree • Huckleberry Meadow • Squatter's Cabin • Washington Tree • General Lee Tree • Moro Rock • Monarch Lakes • Crystal Lake

ACCESS: From Visalia, 35 miles east via California 198.

HOURS: Daily, year-round. Some park roads closed during winter.

FEES: Per car and for camping. Golden Eagle pass accepted.

PARKING: Throughout park.

GAS: At Lodgepole and Three Rivers.

FOOD: At Giant Forest (summer only), Three Rivers, and general store at Lodgepole, year-round.

LODGING: At Giant Forest (summer only).

All facilities at Giant Forest were scheduled to close by 1998; inquire at park about new facilities at Wuksachi Village.

VISITOR CENTER: Foothills Visitor Center at Ash Mountain offers information, visual program, permits, exhibits, books, and maps. Lodgepole Visitor Center offers audio-visual program, natural history and history exhibits, permits, books, and maps.

PETS: Permitted on leash in developed areas. Not permitted on trails.

PICNICKING: At designated sites throughout park.

HIKING: Trails available.

BACKPACKING: Permitted on more than 700 miles of trails with permit. Water available but must be treated.

CAMPGROUND: At Potwisha, Buckeye, Lodgepole (reservations available during summer from MISTIX), Dorst, South Fork, Cold Springs, and Atwell Mill. Fires are permitted in pits only. Showers at Lodgepole. No hookups.

TOURS: In summer, free naturalist-guided walks are given daily. In winter, free snowshoe walks are given weekends and holiday periods (snowshoes provided for nominal fee). In English.

OTHER ACTIVITIES: Horseback riding, cross-country skiing, fishing (license required), and wilderness hiking (permit required).

FACILITIES FOR DISABLED: Restrooms, campgrounds, picnic areas, and campsites at Potwisha and Dorst.

For additional information, see also Sites, Trails, and Trips on pages 274–282, the map in Kings Canyon National Park on pages 182–183, and the map on page 277.

ON A CLEAR SUMMER DAY IN 1861, HALE D. Tharp and his two grown stepsons, John and George Swanson, dismounted from their horses at the base of a massive granite dome perched on the high north rim of the Middle Fork of the Kaweah River—the protuberance later would be named Moro Rock—and began to climb. One motive was the human urge to stand high. Beyond that was a quest for orientation. The trio had spent the greater part of this 1861 trip, and of earlier ventures as well, zigzagging out of the immense canyon of the Kaweah's Middle Fork into a forest of conifers that were gigantic beyond their previous imagining. Now they felt a need to fit the marvels they encountered into a coherent whole, here on the rough western slope of the southern Sierra Nevada.

Since that day, uncounted thousands of other people have made the same 300-foot ascent of Moro Rock's back side. It is easier now—concrete steps are guarded by steel handrails. But the view from the bald summit, 6,725 feet above sea level, remains as overwhelming, *on clear days*, as when Tharp and the Swanson brothers first saw it.

Scarcely 12 miles to the east rise the snow-streaked peaks of the Great Western Divide, some of them more than 12,000 feet high. (The Great Western Divide is a spur of the main Sierra Nevada.) From the snow streaks on the divide, converging streams plunge into the Kaweah's Middle Fork. By the time the combined waters have roared past the canyon wall on which Moro Rock sits, they have dropped to an elevation of 4,000 feet—a descent of 1.5 miles in the span of a glance. And still the river has to descend another 3,000 feet before emerging into California's San Joaquin Valley.

At first that dramatic panorama holds the viewer in thrall. Then, slowly, ecological variations wrought by changes in altitude command attention. At one end of the spectrum are the pastel colors of the wild oaks and chaparral of the foothills; at the other, the pale rock of the barren summits. In between, rolling north and south along the waist of the Sierra, is the dense, dark-green canopy of what the naturalist John Muir called "the grandest and most beautiful" coniferous forest in the world. Rising here and there out of that canopy are the huge, rounded tops, some decorated with snags as arrogant as spikes on a helmet, of the bulkiest trees now alive: the giant sequoias, or, in botanical terms, *Sequoiadendron giganteum*.

Overleaf: Sunset Rock, west of Giant Forest, is famous for its view of the San Joaquin Valley.

Native American Settlers

Hale Tharp, the first non-Indian to view the magnificence of this land, had brought his family to the foothills near the lower Kaweah River in 1856, looking for cattle range. About 2,000 Indians, he said later, were living in the district. They were Potwishas, a subtribe of the Monaches, or Western Monos, whose homeland had once lain at the eastern base of the Sierra. At some time between A.D. 1000 and 1500, small groups of Monaches had drifted west. Over the course of many years, they scattered. One subgroup, the Tubatulabals, settled beside the turbulent, southward-flowing Kern. From that new homeland they ranged, on occasion, as far up the river as its headwaters in the vast horseshoe of peaks formed by the Great Western Divide and the outliers of Mount Whitney—at 14,494 feet the highest point in the lower forty-eight states, and since 1926 a part of Sequoia National Park.

Others of the nomads moved north from the Kern along the western base of the mountains. Avoiding the heart of the San Joaquin Valley, which was occupied by Yokut Indians, they settled in extended family groups near the points where the Tule, Kaweah, and Kings rivers break from the mountains. Though all were Monaches—that is, Monos who had moved west—the different groups were given different names, probably by the Yokuts: Potwisha, Woksaki, and Wobonuch.

In their new homes, they were introduced to the staple food of most California Indians—acorns. The nuts existed in such quantities that long wanderings in search of sustenance were no longer necessary. After carrying home a harvest in baskets on their backs, the women hulled the acorns, put the kernels into small holes in slabs of flat-lying foothill granite, and pulverized them with stone pestles. As many as fifty grinding holes, arranged close together so that the women could work in company, have been found at Hospital Rock beside the Middle Fork of the Kaweah River in Sequoia National Park. The pulverizing finished, the meal was dumped into a small basin of sand lined with grass. It was then covered with cedar boughs that acted like spreading screens, and water was poured through to leach away the acorns' bitter tannic acid. The product was then ready for boiling into mush or baking into cakes.

The Indians also feasted on dried manzanita berries, rats, rabbits, squirrels, and occasional deer. Instead of making temporary houses out of brush and gnarled pinyon sticks, as did the Monos east of the mountains, the Monache groups built semipermanent homes by erecting a conical frame of willow poles and covering it with strips of cedar bark. Temperature rather than the availability of food controlled group movements. Winter was the time for congregating along the lower edges of the foothills, where snow seldom fell. But summer could be hot in the foothills, and then the families sought the shade of the forest belt, where deer abounded. Long before Europeans had reached California, the Monaches, and undoubtedly the Yokuts, were familiar with the ruddy-barked sequoia trees that were scattered grandly among other conifers.

Trade kept the Monos east of the mountains in touch with the Monaches to the west. The eastern Indians seem to have been the most active, carrying with them on their journeys pine nuts, the dried larvae of flies taken from the alkaline lakes of their homeland, salt, rabbitskin blankets, and obsidian; the last was in demand for making arrowheads and cutting tools. These goods were exchanged for acorn meal, shell beads, deerskin, and arrow shafts of strong, straight tule. Some of this trade extended to the Yokuts as well.

Mostly the merchants traveled by way of Walker Pass, but during the few weeks in summer when the high country was free of snow, venturesome traders clambered up one side of the mountain crest and down the other. Enough traces of their passing have survived to show that the land's native inhabitants had begun using the high mountain trails and passes of the southern Sierra centuries ago.

American Settlement

The Spanish, who made their first settlement in California in 1769, knew none of this. Only rarely did they and the Mexicans who suc-

The entrance to the park around 1900.

ceeded them venture far enough inland to glimpse in the distance the long white line of mountains they named Sierra Nevada. Later, when American trappers, explorers, and, finally, settlers were seeking the Pacific, the rugged loftiness of the southern Sierra deflected them down toward Walker Pass or to other low crossings well to the north. Thus the foothill Indians were able to continue their ways.

The gold rush ended the isolation, even though the only placer diggings in Monache land were shallow gravels along the lower Kern. But miners needed food. Farmers drifted into the fertile San Joaquin Valley, and, in 1850, some of them founded the town of Visalia not 30 miles from the Potwisha villages along the Kaweah. In 1856, Hale Tharp followed with his herd of cattle.

He got on well with his Indian neighbors. Wondering about cool summer range for his animals and eager to see the huge red-barked trees that the Indians talked about, Tharp persuaded two of them to guide him, in the summer of 1858, to their favorite flower-jeweled, forest-girt meadows. The group probably started from the Indian village at Hospital Rock (so named because the Potwisha had treated one of Tharp's stepsons there) and zigzagged upward, much as the modern road does, past Moro Rock and into what is now known as the Giant Forest: 18,657 massive trees (8,411 of them more than 1 foot in diameter at breast height) scattered with an array of tall firs and pines across 3,200 cool acres, one of the most extensive grove of big trees—or series of groves, depending on how one defines *grove*—in the world.

Tharp's initial trip was followed by a longer one in 1860. The next year—the year that he and his two stepsons climbed Moro Rock—he established a squatter claim to the area by pasturing his horses in the vicinity of Crescent Meadow. But he did not take cattle up the rough hill until 1869, after he had hewn a trail that was wide enough to accommodate livestock. Needing living quarters while he watched the animals, Tharp found a huge log that had been hollowed out by fire and capped its cavernous end with a shed fitted with a door and window!

The Native Americans of the area fared less well. Following a clash with Visalia settlers in 1859, fragmented groups of Monaches—those who had not succumbed to measles and smallpox introduced by the invaders—fled across the Sierra to join their relatives in the Owens Valley. There they became allies of the Monos and other Paiute groups that were waging a fierce guerrilla war against miners who were pushing into the Coso Mountains, southeast of Owens Lake, where silver had been discovered in 1860. To protect the miners, the army on July 4, 1862, established Camp Independence in the Owens Valley.

Hoping to shorten travel time between Visalia and Camp Independence, an entrepreneur named John Benjamin Hockett obtained a franchise to build a toll trail. Reporting to the county supervisors that he had completed the task during the summer and fall of 1863 at a cost of $1,000, Hockett prepared to collect tolls. The army, however, found his work substandard and took over maintenance of the trail in 1864.

One user of the Hockett Trail that summer was young Clarence King of the California State Geological Survey; King was afire with ambition to scale Mount Whitney, recently named for his boss, Josiah Whitney. (King later became the first head of the far bigger U.S. Geological Survey.) Because of his penchant for wandering into cul-de-sacs, he failed in the attempt. When he tried again in 1871, he got lost in swirling clouds and, without realizing the mistake, landed on Mount Langley. So the actual first ascent of the tallest peak in the coterminous United States was made on August 18, 1873, by three fishermen who had been camping in the upper Kern River Canyon. King refused to believe their reports until he had once again followed the Hockett Trail into the high country, and on September 19, 1873, stood belatedly and dejectedly on the peak that he thought he had conquered two years before. One month later, John Muir reached the top alone on a difficult route out of Owens Valley.

By the time Whitney had been scaled, lumbermen were edging into the lower parts of the forest belt. Sheep ranchers were keeping pace. Large numbers of sheep were held on the winter grazing and spring lambing grounds of the southern half of the San Joaquin Valley. There was not enough summer grass to go around, however, and more and more ranchers looked toward the mountains. But the owners did not like the hard, dirty, lonesome work of herding, and so they imported expert Basque workers from the Pyrenees of Spain and France. These herders, most of whom intended to return home after making a stake, had no interest in protecting the land. To keep the animals from getting lost, they herded them in tight bands, with the result that they trampled even more grass and tree seedlings than they ate. The herders also set fire to the underbrush so that increased sunlight would produce thicker crops of grass the following year. Some of the fires swirled out of control.

John Muir wrote articles excoriating the practices—he called sheep "hoofed locusts"—and Clarence King reported angrily, after his 1873 ride along the Hockett Trail, that the once lovely Kern plateau had been devastated. "The indefatigable shepherds have camped everywhere, leaving hardly a spear of grass behind them." No remedies followed; it was not the American way, in those days, to check the exploitation of natural resources.

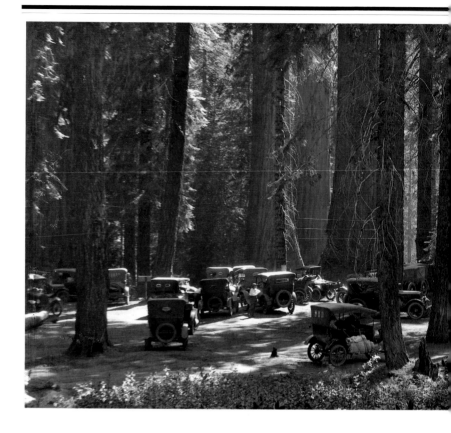

Establishment of the Park

In October 1885, fifty-three members of a San Francisco-based socialistic group filed claims to several plots of timberland in the Kaweah River's watershed. Notice of the filings was published in the Visalia *Delta*, as required by law. So many simultaneous claimings by men from the same city (several used the same street address) roused the suspicions of the *Delta*'s editors, for timber companies, anxious to sidestep the laws that limited the amount of public land they could acquire, often hired out-of-work panhandlers to make the entries and then transfer title.

Apprised by the paper of the activity, the government withdrew several key townships from entry pending investigation. The colonists took the situation in stride. They had acted in good faith, and nothing in the nation's land laws prevented like-minded groups from working as associations on community projects. Confidently they went ahead with their plans to ship timber all over the world and to develop from the proceeds a flourishing settlement that

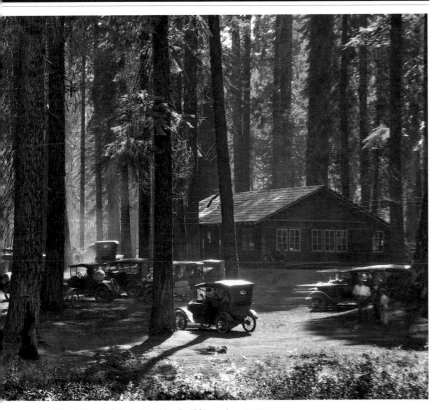

Giant Forest Administrative Building, circa 1922.

would show the superiority of communal societies over capitalistic ones. The government did nothing to investigate the colony.

All this took place at a time when conservationists, led by George Stewart of the Visalia *Delta*, were agitating for a national park that would protect the valley's watersheds by ending ruinous grazing and lumbering practices. John Muir brought his trenchant pen to the crusade; the American Association for the Advancement of Science joined the fray. More weight came from the Southern Pacific Railroad, which wanted, in addition to tourist traffic to the park, an assured supply of water for the many acres of grant land it hoped to sell to farmers. But when President Benjamin Harrison finally signed, on September 25, 1890, a congressional bill creating Sequoia National Park—the second in the nation, after Yellowstone—the agitators were dismayed. They had dreamed of an Eden-like reserve extending from present Yosemite National Park south to the Kern and from the foothills to the Sierra crest. What they received amounted to about 50,000 acres along the watershed of the Kaweah's South Fork far from Giant Forest and even farther from Mount Whitney and its adjoining 14,000-foot peaks.

No one can prove what happened next, but apparently a Southern Pacific land agent approached some of California's delegation in Washington and showed them the light. A pending bill to create Yosemite National Park was revised in such a way as to create small (2,560-acre) General Grant National Park and enlarge Sequoia National Park to 160,000 acres. None of this land touched the high country—but it did deprive the colonists of many of their claims without recompense and without a hearing. No other marked change came until the creation, in 1916, of the National Park Service under the direction of Stephen Mather. He knew that Sequoia National Park embraced about 4,000 acres of private holdings that might be logged over or subdivided for summer cabins. When government appropriations fell short of the amount needed to purchase the tracts, Mather sought funds from private sources. Gradually the geographic integrity of the park was achieved.

In 1926, years of agitation for a park that would include at least some of the high country east of the original reserve bore fruit, and the boundary was rolled east to the Sierra crest.

The Sierra Club fought and won a long legal and public-relations battle that brought the Mineral King area into the park. Mineral King contains open subalpine meadows and high peaks of great visual appeal. In the 1940s, the Club had agreed in principle to support construction of a rustic ski resort on what was then Forest Service land. In 1965, the Forest Service approved a Disney Corporation bid to build a humongous complex that included 27 ski lifts and a ten-story garage, restaurants, and hotels able to accommodate 14,000 people at one time.

The U.S. Interior Department agreed to upgrade a road that cut across the park, to allow access to the resort. This triggered a federal lawsuit in 1969 by the Sierra Club, which obtained an injunction against construction. The dispute went to the U.S. Supreme Court, which held that the Club, as its case had been presented, had no legal standing; the Court added, however, that the Club could argue its case again if it showed how the resort would damage its interests and those of its members.

Meanwhile, Club volunteers initiated an aggressive lobbying and public-relations campaign in opposition to the resort. Disney abandoned the struggle, and in 1978 Mineral King, by act of Congress, was included in Sequoia National Park.*

*For a discussion of the geology of Sequoia, see Kings Canyon National Park, pages 189–193.

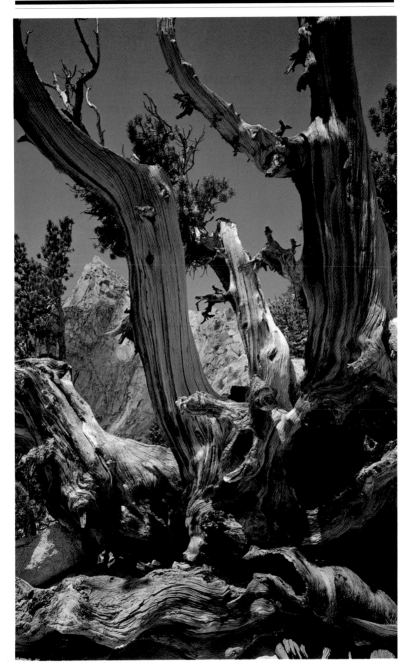

Whitebark pine is able to grow in the high altitudes of the Sierra Nevada.

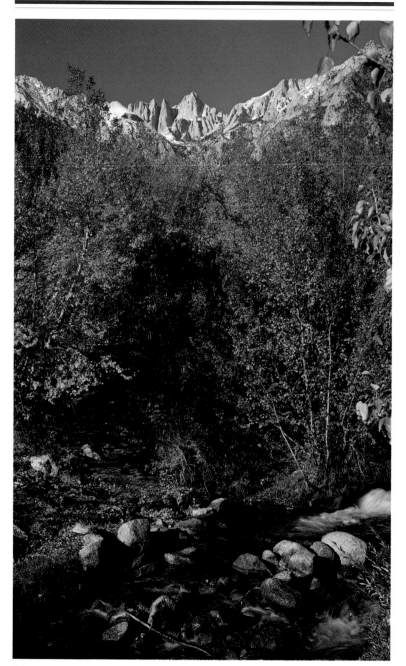

Mt. Whitney, at 14,494 feet, towers above the autumn trees at Lone Pine Creek.

The Sierra Nevada is a classic fault-block mountain range. Powerful movements in the earth's crust, occurring intermittently during many millions of years, thrust its eastern edge upward more than 2 miles—a phenomenon strikingly visible in the erosion-clawed escarpment that lines the section of the Owens Valley that is directly opposite Sequoia and Kings Canyon National Parks. Westward, the tilted Sierra block, incised by enormous canyons, drops more gently toward the Pacific. These geographical circumstances make the growth of a belt of big trees, sequoias among them, all but inevitable.

Climate and Precipitation

Beginning in October or November and continuing until May, massed storm clouds float out of the North Pacific to deluge the California coast. The densest portion of them strikes the northern part of the state, but strong flankers swing southward. As the oncoming front is forced upward by the Coast Range, the water vapor cools and rain begins. The obstacle is not very high, however; the storm passes easily over it and then sags again, growing warm enough to reabsorb the water droplets as vapor. As a consequence, the San Joaquin Valley lies in a "rain shadow," where precipitation is slight.

Immediately east of the valley, the Sierra slope forces the cloud cover to rise much higher than before. Again precipitation falls as rain in the oak and chaparral belt of the foothills and as snow in the higher elevations. Then, at an elevation of 8,000 to 9,000 feet, intensity tapers off, for the clouds have dropped the bulk of their freight. Dry winds howl, and the high, cold plateaus and basins above timberline are actually deserts, although drifts piled by blizzards and evaporating slowly because of the cold tend to disguise the reality.

Latitude adds another element to the equation. The southern foothills are warmer on average than the northern. Tree lines are higher. Evergreens start growing at an elevation of about 1,200 to 1,500 feet near Lassen Peak, but at 2,500 feet or so in the south. Arctic-zone timberline conditions appear at about 8,000 feet on Lassen Peak, but at about 11,000 feet on the Kings–Kern Divide near Mount Whitney.

Then add this: winter storms from the Pacific are relatively warm. When the rain turns to snow—generally at 4,000 or 5,000 feet in Sequoia National Park—it is moist and heavy, not the insubstantial powder of the peaktops. It clings stickily to the trunks and boughs of the conifers and presses the latter sharply downward, giving the forest belt an extraordinary whipped-cream appearance that delights cross-country skiers. Thermometers seldom dip to 0° F at Giant Forest, and the 10 to 20 feet of snow on the ground are an ideal insulator. The porous soil beneath the blanket absorbs enough water to last throughout the dry, warm summer that follows, and the impervious granite beneath the soil is frequently close enough to the surface to keep that moisture within reach of even the sequoias' shallow roots. Thus, because of equitable year-round temperature and adequate moisture distribution, the Sierra forest belt has produced, in addition to the giant sequoias, some of the tallest sugar pines, lodgepole pines, and red firs ever recorded.

Watch the beginning of nature's annual surge as you drive, in the spring, from park headquarters above Three Rivers to Giant Forest. The new leaves of the willows, sycamores, alders, and occasional cottonwoods that line the Middle Fork of the Kaweah River shine like sequins. Gnarled oaks and matted chaparral cover the hillsides. A bend in the deepening canyon opens a sudden view of the Great Western Divide, its peaks still covered with snow. Down here a different white appears—plump, creamy fingers swaying at the tip of almost every branch of the big, sprawling bushes called California buckeye, and tall, candle-straight yucca marching like white-uniformed acolytes up a rocky ridge toward the dome of Moro Rock.

The road leaves the stream to twine upward along the steep, arid, south-facing canyon wall. Soon the first ponderosa (yellow) pines appear, sunlight glowing on long, green needles and on thick, orange bark, which on the trunks of mature trees is divided into massive plates separated by deep black or brown grooves. Then, still higher, as the land flattens somewhat, appears a mixture of other conifers—sugar pines, incense-cedars, white firs, a few red firs, and, most prominently, the commanding, cinnamon-red boles of the sequoias.

Sequoiadendron giganteum

They are giants indeed, relics of the Age of Dinosaurs. Once they grew throughout northern Europe and North America, but environmental changes slowly strangled them. Ten million or more years ago, only a few survivors remained in what is now southern Idaho and western Nevada. They, too, seemed doomed, for the gradual rise of the Sierra Nevada was draining water from Pacific storms and creating more aridity to the east than the ancestral sequoias could tolerate. Yet somehow, in the geologic nick of time, seeds managed to reach the moist western slope.

Tiny seeds. The ones we know today are paper thin and no big-

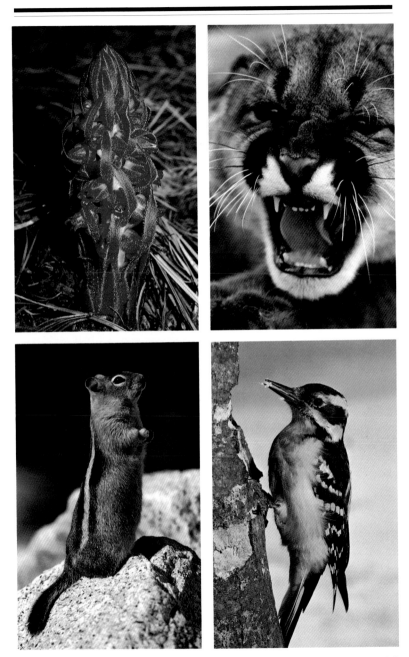

Clockwise from top left: Snow plant; mountain lion; hairy woodpecker; golden-mantled ground squirrel.

ger than an oatmeal flake. About 90,000 of them weigh 1 pound. Even so, it is not difficult to find a few by brushing your hand across unlittered soil near a big tree. The thin black line that contains the embryo divides the seed into two tannish "wings." Under propitious conditions, those wings can carry a sequoia embryo as much as one third of a mile from its birthplace. Could similar seeds have been blown across relatively low Sierra passes 10 million years ago? Or did birds and small animals, which today pay scant attention to the seeds, act as carriers in ancient times? No one knows.

No one knows, either, the extent of the ancient relocated forest of *Sequoiadendron gigantea*. Today the trees are scattered in groves of varying size over a span of 260 miles. Most are clustered in the southern Sierra at elevations of 5,000 to 7,000 feet. They favor "platforms" on or near the tops of the heavy-shouldered ridges that rise between profound canyons. This is a very different environment from that of the coastal hills of northern California, where another redwood (*Sequoia sempervirens*) flourishes within sound of the surf. Although thinner than the Sierra tree, mature coast redwoods are taller and grow in dense stands of their own kind. *Gigantea*, by contrast, are always mixed, very sparsely, with a retinue of other species.

Because their reproduction is so difficult and uncertain, *Sequoiadendron gigantea* generate floods of seeds. In a normal year, a mature tree produces about 2,000 cones the size and shape of a hen's egg. These bright green cones hang on the upper branches of the tree for several years. Meanwhile, more keep coming along—and some drop, too—so that it is not unusual for a medium-sized sequoia to hold 15,000 or more cones at once. Each cone contains an average of 200 seeds. Three big trees standing close together are potentially able to put 1 million seeds on a single acre in a year.

The seeds sometimes are released by the larvae of a minute beetle that chews through a cone in such a way as to cut its water supply; the scales then dry and shrink, freeing the seeds. But the indefatigable sower is a small and frantically energetic squirrel. The chickaree has a bushy tail, a brownish back, a light-colored belly, and a white ring around each bright, black eye. Although chickarees prefer pine nuts and disdain sequoia seeds, they do relish the inside fibers of sequoia cones, which they store in great numbers for winter use. After scampering up a tree and tearing open a few cones for breakfast, scattering seeds the while, the animals start a frenzied clipping; one observer tells of 538 cones, severed by a single squirrel, plumping to the ground in 31 minutes. The cones are carried one by one to storehouses, where more seeds will be strewn about during winter banquets.

About 75 percent of a cone's seeds are viable when shed. If living embryos fall onto a spot where full sunlight dehydrates them quickly or if they land in dry duff, they perish—the fate of more than 90 percent of them. Those that survive are the few that land on dampish mineral soil that recently has been disturbed by the falling of a tree, by logging or road-building activities (outside the park), or by fire, which by burning away the organic matter in the topsoil creates, for a short time, tiny cavities that act as refuges. Fire also eliminates the forest's understory of brush and smaller trees, white fir in particular, that otherwise would cut off the sunlight that the seedlings need once they have sprouted. Indeed, fire is so beneficial that when conditions are favorable, the National Park Service itself starts fires to improve the forest ecology.

Except for characteristic tiny, overlapping, pointed leaves that cling tightly to each twig, a young sequoia bears scant resemblance to a mature tree. The numerous branches of the younger tree point downward; its shape is sharply conical. But as competition for sunlight increases, the lower branches die and fall off, exposing 100 or more feet of the magnificent trunk that so rivets the attention of park visitors. Now the bulky crown may become lopsided because fire scars have cut off part of the sap supply or because lightning has killed a huge upper branch, leaving behind a hoary snag. Also, many of the high branches twist about and grow upward, reaching for the sun. The cone shape vanishes, and what is left is a gnarled embodiment of serene power.

The essence of this impression does not come from height alone. Although the General Sherman Tree in Giant Forest is 274.9 feet tall, many coast redwoods stand higher. Although the Sherman's circumference at the ground is 102.6 feet, a genus of cypress in Mexico is much bigger around. Age? Bristlecone pines live almost 2,000 years longer than the General Sherman's estimated age of 2,300 to 2,700 years. But because there is relatively little taper in the Sherman's trunk, it emerges as the largest living thing on earth; its great bole alone weighs an estimated 1,385 tons—a truly remarkable figure because sequoia wood is light, 13 pounds per cubic foot, compared, for example, with the 53 pounds of a live oak. Any living object that is capable of sustaining such overwhelming volume is bound to be regal.

Amazement increases when one realizes that although the giant's root system may reach out more than 100 feet from the trunk, it goes down only 3 to 6 feet. To keep standing, the tree must be well balanced. Hence the marvelous straightness of most of them. Further buttressing is provided by a basal swelling that time

Overleaf: Manzanita bush in Giant Forest.

carves into knobs that look like elephant feet. Eventually, though, imbalance comes. Every old sequoia has lived through many blazes—thanks to the resistant qualities of its thick, low-resin, and tannin-filled bark—but sooner or later fire will take its toll on a tree. Snow will overweigh one side or the other. If the ground is soggy at the time, and if gales roar across the ridges, there may be a thunderous toppling. Then silence. And a shattered trunk—sequoia wood is very brittle—whose pieces will be almost as long in decaying as the tree was in reaching its prime.

Sites, Trails, and Trips

Giant Forest

Many of those who know the sequoias believe that no other grove of trees on this planet is so beautiful and awesomely impressive as the Giant Forest; and, some say, only the words of John Muir, who saw them in the waning days of the nineteenth century, can describe them. Although he spoke eloquently, even Muir failed to capture the majesty that is revealed to each visitor, who, when encountering a sequoia for the first time, is stunned by its magnificence. One must find his or her own way to accept what nature has done here. And along the almost 40 miles of footpaths in the 5 square miles of Giant Forest there is no better place. An excellent trail folder with map is available through the Sequoia Natural History Association at any park Visitor Center.

Hazelwood Nature Trail. The Hazelwood Nature Trail is an easy, 1-mile loop that wraps up the whole story of the sequoias for those with little time or some physical disability. Trail-side exhibits lead the visitor over gentle grades through excellent stands of the giant trees. The trail begins and ends opposite the Giant Forest Lodge/Round Meadow Turnoff and takes about 1.5 hours.

Huckleberry Meadow Loop Trail. The 5-mile Huckleberry Meadow Loop Trail goes through the central portion of the Giant Forest, which begins near the lodge, and leads to some of the lesser-known features of the park: Huckleberry Meadow; the historic Squatter's Cabin; and the 250-foot-tall Washington Tree, one of the finest examples of a truly giant sequoia. The trail is signed and takes about 3 hours to complete.

Crescent Meadow and Log Meadow Loop Trail. The gentle meadows of Sequoia National Park are as much a part of the whole picture as the trees, and the Crescent Meadow and Log Meadow Loop

Crescent Meadow is in the southeastern portion of Giant Forest.

Trail is one of the easiest trails that reveals these treasures. A 2- to 3-hour walk around the two meadows offers wonderful views of giant sequoias, the oldest pioneer cabin in the park, and, in the right season, blankets of wildflowers. The 1.8-mile trail begins and ends at the Crescent Meadow parking area and is signed.

Congress Trail. Take a folder with you; you can buy one at the trail head or at any Visitor Center. This is a fascinating place, filled with trees with interesting names, not the least of which is the famous General Sherman Tree and its companion, the General Lee Tree. There are others: Lincoln, McKinley, and the House and Senate Group. The Congress Trail is easy, a 2-mile loop, and it takes about 1 to 2 hours to enjoy. Follow the signs.

Trail of the Sequoias and Circle Meadow Loop Trail. The 6-mile Circle Meadow Loop Trail explores the east portion of the Giant Forest and visits Log and Circle meadows as it wanders through some of the finest giant sequoia stands. Signs lead off the Congress Trail to Crescent Creek and the open, grassy Log Meadow. Allow approximately 4 hours for some moderately difficult hiking.

Moro Rock and Soldiers Trail Loop. Beautiful groves of giant sequoias and an exciting climb up Moro Rock highlight this 3- to 4-

TRAILS OF SEQUOIA NATIONAL PARK

GIANT FOREST AREA

HAZELWOOD NATURE TRAIL: Starts and ends at south side of Generals Highway, opposite the Giant Forest Lodge registration office (follow purple-lettered signs); 1 mile; 1.5 hours; an easy loop trail that wanders on gentle grades through great stands of giant sequoia; trailside exhibits.

HUCKLEBERRY MEADOW LOOP TRAIL: Starts and ends at south side of Generals Highway; opposite the Giant Forest Lodge registration office (follow purple-lettered signs of the Hazelwood Nature Trail for approximately .5 mile to the junction of the Hazelwood, Alta, and Soldiers trails; then follow blue-lettered signs); 5 miles; 3 hours; loop trail through the central portions of the Giant Forest to the Squatter's Cabin, and Huckleberry and Circle meadows, past the 250-foot-tall Washington Tree and other sequoias nearly 300 feet tall.

CRESCENT MEADOW AND LOG MEADOW LOOP TRAIL: Starts and ends at Crescent Meadow parking area (follow orange-lettered signs); 1.8 miles; 2 to 3 hours; begins on a short section of the High Sierra Trail, then follows the fringe of Crescent Meadow to Tharp's Log and Chimney Log.

CONGRESS TRAIL: Starts and ends at General Sherman Tree (follow yellow-lettered signs); 2 miles; 2 to 3 hours; ascends gently into Alta Plateau section of Giant Forest, past the President, Chief Sequoyah, General Lee, and McKinley trees, as well as the House and Senate groups.

TRAIL OF THE SEQUOIAS AND CIRCLE MEADOW LOOP: Starts and ends at General Sherman Tree (follow yellow-lettered signs of the Congress Trail for .7 mile to the junction of the Congress, Alta, and the Trail of the Sequoias; then follow green-lettered signs); 6 miles; 4 hours; steady, moderate climb to Crescent Creek in the Giant Forest; at first junction past the creek (about 1 mile), trail branches off and meets the Circle Meadow Loop, at an elevation of approximately 6,700 feet, which passes the historic Tharp's Log and Chimney Tree.

MORO ROCK AND SOLDIERS TRAIL LOOP: Starts and ends at Giant Forest Village (follow red-lettered signs); 4.6 miles; 3 to 4 hours; loop trail to the granite dome Moro Rock; spectacular views from the summit, 300 vertical feet up Moro Rock; trail changes name and returns by the Soldiers Camp, where the United States Cavalry lived in 1913.

MINERAL KING AREA

TIMBER GAP TRAIL: Starts at Sawtooth Pass parking area; 4 miles round trip; 1,400-foot ascent; climbs steadily on an old mining route into a dense red fir forest and then onto an open slope; wildflowers are in abundance in the summer.

CRYSTAL LAKE TRAIL: Starts at Sawtooth Pass parking area on Timber Gap Trail (junction with branch to Crystal Lake is 3.2 miles from Monarch Lakes trail head); 9.8 miles round trip; 3,000-foot ascent; trail through the remnants of the old Chihuahua Mine and into an avalanche-prone basin; some steep climbing through foxtail pine and over broken talus to Crystal Lake; magnificent views of Mineral Peak and Rainbow Mountain.

EAGLE LAKE TRAIL: Starts at Eagle–Mosquito parking area; 6.8 miles round trip; 2,200-foot ascent; leads past Eagle Basin and the mysterious Eagle Creek, and through a boulder field to Eagle Lake.

GIANT FOREST TRAIL MAP

Campground ━━━━━━
Picnic Area ━━━━━━

ROAD ━━━━━━
TRAIL • • • • • • • • • • • •

N

GENERALS HIGHWAY

Wuksachi Village •

Visitor Center

El. 6720'
LODGEPOLE

Lakes Trail

WOLVERTON
El. 7250'

LONG
MEADOW

Alta Trail

**General
Sherman
Tree** El. 6800'

Congress
Trail

Marble Fork

Sunset
Rock △
El. 6365'

Wolverton
Cutoff Trail

ROUND
MEADOW

Little Creek

Lodge

CIRCLE
MEADOW

Trail of the
Sequoias

Village
El. 6500'

Hazelwood
Nature
Trail

CRESCENT
MEADOW El. 6800'

Squatter's
Cabin

Four
Guardsmen

Huckleberry
Meadow
Loop Trail

High
Sierra
Trail

HUCKLEBERRY
MEADOW

Auto
Log

Moro
Rock
Trail

Tunnel
Log

Crescent
Meadow
and Log
Meadow
Loop Trail

Eagle
View

Crescent Creek

To Ash Mountain

△ Moro
Rock
El. 6725'

M I L E S

0   ½   1

SEE MAP ON PAGES 182–183.

hour, 4.6-mile loop trail. From Moro Rock summit, to which there is a 300-foot vertical climb, there are spectacular views of the foothills of Sequoia National Park, the town of Three Rivers, the San Joaquin Valley, and, if there is no smog, even the Coast Range, more than 100 miles to the west. Follow signs that begin just west of the cafeteria at Giant Forest Village.

Mineral King

The Mineral King area of Sequoia National Park gets its name from the optimism that spurred the mining investments here in the late 1870s. For a few short years, this quiet mountain valley promised to become the answer to dreams of wealth—rich silver ore as limitless as that taken from Nevada's great mines. Nearly a decade later the dream had vanished, but the greatest treasure, which most of the miners missed completely, was still there. Nearly lost a second time, when recreation developers almost added their scars to the landscape, Mineral King is now an integral part of Sequoia National Park, and its trails reveal some spectacular scenery.

Most trails in the Mineral King area begin at 7,500 feet. Hiking at this altitude can be strenuous and potentially dangerous. All trips should be gauged to the least fit member of the party. A trail folder with excellent information is available. The road up the valley is open only in the summer.

Timber Gap Trail. The 4-mile round-trip Timber Gap Trail begins at the Sawtooth Pass parking area and climbs a total of 1,400 feet through a dense red fir forest to Timber Gap. At the gap are views of the valley of the Middle Fork of the Kaweah River.

Monarch Lakes Trail. The Monarch Lakes Trail leads through Ground Hog Meadow, 1 trail mile and 920 vertical feet from Mineral King, and then through a long series of switchbacks in the climb to the Monarch Lakes. At the higher levels, the trail goes through Sawtooth Pass, which offers one of the most magnificent views in the southern Sierra. The total elevation gain in this 4.2-mile one-way hike is 2,580 feet.

Crystal Lake Trail. The Crystal Lake Trail ascends 3,000 feet along the 4.9 miles that lead from the Sawtooth Pass parking area to the termination at a Southern California Edison dam site. The trail branches from the Monarch Lakes Trail 3.2 miles from the trail head; it is easy to miss. There are campsites on the terrace just below Crystal Lake. Although there is no trail beyond this point, a short scramble up the bluffs to the northeast leads to Little Crystal Lake.

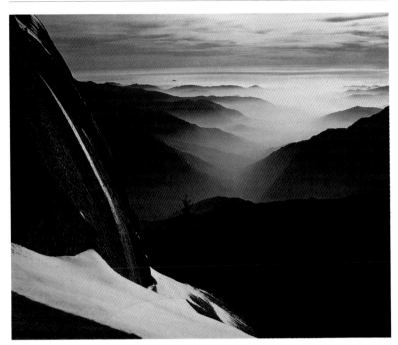

Kaweah River Canyon as seen from the summit of Moro Rock, 6,725 feet above sea level.

Franklin Lake Trail. When hikers reach Franklin Lake, they are at an elevation of 10,327 feet, in the "High Sierra." The Franklin Lake Trail begins at the Eagle–Mosquito parking area, fords the Kaweah River, and then follows an old road and some short switchbacks to Farewell Gap. From the gap, the lake route leads through the prospecting country of an 1870s mining operation, across Franklin Creek, and on to a rock and masonry dam built in 1904/05. The hike is 5.4 miles, and the total elevation gain is 2,527 feet.

White Chief Trail. During midsummer the White Chief meadows are filled with wildflowers, just one thing that makes this hike so attractive. The steep but very scenic trail to White Chief Canyon begins at the Eagle–Mosquito parking area and terminates some 3 miles later at the old White Chief Mine. Although it becomes increasingly faint, the trail continues another mile above the mine until it disappears in the giant glacial cirque that forms the head of the canyon. The total distance is 4.1 miles, and the elevation gain is 2,200 feet.

Eagle Lake Trail. The Eagle Lake Trail follows the same route as the White Chief Trail for the first mile, then branches to the right toward Eagle Canyon. In early summer, the canyon is abundant with flowers—lupine and snow plant in shady areas, and orchid, leopard lily, Indian paintbrush, and shooting star in the meadows. Surrounded by mountain crests, Eagle Lake is a typical glacially formed lake called a tarn. The distance is 3.4 miles, and the elevation gain is 2,200 feet. Along the way, the trail passes Eagle Creek sink hole, where the creek disappears; where the water goes, no one really knows for certain.

Mosquito Lake Trail. Take the right-hand trail about 1 mile from the White Chief and Eagle Lake trail head. The Mosquito Lake Trail is a 3.4-mile hike up and over Miner's Ridge and down to Mosquito Lake 1. There are four other lakes, but no real trail to them; a steep climb leads to Lake 2, but there is no elevation change from there on. The distant lakes are excellent for brook and rainbow trout fishing. The total elevation gain to Lake 1 is 2,200 feet. To allow for revegetation, camping is not permitted at Mosquito Lake 1.

High Country

Some of the best hiking trails in all the national parks are found in the high country of Sequoia National Park. For the sturdy and dedicated, there are no better.

High Sierra Trail. For good reason, one branch road and several winding forest trails converge on lovely Crescent Meadow in the southeastern corner of Giant Forest. For here is the starting point of the High Sierra Trail, which ultimately joins the even more famous John Muir Trail on Wallace Creek, 49 miles away. Add another dozen miles for the push to the top of Mount Whitney, and the young in limb and heart are able to take in, on foot or on horseback, a full cross section of the park. Popularity is such that limits have had to be placed on daily use.

   Construction of the trail began in 1928, two years after the park's boundaries had been rolled east to include the Sierra's crest. The need for extensive blasting and the placing of suspension bridges across reverberating chasms delayed completion until 1932. The engineering returned high rewards. One lofty point after another opens sweeping panoramas. Environments change constantly as the trail slants across slopes matted with slow-growing chinquapin and red-barked manzanita, and then dips into the forested bottoms of the glaciated troughs of the Big Arroyo and the awesome Kern. Avalanche chutes scar the steep granite sides of the Angel Wings. There are meadows and lakes, and creeks where

A fallen sequoia in Giant Forest.

gray water ouzels flit across the glinting water before disappearing into a curtain of spray. The song of canyon wrens cascades; clumps of red penstemon burst out of unlikely cracks in the rock.

Tree species change with altitude. Among them are Jeffrey pines, which resemble ponderosas but favor higher places; soaring sugar pines, whose cones, up to 18 inches long, dangle like ornaments from the tips of the uppermost branches; lodgepoles as straight as if they had been set by a plumb line; and massed red firs that cast a cathedral shade. Near timberline the forest thins, and the junipers, foxtail pines, and white-bark pines are often cruelly deformed, flattened, and stripped of much of their bark and foliage by the arctic weather.

The View From On High. The long rumple of peaks on the Kern–Kaweah Divide looks like a sea of choppy water turned to stone. The somber colors of lofty Black Kaweah contrast strikingly with the pale granite of most of the other summits. Somewhere on almost every peak is a horseshoe-shaped cirque, the rims of its sheer walls often sculptured by erosion into formidable spires. The steely sheen of ice-scoured stone, the vast tongues of talus and scree—it would be a forbidding land were it not for the enchant-ment of bright turquoise lakes and the dwarfed flowers that bloom in a frenzy of exuberance to complete their life cycles within the six or seven weeks allowed them.

There are signs of trouble, too. Although venturesome back-packers can work their way across country to seldom-visited glens, most campers cling to the trails and gravitate toward familiar campsites. Meadows suffer, especially from horses. Some swales have been closed to grazing, and a few to any camping. To preserve the last bits of timberline wood—and to do away with ugly circles of smoke-blackened rocks—campers must use only gas stoves in some areas at higher altitudes. To halt the steady degradation of water purity, visitors must camp well back from streambanks and lakeshores. But the main defense has to be the consideration and cooperation of those who love the backcountry enough to want to keep it as free as possible from the pressure of their own numbers.

Worse things may be lying in wait. A century ago, travelers in the San Joaquin Valley used to exclaim over the view of the moun-tains. That view is seldom visible now, except after winter rains. To understand why, shift viewpoints. On a day of summer atmospher-ic inversions, look from the top of Moro Rock down the Middle Fork of the Kaweah River. The murk that obscures the canyon has in it some dust and smoke from agricultural activities, but much is smog that has leaked out of the San Francisco–Oakland region to mingle with fumes generated by the valley's own cities. Prevailing winds sweep the miasma inexorably up the Sierra's gentle slopes. Concern is growing about the possible effect of acid rain on the trees. Ponderosa and Jeffrey pines are particularly vulnerable; characteristically, the enduring sequoias seem more resistant. Research is being conducted.

But they are so very rare. They make up less than 1 percent of the southern belt of mixed conifers. Perhaps that is why they take on an air of individuality for those who spend time with them—rap-port is difficult to achieve with a crowd. But with them you can sit still and let the scope of their grandeur unfold slowly, which is the only approach it will yield to. You may even sense a timeless wis-dom there. Having so narrowly escaped extinction themselves, the sequoias have much to say to us now.

Opposite: Cloud-shrouded Mt. Whitney as seen from the summit of Mt. Langley.

YOSEMITE
NATIONAL PARK

El Capitan towers almost 4,000 feet above the floor of Yosemite Valley.

YOSEMITE NATIONAL PARK, P.O. BOX 577
YOSEMITE NATIONAL PARK, CALIFORNIA 95389
TEL.: (209) 372-0200

HIGHLIGHTS: Yosemite Valley • Half Dome • Yosemite Falls • Bridalveil Fall • Indian Cultural Museum • Happy Isles • John Muir Trail • Mariposa Grove • Tuolumne Meadows • Tioga Pass

ACCESS: From Merced, 81 miles to Yosemite Valley via California 140. From Fresno, 94 miles to Yosemite Valley via California 41.

HOURS: Daily, year-round.

FEES: For all visitors (less for those in bus, on horseback, foot, or bicycle).

PARKING: At Yosemite Valley and Mariposa Grove; in summer, at Glacier Point, Wawona, Crane Flat, and Tuolumne Meadows.

GAS, FOOD, LODGING: Year-round at Yosemite Valley. Gas year-round at Wawona. Other areas during summer.

VISITOR CENTER: Yosemite Valley Visitor Center offers information, maps, exhibits, backcountry permits, park publications, orientation slide program, and films. Tuolumne Meadows Visitor Center (summer only) offers information, maps, books, and exhibits. Big Oak Flat entrance information station.

MUSEUM: In Yosemite Valley Visitor Center, Happy Isles Nature Center; also Indian Cultural Museum nearby, Hill's studio at Wawona, and Sequoia Ecology Museum at Mariposa Grove.

GIFT SHOP: Several in Yosemite Valley; also at Wawona, Glacier Point, Mariposa Grove, and Tuolumne Meadows.

PETS: Permitted on leash in developed areas, but not allowed in public buildings and wilderness areas, or on trails. Kennels available (summer only).

PICNICKING: At designated sites in Yosemite Valley and other areas of park.

HIKING: Throughout park. Water available in some areas, but must be purified.

BACKPACKING: Throughout backcountry except where prohibited; wilderness permit required.

CAMPGROUNDS: Many sites throughout park. Yosemite Valley, reservations required in summer. Tents and trailers; showers.

TOURS: Guided walks, hikes, and bicycle tours.

OTHER ACTIVITIES: Horseback riding, skiing, swimming, boating, fishing (license required), and mountain climbing.

FACILITIES FOR DISABLED: Parking, some lodging, restrooms, Visitor Center, some trails, special interpretive programs, and sign-language interpreter in summer.

For additional information, see also Sites, Trails, and Trips on pages 305–320 and the maps on pages 288–289 and 312–313.

YOSEMITE VALLEY, ONCE SEEN, IS NEVER forgotten. It is one of the few places in the world where the scenery seems to be in perfect, harmonious balance: the towering granite cliffs and domes surrounding a grassy valley floor; the dark forests and shining rocks; the movement of water everywhere, falling from the cliffs in rushing waterfalls and flowing through the length of the valley in the Merced River—and all touched with sunlight and shadow. There is no temptation to rearrange the elements—to move a waterfall or readjust a pinnacle—the scene has the memorable beauty of completeness.

Yosemite Valley is also a living place; most of the geological forces that shaped it are still at work, and the changing seasons bring a constant renewal of grass, trees, and flowers.

But Yosemite Valley is only a small part—less than 1 percent—of Yosemite National Park's 1,169 square miles. In the park's backcountry the scenery may not be as concentrated, but it is no less magnificent. There are dense forests and glowing fields of wildflowers, alpine meadows and lakes, deep canyons and snow-capped peaks, and groves of centuries-old giant sequoias.

The grandeur of the scenery is reason enough to visit Yosemite, but there are millions of years of history here too. It is almost impossible to spend any time at Yosemite and not wonder what powerful natural forces could have shaped and sculptured the great rocks. Some colorful theories have been proposed over the years; Galen

Water plummets down glacier-made Vernal Fall throughout the year, even during the summer

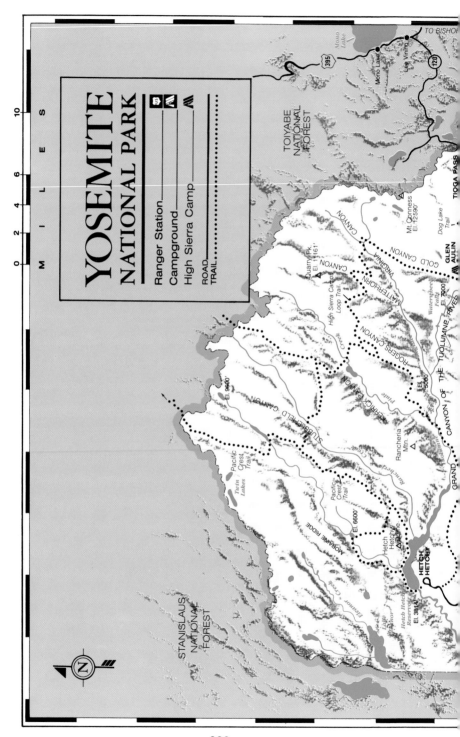

YOSEMITE
NATIONAL PARK

Ranger Station
Campground
High Sierra Camp

ROAD
TRAIL

MILES
0 2 4 6 10

N

STANISLAUS
NATIONAL
FOREST

TOIYABE
NATIONAL
FOREST

TO BISHOP

Mono Lake
Lee Vining
395
120

Mono Lakes

TIOGA PASS

Mt. Conness
El. 12,590'

Dog Lake
Trail

GLEN
AULIN

GOLD CANYON

VIRGINIA CANYON

Quarry Pk.
El. 11,161'

High Sierra Camp
Loop Trail

MATTERHORN CANYON

ROGERS CANYON

Waterwheel
Falls

El.
5000'

CANYON OF THE TUOLUMNE RIVER

GRAND

El. 9600'

STUBBLEFIELD CANYON

MERRICK CANYON

Pacific
Crest
Trail

Twin
Lakes

Rancheria
Mtn.

Rancheria Creek

Pacific
Crest
Trail

MORAINE RIDGE

El. 6600'

Hetch
Hetchy
Dome

HETCH
HETCHY

Eleanor Creek

Lake
Eleanor

Hetch Hetchy
Reservoir
El. 3814'

Clark, the first Guardian of the Yosemite Grant, thought that the domes were "great, frozen gas bubbles." Scientific thought has refined Yosemite's geological history since then, but it is still a fascinating story, as are Yosemite's natural history and human history. As John Muir, conservationist and celebrant of Yosemite, said, "This one noble park is big enough and rich enough for a whole life of study and aesthetic enjoyment . . . its natural beauty cleanses and warms like fire, and you will be willing to stay forever in one place like a tree."

HISTORY

Indians of Ahwahnee

The first humans to live in the Yosemite region probably arrived more than 4,000 years ago, crossing the Sierra from the Great Basin country to the east of the mountains. Over the centuries, Miwok-speaking people from central California gradually moved into the area, living in villages along the Merced River and in Yosemite Valley itself. They called the valley Ahwahnee, loosely translated as "deep grassy valley," and themselves, the Ahwahneechee.

These early Indians were hunter-gatherers, dependent mainly on the valley for food, shelter, and other needs. In late spring and summer they moved into the high country to hunt for deer, and carried on trade with Mono Lake Paiutes across the mountains.

A staple of the Ahwahneechee diet was the acorn of the black oak. Women collected acorns and stored them inside free-standing granaries *(chuck-ah)* woven from branches of deerbrush, grapevine, and conifer. When needed, the acorns were removed from the chuck-ah, shelled, pounded into a fine flour, leached repeatedly to remove the bitter tannin, and cooked into soup, mush, and cakes.

A delicacy was the *ka-cha-vee*, a small insect larva collected by the millions by Mono Lake Paiutes and traded to the Ahwneechee. Mushrooms, camas and brodiaea bulbs, and greens of miner's lettuce, bracken fern, and clover were gathered and eaten in season. To this diet was added rainbow trout that the men speared or trapped in the Merced River, deer and other large wildlife killed with bows and arrows, and squirrels, flickers, and other small animals caught with snares.

The Ahwahneechee cold-weather shelter was the *umacha*, a cone of poles overlaid with bark from incense cedar trees. In warm weather, the Ahwahneechee slept outdoors. Using earth, brush, grapevine,

Opposite: President William Howard Taft, behind driver, and conservationist John Muir, to Taft's left, visit Mariposa Grove in 1909.

poles, and cedar bark, the men also built sacred meeting lodges (roundhouses) and sweathouses. Authentic models of these structures stand today behind the Visitor Center in Yosemite Valley.

The Mariposa Battalion

The first documented entry of non-Indians into Ahwahnee took place in 1851, although the valley may have been seen from the rim in 1833 by members of the Joseph Walker trapping party. The discovery of gold in the Mother Lode Country of the Sierra foothills had brought thousands of miners and prospectors into what had been for centuries Indian land. Bands of Indians had taken to raiding nearby trading posts in retaliation for this invasion, so in the spring of 1851, the state-sanctioned Mariposa Battalion was sent into Yosemite Valley to rout the Indians and move them to a reservation. The expedition was a failure; the Indians easily eluded the battalion. Other expeditions were dispatched to the valley, and, several skirmishes later, most of the Ahwahneechee were taken to a reservation on the Fresno River. Although some Indians later returned to Yosemite, their lives had been irrevocably changed.

Establishment of the Park

The Mariposa Battalion may not have been particularly effective against the Ahwahneechee, but its visit was to change Yosemite forever. The descriptions that the soldiers brought back of the incredible natural wonders of the valley aroused the curiosity and excitement of the public, and within a few years the first trickle of what was to become a flood of tourists had begun.

By 1864, the press of tourism and private entrepreneurs was becoming a threat to the beauty of the valley; overdevelopment and overgrazing were already a severe problem.

In that year, a bill was passed in Congress and signed by President Abraham Lincoln requiring the state of California to preserve and protect Yosemite Valley and the Mariposa Grove of Giant Sequoias in a natural, undisturbed condition. This was the first practical application of an idea that resulted in today's national park system.

During the twenty years that followed, toll roads were built, a stage line was started, and hotels sprang up to cater to the increasing numbers of visitors. Largely through the efforts of John Muir, who would soon become the Sierra Club's first president, Congress acted in 1890 to create Yosemite National Park. The national park was composed of lands surrounding the original state park. In 1906, after a decade of lobbying by Sierra Club secretary William Colby,

California ceded its part to the federal government, and the two segments were combined.

The Fight Over the Hetch Hetchy Dam

Many national parks have been embroiled in controversies, but no nationwide debate has been more intense than the one that focused on Hetch Hetchy Valley, within Yosemite National Park, in the early years of the twentieth century. John Muir regarded Hetch Hetchy, which lies 10 miles north of Yosemite Valley, as a rival in wild beauty to Yosemite itself. He was stunned when the city of San Francisco, some 150 miles to the west, announced that it wanted a dam built in Hetch Hetchy Valley so that its growing population would be assured of a fresh water supply.

Support for the dam increased after the devastating 1906 earthquake engendered widespread sympathy for the City by the Bay. The U.S. Department of the Interior approved the dam application in 1908.

With Hetch Hetchy serving as a catalyst, the U.S. "conservation" movement became bitterly divided between those who believed that large tracts of pristine land should be preserved in or close to a wilderness condition in perpetuity and those, on the other hand, who thought that natural resources should be utilized in a way that would be most beneficial to mankind.

A report by engineers declared that the deep, narrow lower end of Hetch Hetchy was the best answer to San Francisco's needs, while opponents of the dam contended that other sites should be considered, even if the cost would be somewhat greater.

With Congressional approval required, the debate continued for years. Muir and his allies in and outside the Sierra Club organized a national effort to block passage of the dam bill. Influential newspaper and magazine editors published articles and editorials that generated a flood of mail to Washington. Muir himself thundered in print, "These temple destroyers, devotees of ravaging commercialism, seem to have a perfect contempt for Nature, and instead of lifting their eyes to the God of the Mountains, lift them to the Almighty Dollar." He raged on, "Dam Hetch Hetchy! As well dam for water-tanks the people's cathedrals and churches, for no holier temple has ever been consecrated by the heart of man." Congressman Horace Tower of Iowa declared that "dishwashing is not the only use for water, nor lumber for trees, nor pasture for grass."

In rebuttal, Gifford Pinchot, former chief of the United States Forest Service, testified before Congress that "the fundamental principle of the whole conservation policy is that of use, to take every part of the land and its resources and put it to that use in which it will serve the most people."

Top: The naturalist John Muir regarded Hetch Valley, in the park, as comparable in beauty to Yosemite Valley.
Bottom: After a long fight, preservationists failed to stop construction of a dam that flooded Hetch Hetchy.

In 1913, Congress approved the creation of a reservoir, and O'Shaughnessy Dam now rises in the gorge of the Tuolumne River within the park. But, as the excellent account by Roderick Nash in his perceptive study, *Wilderness and the American Mind*, shows, the American preservation movement had come of age, and it would be better prepared when future efforts were made to construct dams in units of the national park system.

Yosemite was administered by the cavalry until 1916, when the National Park Service was established in the Department of the Interior, and the park was finally put under civilian management. Tourism grew steadily in the years that followed as Yosemite's fame spread: by the 1940s, Yosemite had 500,000 visitors a year; by the mid-1990s, more than 4 million people from around the world visited the park annually.

GEOLOGY

Yosemite National Park lies midway along the 400-mile-long range of "snowy mountains," the Sierra Nevada, poetically described by John Muir as "the range of light." To the west and paralleling the Sierra Nevada is California's Central Valley, and to the east is the vast desert of eastern California and the basin and range country of Nevada.

El Portal, near a west entrance to the park, is at an elevation of 2,100 feet; the land climbs steeply along the Merced Canyon to 4,000 feet, the level of the floor of Yosemite Valley. Most of the park—the high country—is the rugged granite terrain of forests, alpine meadows, and bare rock that surrounds the valley. Much of this area is 5,000 to 10,000 feet in elevation, with major peaks like Mount Lyell, Mount Dana, Mount Clark, and Mount Conness reaching into the thin air above 11,000 feet to more than 13,000 feet. Tioga Pass, the park's east entrance, is almost 10,000 feet high.

Two major rivers drain Yosemite. The Merced—mostly placid as it winds through Yosemite Valley, but wild and foaming both above and below this stretch—channels rain water and snowmelt from the park's southern half. The Tuolumne drains the northern half. Both rivers head near the park's eastern boundary—along the Sierra crest—flowing westward down the range's less-steep western slopes and out to the San Joaquin River in the Central Valley.

Most of the park has been chiseled out of granite by erosion. This bedrock, which appears buff to gray from a distance and salt-and-pepper close up, is partly clothed by variously colored lichen, evergreen forests, and flower-filled meadows. In winter, almost all the high country is covered by snow, but the valley walls are too steep for snow to collect, and the valley floor is low enough that its

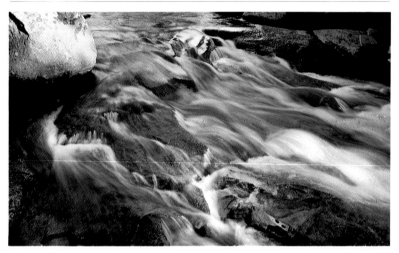

The Tuolumne River and its tributaries drain much of the high country.

snow cover is intermittent.

But snow and vegetation only partly hide the granite; exposed slabs, boulders, ridges, ledges, cliffs, domes, and peaks abound, many of which are entirely treeless. From numberless vantage points, visitors can look out on vast "seas of granite." This is a park of grand vistas, huge in scale and evoking a sense of eternity.

Ancient Beginnings

Ageless as they seem, Yosemite's granites are not the Sierra's oldest rocks—not by some 200 million years. Some of the beds of slate exposed in Merced Canyon along California 140 to the west of the park were deposited in an ancient ocean as layers of mud and sand roughly 450 million years ago. Later they were twisted and metamorphosed within mountain ranges ancestral to the present Sierra. Only the contorted layers and a few ancient marine fossils document this distant beginning.

The next chapter written in the rocks is related to the drifting apart of North America and Europe, which began about 200 million years ago. As one of the earth's crustal plates slowly carried North America westward, the Atlantic Ocean opened and the Pacific coast was crumpled by mountain building. Since oceanic crust is generally heavier than continental crust, the Pacific plate buckled beneath the North American plate, creating a deep oceanic trench. The adjacent continental crust was folded and fractured, and molten rock from below squeezed upward to form a volcanic mountain range similar to the present-day Andes in South America.

Much of the molten rock, or magma, that fed these ancient Sierran volcanoes cooled slowly, deep underground, forming the vast granite core that is exposed in the present Sierra Nevada. All this activity occurred on a time scale that was slow, even in geologic terms. The granites of Yosemite and the neighboring Sierra have been dated by geologists to be as old as 200 million years and as young as 60 million years, with many in between. As a result, Yosemite's many distinct granites are of a wide range of colors, textures, and mineral ingredients, evident in the cliff walls of the valley.

The gold veins in the foothills of the Sierra, like those in the Mother Lode Country to the west of the park, formed from the distilling action of hot waters associated with the volcanism of this same granite-forming period.

Uplift and Erosion

Granite is formed deep in the earth, perhaps 7 miles beneath the overlying volcanoes. The granites of Yosemite have been uplifted some 7 miles, and 4 to 5 miles of rock have been eroded from above them to expose the granite core. This is not to say that the Sierra was ever 7 miles high. The process of uplift, with its attendant earthquake activity, was slow and episodic; 7 miles up in 60 million years is an average of only 7 inches every 1,000 years. Erosion by rain and streams kept pace with much of the uplift, and the Sierra is probably higher now than it was earlier in its history.

One of the interesting aspects of the last 3 million years of uplift of the Sierra is that it was not symmetrical. Instead, the major uplift was on the eastern scarp of the range. The western flank was tilted toward the Central Valley of California. This westward tilting accounts for the less-steep western slopes and for a Sierra crest that is nearer to the eastern side of the range.

Glaciation

Fire and ice have been Yosemite's major creators. The earth's internal fires melted the magma that cooled to form granite, and rivers of glacial ice carved the present peaks and valleys.

During the last few million years, the earth's climate has cooled enough that great ice sheets have formed and melted several times. Apparently the uplift of the Sierra has also accelerated, raising the peaks to higher cooler elevations. The result has been several periods of major mountain glaciation. Ice caps as much as 1 mile thick accumulated in the high country, sending slow-moving rivers of ice down the preexisting valleys. The major glaciers that ground down the Merced and Tuolumne canyons were thick and heavy, and several generations of ice carved the deep U-shaped valleys seen today.

The work of the glaciers was aided by great bedrock cracks—called joints by geologists—that formed as the granite cooled and was exposed by erosion. Sometimes these joints are flat or convex, and exfoliate (flake off) to form the great granite domes. In other places they are almost vertical and helped form the massive cliff of El Capitan in the valley and the steep-sided summits of Cathedral and Unicorn peaks in the Tuolumne Meadows area. A combination of exfoliation and vertical joints, and the patient carving of glacial ice, formed Half Dome.

With each ebb and flow of the erosive ice, Yosemite's face was sculptured closer to its present form. While freezing and thawing water dislodged granite blocks from exposed summits above, glacial ice plucked rocks from the flanks of the high peaks, resulting in the bowl-shaped cirques exposed today. Downslope, aprons and rivers of glacial ice carved and polished the granite. Millions of rocks of all sizes, trapped in the moving ice, engraved scratches on rock surfaces and later were left strewn across the landscape as "erratics" when the ice melted.

In part of Yosemite Valley, ice quarried 3,000 feet or more of bedrock from the valley floor. When the ice melted, only 10,000 years ago, a glacial lake filled the valley, into which hundreds of feet of mud and sand were deposited. These sediments produced the flat floor of the present-day valley.

The twentieth century was a time in which almost all of Yosemite's ice had retreated, leaving mere remnant glaciers on the high peaks. But in the perspective of geologic time, we can expect the ice to return, renewing its sculpture of Yosemite and the great Sierra Nevada.

Waterfalls

Yosemite's magnificent waterfalls and cascades are products of the same forces that shaped Yosemite Valley's distinctive cliffs and domes. While Yosemite Valley was being carved more and more deeply by glacial action, the tributary ice streams like Yosemite Creek cut much more slowly; their valleys were left hanging above the major glacial valleys as the ice melted, and their waters poured down the main canyon walls or leaped into space where the walls were steepest.

The classic example of this hanging valley type of fall is Yosemite Falls; the Upper Fall plummets 1,430 feet and, after a series of cascades for 675 feet, the Lower Fall plunges 320 feet more. Yosemite Falls, at 2,425 feet, is the highest waterfall in North America and the second-highest in the world after Angel

The often-photographed Jeffrey pine on 3,073-foot-high Sentinel Dome.

Fall (3,212 feet) in Venezuela. Indeed, five of Yosemite's waterfalls are among the ten highest on earth; even Vernal Fall, at 317 feet, is almost twice as high as Niagara.

Bridalveil Fall is another fine example of the hanging valley type of waterfall. Falling 620 feet, its misty waters seem to float in the valley breezes.

A different type of waterfall resulted from the action of glaciers plucking huge blocks out of streambeds where the granite was jointed, thus producing "glacial stairways." Vernal and Nevada are falls of this type; in Merced Canyon, the Merced River drops 2,000 feet in 1.5 miles in a section called the Giant's Stairway, with 317-foot Vernal Fall and 594-foot Nevada Fall pouring over two of the steps.

In many places in Yosemite, falls cascade over irregularly fractured granite or over more gently sloping, smooth cliffs instead of leaping freely. The Cascades in Cascade Creek and the 1,250-foot Royal Arch Cascade are good examples.

Spring is the season to see Yosemite's many splendid falls. The rapid melting of the heavy winter snowpack gives the falls a booming vitality. By autumn, some of the falls are dry, or nearly so. This is in part related to the watershed area that each waterfall drains. For example, Ribbon Fall near El Capitan drains only 4 square miles, whereas Nevada Fall drains 118. In consequence, Ribbon Fall often disappears before summer is over, while Nevada Fall thunders all year round. Even in winter, the waterfalls have a stark

beauty. Yosemite Falls grows a huge curtain of frost and a great ice cone at the base of the Upper Fall, reminders of the glacial origin of its hanging valley.

NATURAL HISTORY

Climate and Precipitation

Yosemite's mild climate makes travel a pleasure in almost any season. In summer, days are warm and dry; temperatures sometimes reach as high as 100° F in the valley and 75° F in the high country, but nights are always cool. Summer skies are usually blue and cloudless, with an occasional thundershower in the afternoon.

Winter temperatures can fall as low as 5° F to 10° F, although the usual range is from 20° F to 40° F and sometimes as high as 65° F or so. The first snowfall usually comes to the valley before Christmas; snows in the high country come earlier and are so heavy that the cross-Sierra Tioga Road is closed to cars for six to nine months of the year, even though the floor of Yosemite Valley may be largely snowless much of the winter. Even in winter, the skies are brilliantly clear between storms; the icy beauty of Yosemite's snow-crowned cliffs and trees shining under the deep-blue sky is an unforgettable sight.

Trees, Plants, and Flowers

At first glance, Yosemite's shining granite domes and leaping waterfalls seem to be its most spectacular attractions. At a closer focus, though, the diversity of Yosemite's plant life is just as intriguing. With altitudes ranging from 2,000 feet on the western boundary to 13,000 feet at the eastern summit, there are innumerable local environments hospitable to plants with differing needs. Thirty-seven kinds of native trees grow in the park (both broad-leaved and cone-bearing evergreens) and more than 1,400 flowering plants, as well as innumerable shrubs, grasses, sedges, ferns, and fungi. They are distributed in broad vegetation zones or belts, overlapping in places, that are determined largely by altitude.

While most of Yosemite is at a high elevation, the park boundary at El Portal and parts of the Wawona and Big Oak Flat roads are in the foothill woodland zone of 2,000 to 3,000 feet. At this elevation, the most conspicuous trees are the digger pine, a spreading rangy tree with grayish needles, and the handsome, tall ponderosa,

Opposite: A winter frost in Yosemite Valley.

or yellow, pine. There are live oaks here, too, and California buckeye, which in early summer is covered with long clusters of white blossoms. In spring this zone is blanketed with blue and purple lupine, orange-gold California poppies, and dozens of other wildflowers, and dotted with western redbuds, small shrubs that are completely swathed in brilliant magenta blossoms. Hillsides are covered with dense brush or chaparral, mostly the hardy California lilac and purple-barked, gnarled manzanita.

Beginning at about 3,000 feet is the mixed-conifer forest, a broad zone of diverse tree species extending to about 7,000 feet in elevation. In this zone, depending on rainfall and suitable soil, are mixtures of ponderosa pine; Jeffrey pine; sugar pine, with its foot-long cones; incense cedar, a large tree that is often mistaken for a giant sequoia, and is in fact not a cedar but a member of the cypress family; and Douglas-fir, which is not really a fir and, just to complicate matters, looks like a spruce. Also in this zone, which includes Yosemite Valley, are fine stands of black oak and, scattered through the forest and along the Merced River, lovely California dogwood, which in May and June blooms lavishly with large, creamy white flowers.

The magnificent giant sequoias—the largest living things known—grow best at this elevation. There are three groves within the park: the Mariposa, Tuolumne, and Merced Groves of Giant Sequoias. These trees—some of which are almost 3,000 years old—average 250 feet in height and 15 to 20 feet in diameter. A "big tree" is so massive that it is almost impossible to comprehend that it is a living, growing plant. These huge trees have cinnamon-colored bark that is sometimes 2 feet thick, and bear tiny cones about the size of a hen's egg.

The lavish wildflowers of this zone vary as the seasons progress, from the brilliant red snow plant that pushes through the forest floor just as the snow is retreating, to the autumn-blooming meadow goldenrod. The lovely western azalea blooms in the valley

Counterclockwise from opposite top: Pygmy owl on cow parsnip; Anderson thistle; shooting stars; monarch on a milkweed; raccoon.

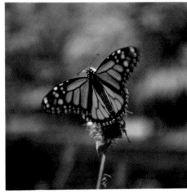

meadows in June, as do the tall, showy cow parsnip, milkweed (which harbors the monarch butterfly), and such small flowers as violets, pussy paws, and brodiaea.

The most extensive of Yosemite's forests grow between 6,500 and 9,000 feet; this is sometimes called the lodgepole pine–red fir belt. In areas of suitable moisture and soil, the stately red fir grows in almost pure stands; where soils are too soggy or too thin for red fir, the smaller lodgepole pine dominates.

Along the trails and in mountain meadows in this zone are an abundance of wildflowers, including the shooting star, monkey flower (yellow, pink, and red varieties), larkspur, and paintbrush. Occasionally it is possible to find the rare Washington lily, a large white blossom on a 6-foot stalk.

Above 9,000 feet, the forest thins out to small groves and scattered trees: western white pine, mountain hemlock, and, at the highest elevations, whitebark pine. Among the few struggling whitebark pines that grow above timberline there is still a fine community of wildflowers, among them mats of spreading phlox, bell-shaped white heather, alpine pentstemon, and Dana's lupine.

Wildlife

The most conspicuous animal in Yosemite National Park is the mule deer, which is often seen browsing in meadows singly or in small bands. They are the only hoofed animals in the park, although the Sierra bighorn once lived in the high country. Gentle and inquisitive, mule deer are nonetheless wild animals and should not be touched or fed.

The same caution applies to the Sierra black bear, which in spite of its name can vary in color from light yellow through brown to black. This is the only species of bear still found in the park.

It is sometimes possible to catch sight of a coyote, raccoon, gray fox, or porcupine and, rarely, a bobcat or mountain lion. Squirrels are very common; the gray squirrel with its long, bushy tail is active almost all year. There are five species of chipmunk in the park, as well as the Sierra chickaree, or red squirrel, which lives at the higher altitudes.

Other high-mountain animals include the Sierra marmot, the largest local representative of the squirrel family; the grayish yellow California badger; and the cony or pika, a small, elusive creature that resembles a rabbit and is more often known by its high nasal chirp, than by sight.

Birds are abundant in Yosemite, with a population of more than 220 species. The most immediately obvious in the valley are the crested Steller's jay, a brash "camp robber"; several kinds of woodpeckers

Tuolumne Meadows is the largest high-mountain meadow in the Sierra Nevada.

and flickers; and the western meadowlark, with its beautiful song.

The birdlife also varies with elevation; at higher altitudes are found (among many others) the mountain bluebird, Clark's nutcracker, and mountain chickadee. A most unusual bird that sometimes can be seen along fast-moving mountain streams is the water ouzel, or dipper; it bobs up and down on a streamside rock for a few moments and then makes a dash into the stream, going completely underwater to hunt for larvae on the bottom.

SITES, TRAILS, AND TRIPS

Yosemite National Park is so large and so scenically varied that the problem for the visitor is not finding something to see or do, but choosing among the riches. Much of the best scenery can be seen from the park's roads, but to experience more fully this extraordinary mountain environment, try to sample at least a few of the more than 750 miles of trails available to hikers and horseback parties.

Yosemite Valley

Yosemite Valley is a logical starting point for a tour of the park; for many, this "Incomparable Valley" is a destination in itself. Because of the very heavy summer visitation to the valley, it is a good idea to make camping reservations early.

The roads in Yosemite Valley are arranged in a one-way system, with those in the eastern part of the valley closed to cars. However, a free shuttle bus operates in the eastern end, including the restricted Mirror Lake Drive, making frequent stops at scenic spots.

The Yosemite Valley Visitor Center, in Yosemite Village, has exhibits on the park's natural features and human history. Here also is information on trails and campgrounds, and many publications about Yosemite National Park and the Sierra. The collections of the *Indian Cultural Museum* and the model Ahwahneechee village show how Yosemite's early inhabitants lived.

The road leads west from the Visitor Center, and in about .5 mile reaches the Yosemite Falls parking area. A short trail (.2 mile) goes to the bridge at the base of 2,425-foot *Yosemite Falls*. In the spring, the bridge shakes with the thundering drop of water, and sightseers are sprayed with the fine mist. In late summer, the falls wane and in some years are dry by autumn. In winter, a beautiful ice cone (really frozen spray from the falls) builds up at the base of the Upper Fall.

The *Yosemite Falls Trail* starts from a point .5 mile farther along the loop road. This steep (2,700-foot ascent in 3.5 miles) trail offers unrivaled views of Yosemite Falls and Yosemite Valley.

The loop road follows along the Merced River with fine views of Yosemite's cliffs, spires, and domes. The prominent peaks rising one above the other on the right are the *Three Brothers*. These are named for the three sons of Tenaya, who was chief of the Yosemite Indians at the time Yosemite Valley was first entered by white explorers.

The low ridge that the road crosses in this area is the terminal moraine of the last glacier in Yosemite Valley; it is a line of rock rubble, left when the glacier melted.

Just before the Pohono Bridge is *Valley View*, or The Gates of the Valley, with a panoramic vista of Yosemite's granite peaks and domes, Bridalveil Fall, and, in the foreground, tranquil Bridalveil Meadow and the Merced River.

Turn left at the next intersection; the road crosses Pohono Bridge and then the meadow where the Mariposa Battalion camped during its foray into Yosemite Valley in 1851.

At the next intersection, jog a few hundred yards to the right on the Wawona Road to the Bridalveil Fall parking area, for a view of this ethereal waterfall. *Bridalveil Fall* was called Pohono, or "puffing wind," by the Indians. A short (.2 mile) trail leads to the base of the fall.

Backtrack to the valley loop road, for another fine view across the river to *El Capitan*, a sheer, granite promontory that rises almost 4,000 feet above the valley floor. On the right loom *Cathedral Rocks* (sometimes called the Three Graces) and then *Cathedral Spires*, two towering shafts of granite 2,300 and 3,000 feet above Yosemite Valley.

Past Cathedral Spires, the next huge granite tower is 3,073-foot *Sentinel Rock*. To the right of the rock, *Sentinel Fall* cascades down the cliffs in springtime. Near the base of Sentinel Rock is the

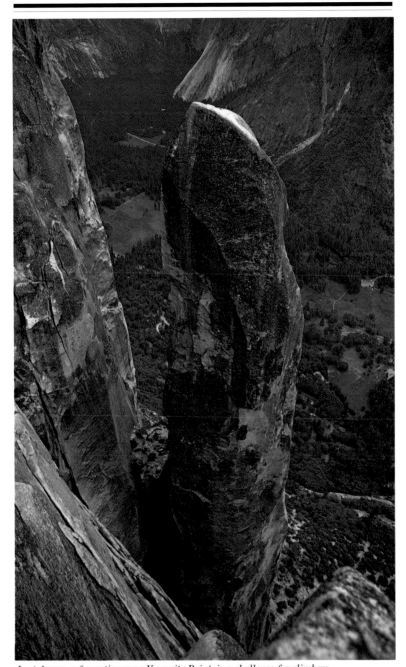

Lost Arrow, a formation near Yosemite Point, is a challenge for climbers.

start of the *Four-Mile Trail* to Glacier Point, a steep but scenic trail that, in spite of its name, is almost 5 miles long.

Past Sentinel Rock, the road breaks out of the forest into an open meadow, with another view of stately Yosemite Falls. Continue right at the next intersection to visit the Sierra Club's *LeConte Lodge*, a memorial to geologist Joseph LeConte, with exhibits and a library (open only in the summer). About 1 mile farther is Curry Village. A large parking area is located here; the roads to Happy Isles and Mirror Lake are open only to the shuttle buses that leave from Curry Village and to bicyclists and foot travelers.

At *Happy Isles*, 1 mile past Curry Village, the Merced River reaches the valley floor in a tumble of white water, branching into several channels. A pleasant trail crosses bridges among the small islands in the river, and a nature center nearby features exhibits about Yosemite's ecology.

Happy Isles is the trail head for many of Yosemite's finest trails, the most notable being the *John Muir Trail*, which starts here and leads to Tuolumne Meadows, then south through the Sierra to Mount Whitney, 212 miles away. Many shorter hiking trips begin here too, starting along the same trail. Just .9 mile up the John Muir Trail is Vernal Fall Bridge, from which there is a magnificent view of this 317-foot waterfall and the tumultuous waters at its base. The steep, 1-mile *Mist Trail* leads to the top of *Vernal Fall*, and another 2.4 miles to the top of 594-foot *Nevada Fall*.

As the trail continues 1.2 miles through Little Yosemite Valley, a 2.1-mile trail to the top of Half Dome branches off to the left. The last part of the *Half Dome Trail* is via a cable-stairway up the rounded northeast side of the dome—a strenuous but exciting climb, rewarded by dramatic views of Yosemite Valley and the High Sierra. *Half Dome*, a huge granite rock formation, towers almost 1 mile above the valley floor. A rounded dome, its west side (facing Yosemite Valley) is a sheer, 2,000-foot cliff. John Muir called Half Dome "the most beautiful and most sublime of all the wonderful Yosemite rocks." (Winter conditions require closure of portions of these trails; closed areas are posted. Inquire at the Yosemite Valley Visitor Center before starting the trip.)

From the valley loop road once again, 1.6 miles from Happy Isles is *Mirror Lake*. Silting in now, so it continues to get smaller, Mirror Lake still reflects the mountains and domes that surround it. The *Mirror Lake Trail*, a 3-mile loop, circles the lake.

From the west edge of Mirror Lake are striking views of the cliffs and domes, the most imposing of which is Half Dome. Across Mirror Lake to the north is Mount Watkins. On windless mornings

Opposite: The west side of Half Dome is a sheer, 2,000-foot cliff.

when the lake is still, a perfect reflection of Mount Watkins can be seen on its surface. As the road turns back to the west, it passes pillarlike *Washington Column* and above it the finely modeled *North Dome*. On the granite walls of the valley are the sweeping curves of the *Royal Arches*, a product of glaciation and exfoliation.

The road crosses the Ahwahnee Meadow near the historic Ahwahnee Hotel, and from here is one of the best views of *Glacier Point*, a stark cliff of granite soaring 3,242 feet above the valley. From the Ahwahnee Meadow, it is .6 mile back to the Visitor Center.

Glacier Point, Wawona, and the Big Trees

The Wawona Road (California 41) leaves Yosemite Valley from the road junction near Bridalveil Fall. It first climbs 1.5 miles to the eastern end of the Wawona Tunnel, where a point called *Discovery View* provides one of the most memorable panoramic views of Yosemite Valley: cliffs, domes, and forested floor, with Bridalveil Fall in the foreground. An interpretive sign identifies by outline the features of Yosemite's profile.

From the Wawona Tunnel, the road winds through lovely forests of ponderosa pine, incense cedar, and black oak for 7.7 miles to the Chinquapin intersection, named for the glossy, green shrub common in this area. Here the Glacier Point Road (16 miles) turns off to the left. This road is usually closed above Badger Pass Ski Area by snow in late autumn, and remains closed all winter.

Five miles past Chinquapin, a short side road turns right to Badger Pass Ski Area, Yosemite's winter sports center, where there are both downhill skiing and the trail heads for some excellent cross-country trips. In the spring, the Badger Pass Meadow is a favorite haunt of wildflower-lovers.

After 3.2 miles, the road crosses Bridalveil Creek, the headwater of Bridalveil Fall. Farther along the road are grand views into the backcountry, with the whole length of the Clark Range in view.

The parking area for the short (1 mile) *Sentinel Dome Trail* is about 5 miles past Bridalveil Creek. After an easy walk, the last part of which is a scramble up the curved side of the dome, the view is a grand 360° panorama of the park. At the top of Sentinel Dome is the famous gnarled Jeffrey pine, a prime subject of countless photographs. Now dead, it was a victim of drought in the late 1970s.

The 1.1-mile *Taft Point Trail* leads from the same parking area to the rim overlooking Yosemite Valley, with superb views of Yosemite Falls and El Capitan. The last several hundred feet of this trail skirt the valley's sheer 3,000-foot rim.

At the end of a series of steep downhill switchbacks is Glacier Point; probably no other easily accessible viewpoint offers the

TRAILS OF YOSEMITE NATIONAL PARK

FOUR-MILE TRAIL: Starts 1.25 miles from Yosemite Village on Southside Drive at Post V18 (Four-Mile Trail parking area) or at Glacier Point; 4.8 miles; 3 to 4 hours one way from Yosemite Valley floor; 3,200-foot ascent; built in 1871 as the route to Glacier Point before roads were available; strenuous, with steep switchbacks; carry water.

MIRROR LAKE LOOP TRAIL: Starts and ends at Mirror Lake; 3 miles round trip; 1 to 2 hours; 60-foot ascent; loop skirts Mirror Lake with magnificent view of Half Dome and continues up Tenaya Canyon; passes glacial polish (.2 mile from start), the Snow Creek Trail (to Tenaya Lake), and at its maximum distance from Mirror Lake (1.3 miles) crosses Tenaya Creek, then passes down opposite side of canyon; level, with a few up-and-down areas.

YOSEMITE FALLS TRAIL: Starts at Sunnyside Campground; 7.2 miles round trip; 2,700-foot ascent; strenuous climb to the top of Yosemite Falls, 2,425 feet above the valley floor; a panoramic view of Yosemite Valley from the world's second highest free-leaping waterfall; steep, with many switchbacks; guardrails at scenic points, but extreme caution should be exercised at all times; summer months are hot and dry; carry water.

PANORAMA TRAIL: Starts at Glacier Point or Happy Isles; ends at Yosemite Valley floor; 3,200-foot descent; 8.5 miles; descends 1.5 miles (1,300 feet in elevation) to pass across top of Illilouette Fall, after which it climbs up and around shoulder above Panorama Cliffs; then descends to valley floor by either horse or foot trail; a popular, though very strenuous, all-day hike is to go up to the Glacier Point Four-Mile Trail and return to the valley via the Panorama Trail; closed in winter.

Yosemite Falls, which sometimes dries up by fall, is best viewed in late spring and early summer.

POHONO TRAIL: Starts at Glacier Point; ends at Wawona Tunnel; 13 miles; 6 to 8 hours; 1,800-foot descent; follows close (within about 1 mile) to the south rim of Yosemite Valley; at Taft, Crocker, and Dewey points, trail comes right to the rim to offer outstanding views of the valley; may be taken in either direction, although it is less difficult from Glacial Point; known for its abundant and varied spring and early summer wildflowers; closed in winter.

HALF DOME TRAIL: Starts at Happy Isles (concrete bridge); 16.8 miles round trip; 10 to 12 hours (many prefer to make hike in 2 days and camp in Little Yosemite Valley); 4,800-foot ascent; follows the Vernal and Nevada Falls Trail to the top of Nevada Fall and on to Little Yosemite Valley, then branches off to follow Clouds Rest Trail around the back side of Half Dome to the base; beyond Nevada Fall, the trail is for both pack animals (which have the right of way) and people; the last 600 feet going up the side of Half Dome is very steep and protected with cables (cables down and trail closed in winter); wilderness permit, obtained at Visitor Center, required for overnight stay.

INSPIRATION POINT TRAIL: Starts and ends at east end of Wawona Tunnel; 2.5 miles round trip; 2 to 3 hours; 1,200-foot ascent; strenuous climb to historic Old Inspiration Point on the old Wawona Road, built in 1875 and used until the new road and tunnel were completed in 1933; steep uphill, with many switchbacks; carry water.

VERNAL AND NEVADA FALLS TRAIL: Starts and ends at Happy Isles (concrete bridge); 1.5 miles to Vernal Fall; 3.4 miles (6 to 8 hours) round trip to Nevada Fall; climb of 1,900 feet requiring only moderate exertion on paved trail for first .8 mile from Happy Isles to Vernal Fall Bridge; .7 mile beyond bridge to top of Vernal Fall via the Mist Trail; strenuous and steep rest of trail; Nevada Fall is start of the 212-mile John Muir Trail to Mount Whitney in Sequoia and Kings Canyon national parks; very wet from spray in early spring and summer; guardrails along steep sections and at top of each fall; caution should be used at all times.

LOWER YOSEMITE FALLS TRAIL: Starts at Yosemite Falls shuttle bus stop/parking area at Post V3 near Yosemite Lodge; ends at bottom of falls; .5 hour.

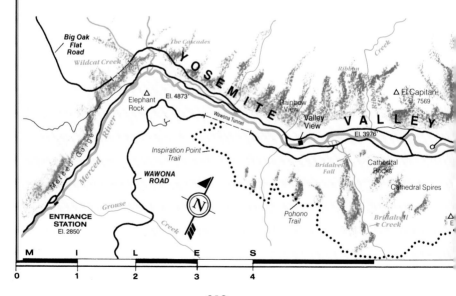

BRIDALVEIL FALL TRAIL: Starts at Bridalveil Fall parking area at Post W1; ends at bottom of falls; .5 hour.

CURRY VILLAGE TO MIRROR LAKE: Starts at Valley Stable or Mirror Lake Junction shuttle bus stops; ends at Mirror Lake; 2 miles round trip; 1 to 2 hours; paved route.

TAFT POINT TRAIL: Starts at Glacier Point Road; ends at Taft Point; 1.2 miles; 2 hours; easy climb; excellent views of El Capitan and Yosemite Falls; no guardrails along 2,000-foot cliffs.

SENTINEL DOME TRAIL: Starts on Glacier Point Road; ends at nearly treeless summit of Sentinel Dome, at 8,100 feet; 2.5 miles round trip; 2 hours; 420-foot ascent; excellent view of Yosemite Valley.

MAY LAKE TRAIL: Starts and ends along Tioga Road at Post T21 (hike begins at end of 1.8-mile road); 2.5 miles round trip; 2 hours; 450-foot ascent; hike among stands of fir and pine; at 9,300-foot elevation.

LEMBERT DOME TRAIL: Starts and ends at Dog Lake trail head just off Tioga Road near Tuolumne River Bridge, at Post T31; 2.4 miles round trip; 2 hours; 850-foot ascent; glacial polish; outstanding views, at 9,450-foot elevation.

HIGH SIERRA CAMPS LOOP TRAIL: Starts and ends at Tuolumne Meadows; traverses about 50 miles of outstanding scenery (passing 5 summer camps, located an average of 8 miles apart, which provide meals and tent accommodations by reservation); elevation range is 7,900 to 10,200 feet.

SEE MAP ON PAGES **288–289.**

scenic splendor found here.

From the parking area, walk 300 yards to Glacier Point for a bird's-eye view of the valley below and the vast expanse of the High Sierra with its polished domes and snow-covered peaks, Vernal Fall and Nevada Fall to the east, and the full drop of Yosemite Falls across the valley.

From Glacier Point, retrace the route to Chinquapin, and turn left on the Wawona Road. The road winds gently downhill through lovely forests of ponderosa pine, incense cedar, and black oak to Wawona, originally a trail-side camp built by Galen Clark, the first Guardian of the Yosemite Grant. Located here is the *Pioneer Yosemite History Center*, where a covered bridge near the camp's original site and several historic buildings relocated to the center from their former settings recreate Yosemite's past. During the summer, a living-history program, including stagecoach rides, helps visitors relive part of the past. Nearby is the beautiful and historic Wawona Hotel, still in operation.

From Wawona, continue south on the Wawona Road, past the turn-off to the south entrance of the park, to the *Mariposa Grove of Giant Sequoias*, 6.6 miles from Wawona.

This magnificent grove contains at least 500 mature giant sequoias, the huge reddish brown trees that are among the oldest and largest living things on earth. One of the largest trees in the grove is the Grizzly Giant, with a base diameter of 30 feet, girth of 94.2 feet, and height of 200 feet. It is thought to be about 2,700 years old.

Most of the grove can be visited only by walking or by riding the tram system (early May to mid-October). Ride the tram round-trip, or get off at one of the stops and walk back along the trails. Near the parking area is the *Pillars of Heaven Nature Trail*, a .5-mile self-guiding loop through part of the grove.

The Tioga Road and the High Country

To many people, the high country—roughly from 7,000 to above 13,000 feet in elevation—is the most exhilarating part of Yosemite National Park. This vast region of sparkling lakes and streams, flowery meadows, and bare granite peaks rising above timberline is accessible by car only during summer and early autumn. In these high altitudes, the air seems clearer and the light more dazzling; the invitation to walk the high trails is almost irresistible.

Leave Yosemite Valley via the Big Oak Flat Road to Crane Flat, where the Tioga Road begins. (Other roads from Crane Flat lead to the *Tuolumne* and *Merced Groves of Giant Sequoias*, and to Hetch Hetchy, a valley that was similar to Yosemite Valley until it was dammed in 1914 to provide a water supply for San Francisco.) The

Yosemite's Cathedral Peak, 10,940 feet, is in the Tuolumne Meadows area.

Tioga Road (California 120) climbs from 6,200 feet through red fir and lodgepole pine forests to Tioga Pass, the park's east entrance, at an elevation of 9,941 feet. It is the highest road pass in California. There are grand views of the high country from many points along the road, and campgrounds in several places provide a more "primitive" camping experience than do those in Yosemite Valley.

At 18.7 miles past Crane Flat, the road crosses Yosemite Creek, the headwater of Yosemite Falls; and 5.1 miles farther is the start of the 3.7-mile *North Dome Trail.*

Two miles beyond is the May Lake Junction. Turn here onto a section of the Old Tioga Road; it winds past Snow Flat, a meadow where some of Yosemite's deepest snows accumulate each winter, and ends at the *May Lake Trail.* This 1.2-mile trail leads to May Lake High Sierra Camp.

On the Tioga Road again, *Olmstead Point,* 2.2 miles beyond the May Lake Junction, provides some of the most breath-taking vistas anywhere in Yosemite. The view to the west is down Tenaya Canyon with its vast expanses of polished and sculptured granite, 9,926-foot Clouds Rest, and the unfamiliar, rounded back view of Half Dome. To the east is Tenaya Lake, a beautiful blue lake

Overleaf: Yosemite Valley and Bridalveil Fall.

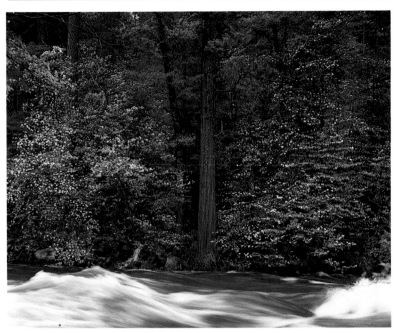

Pacific dogwood grows along the Merced River.

fringed with dark trees and surrounded by glacially smoothed domes and cliffs. The Indian name for Tenaya Lake was Pywiack, or "lake of the shining rocks"; here can be seen some of the best examples of glacial polish.

The road skirts the shore of Tenaya Lake at the base of 9,786-foot *Polly Dome* and passes *Fairview Dome* to reach *Tuolumne Meadows*, the largest high-mountain meadow in the Sierra.

One of the most prominent landmarks of Tuolumne Meadows is *Lembert Dome*, an asymmetric dome of polished granite with a distinctive profile—a good example of the sculpturing effect of ice. It is possible to scramble to the top from a path that branches from the *Dog Lake Trail*, and enjoy a 360° view of Tuolumne Meadows, Unicorn Peak, Cathedral Peak, Mount Conness, Mount Dana, Mount Gibbs, and many high peaks in the distance.

From Tuolumne Meadows, the Tioga Road climbs through lodgepole pine forests and follows along the sparkling Dana Fork of the Tuolumne River to Dana Meadows, ultimately reaching Tioga Pass.

Besides being a place of great natural beauty, Tuolumne Meadows is a favorite starting point for hiking, backpacking, and mountaineering. Many trails into the backcountry originate here, and other trails pass through; the *Pacific Crest Trail* and the *John Muir Trail* meet here and follow the same route to Mount Whitney.

Even a short hike from Tuolumne Meadows can provide a sample of the magic of Yosemite's high country. A loop trail circles the meadows; this is a nice hike to take while adjusting to the higher, thinner air.

A 3-mile trail leads to *Elizabeth Lake*, a lovely subalpine lake nestled at the foot of craggy Unicorn Peak; and a slightly longer trail (part of the John Muir Trail) goes to equally beautiful *Cathedral Lakes*. The first mile or two of one of the longer trails can make a pleasant afternoon's hike. A 2-hour walk eastward along the Lyell Fork of the Tuolumne River on the John Muir Trail affords a fine combination of river, meadow, and mountain; a similar walk westward on the Pacific Crest Trail is an almost irresistible appetizer for a longer hike.

The High Sierra Loop

The High Sierra camps make accessible to the unseasoned hiker some of the most beautiful backcountry in the park. There are five camps arranged roughly in a circle, at distances averaging 8 miles apart. The camps provide beds, restrooms, hot showers, and meals (in a central dining tent). The camps usually are open from early July through early September, and reservations are necessary. The National Park Service also maintains a public campground at each camp.

A High Sierra loop trip starts at Tuolumne Meadows Lodge, the only camp accessible by car. It is a good idea to plan a night or two at Tuolumne Meadows to adjust to the altitude (8,600 feet). In the meadows area you can participate in ranger programs and naturalist-guided hikes, or take guided horseback rides that leave from the Tuolumne Stables.

The trail to Glen Aulin High Sierra Camp from Tuolumne Meadows (7.6 miles) passes through open meadows with views of the Cathedral Range. It follows the Tuolumne River over sparkling expanses of granite and past cascades and waterfalls that signal the beginning of the river's plunge to the Grand Canyon of the Tuolumne River. Glen Aulin Camp is at the foot of *White Cascade* beside a large pool that invites swimming. Follow the trail farther downriver through the Glen Aulin itself—through stands of fir, pine, and aspen—to *Waterwheel Falls*, where, during the early summer, water is tossed backward in "wheels" (arcs) 30 to 40 feet high.

Leaving Glen Aulin, the *McGee Lake Trail* climbs 8.6 miles to May Lake High Sierra Camp, at 9,270 feet. The trail passes McGee Lake, and offers views of Mount Conness to the east, Mount Hoffmann to the west, and Mount Clark to the south. It goes through rock gardens in which grow many Sierra wildflowers like pentstemon, paintbrush, and mountain daisy. The camp sits on the eastern shore of *May Lake* amid mountain hemlocks, with Mount Hoffman (10,850 feet) towering behind. A ridge behind camp offers a panoramic view, from Tenaya Canyon with Half Dome to Tenaya Lake and the many distant peaks beyond.

The next day's hike (8 miles) descends about 1,100 feet and crosses the Tioga Road above Tenaya Lake. The trail then climbs up a series of switchbacks on an exposed slope of granite boulders to Forsyth Pass, eventually reaching three *Sunrise Lakes*, two of which lie directly beside the trail and offer good swimming and fishing. The trail then crosses a pass and drops 1 mile to Long Meadow and Sunrise High Sierra Camp, at 9,400 feet. The camp is on a grassy bench 30 to 40 feet above the meadow, with tents arranged picturesquely among the boulders. The large screen windows in the dining tent frame a view of Mount Clark, bright with alpenglow at sunset, as is Mount Florence to the east. You can stroll by the meandering stream in Long Meadow and watch the deer feed at dusk.

From Sunrise Camp, the trail to Merced Lake follows the Echo Creek drainage down through glens filled with wildflowers to meet the Merced River about 2 miles below camp. The *Merced Lake* High Sierra Camp sits at the east end of Merced Lake in a tall forest of Jeffrey pine, lodgepole pine, and white fir. At the 7,275-foot elevation, nights are comparatively warm. Fishing is good at Merced Lake and at Washburn Lake, 3 miles up the Merced River.

Between Merced Lake and Vogelsang High Sierra Camp there is a choice of trails. One goes up Lewis Creek and over 10,700-foot Vogelsang Pass in 9 miles. This is the steeper trail and affords a stunning view of many of the peaks along the Sierra crest. The other trail follows Fletcher Creek in a more gradual, 7.6-mile ascent, passing through open meadows and near granite domes.

Vogelsang, at 10,160 feet, is the highest camp on the loop. For a fine view, climb Vogelsang Peak (11,516 feet) above the camp. There are numerous lakes in the area around camp, with several kinds of trout, making this camp a favorite of fishermen. Glaciation is much in evidence, with glacial cirques and polished slopes, and the step-formation of the nearby canyons.

The trail back to Tuolumne Meadows (7.2 miles) crosses Tuolumne Pass and follows Rafferty Creek down to the Lyell Fork of the Tuolumne River. Here it joins the John Muir Trail. An alternate route is the longer, more scenic *Ireland Creek Trail* (12.3 miles).

Opposite: Horsetail Falls at sunset.

ANIMALS & PLANTS
OF CALIFORNIA, HAWAII, AND AMERICAN SAMOA

This appendix provides a sample of animals and plants commonly found in the national parks of California, Hawaii, and American Samoa. The two-letter abbreviations indicate the parks in which these animals and plants are most often seen.

AS	American Samoa	HV	Hawaii Volcanoes	RW	Redwood
CI	Channel Islands	JT	Joshua Tree	SQ	Sequoia
DV	Death Valley	KC	Kings Canyon	YO	Yosemite
HL	Haleakala	LV	Lassen Volcanic		

MAMMALS

AMERICAN RIVER OTTER LV, RW, YO

The river otter is one of the largest members of the weasel family, measuring 3–4.25 ft. and weighing up to 30 lbs. Seeing it is really a chance occurrence, but when seen it is a major attraction, distinguished by clownlike actions—floating on its back in the water, sliding in the snow, and generally frolicking about. The river otter has a dark-brown coat, lighter belly, silver-gray throat, and whitish whiskers. Its long tail is thick at the base and tapers to a point, and its feet are webbed. It feeds mainly on fish, but also eats mice and terrestrial invertebrates.

BADGER
DV, JT, KC, LV, SQ, YO

The nocturnal badger is seldom seen in heavily visited areas. Generally a little over 2 ft. long, including a 5-in. tail, it has a flattish body, with short, bowed legs. Its burrow has an 8–12-in. elliptical opening, and is marked by a large mound of earth and debris; the badger can bury itself faster than a person can dig with a shovel. It feeds on rodents.

BIGHORN SHEEP
DV, JT, KC, SQ

Also known as the "mountain sheep" or the "Rocky Mountain bighorn sheep," it is one of the most spectacular animals in the parks. Rams are 3–3.5 ft. in height, 127–316 lbs., and with a horn spread of 33 in. (the horns curve up and back over ears); ewes are 4.25–5.25 ft. in height and weigh 74–200 lbs. Color varies from dark brown to pale tan; generally the belly, rump patch, back of legs, muzzle, and eye patch are white. The bighorn's diet is mostly grasses, sedges, and woody plants, and its habitat is alpine meadows and foothills near rocky cliffs.

BLACK BEAR
KC, LV, RW, SQ, YO

The black bear may be a brownish or cinnamon color, but it can easily be distinguished from the grizzly and brown bears by its straight-profiled face, rather than the dished face of the others, and by its comparatively smaller size (3 ft. at the shoulder, 4.5–6.25 ft. long, 203–595 lbs.) and humpless shoulders. The black bear feeds on grasses, buds, leaves, berries, nuts, bark, insects, rodents, the fawns of deer and elk, and fish, particularly salmon; a scrounger by nature, it will forage near campsites. This is a powerful and potentially dangerous animal despite its clownlike antics; although primarily nocturnal, it is sometimes seen during the day, sometimes "galloping" as fast as 30 miles an hour.

BOBCAT
DV, JT, KC, LV, RW, SQ, YO

The bobcat is North America's most common wild cat; because it is nocturnal and secretive, it is seldom seen. It is tawny in color, with indistinct black spots, a pale or white belly, and a short, stubby tail with 2 or 3 black bars. It weighs 14–68 lbs. and measures 2.3–4 ft. long; the males are larger than the females. In the late winter, the male may be heard yowling at night, much like a domesticated cat. Kits are born in a den, usually in thickets or under rocks and logs. The bobcat feeds on rodents and especially ground-nesting birds.

BRUSH RABBIT
CI, KC, RW, SQ, YO

A small reddish-brown animal mottled with black, the brush rabbit measures 11.5–14.75 in., has short 2.5-in. ears, and a .75–1.75-in. tail. Primarily nocturnal, it nests in thick brushy areas. The brush rabbit's favorite food is clover, but it eats grass and various berries as well as woody vegetation in the winter.

CALIFORNIA
SEA LION CI, RW

The "trained seal" of the circus might be found cavorting much the same way as the sea lion in the waters along Redwood's coast and particularly around the Channel Islands, tossing objects in the air and catching them on its nose, and generally clowning and showing off. The male sea lion weighs up to 660 lbs. and measures 6.5–8.5 ft.; the female is 5–6.5 ft. in length and weighs 100–220 lbs. Although sea lions appear off the shores of all Pacific coast national parks, only Channel Islands has a resident population. An extremely intelligent animal, the sea lion enlisted for a year's training for the circus could have a 12-year show biz career. It feeds on squid, octopus, abalone, and other types of fish, which it usually hunts at night.

COYOTE
DV, JT, KC, LV, RW, SQ, YO

The coyote is the smallest species of wild dog; although resembling a domestic dog, it is often mistaken for a wolf. The coyote is seen fairly regularly in the western parks: its evening "howl" has made it legendary. It weights about 75 lbs., stands about 2 ft. at the shoulder, and is 3.5–4 ft. long, including a tail of 12–15 in. Its fur is brownish- to reddish-gray—at the lower altitudes more tan and red, at the higher altitudes more gray and black. The coyote has a varied diet of deer, elk, rabbit, rodents, snakes, birds, and insects. A typical den is a wide-mouthed earthen tunnel, 5–30 ft. long, which may be the former residence of a fox or badger.

DEER MOUSE
CI, DV, JT, KC, LV, SQ, YO

There are about 100 species of rats or mice in North America, and probably the most common in the Southwest is the deer mouse. A grayish to reddish-brown mouse about 5–8.75 in. long, including a 2–5-in. tail, it feeds on seeds, nuts, small fruits, berries, and insects. It usually burrows in the ground, though some may nest in raised areas or have refuge burrows.

FISHER
KC, LV, SQ, YO

The fisher closely resembles but is larger than both the marten and the mink. Its long, thin body is dark brown with a broad grayish head and a bushy tail. The male may measure up to 40 in. and weigh 18 lbs.; the female is smaller. It preys mostly on snowshoe hares, porcupines, squirrels, and mice. Fishers tolerate one another only during the mating season; for the most part they are loners and thus are rarely seen. Their fur is considered valuable, and for this reason the population has dropped in recent years.

GRAY FOX
JT, KC, LV, RW, SQ, YO

Of the six species of foxes in North America, the gray fox is the most commonly found in national parks; yet, being nocturnal, it is seldom seen. It is gray, with a black stripe running down the top of its tail, stands 14–15 in. at the shoulder, and is 3–4 ft. long, including a 9–17-in. tail. The gray fox feeds on rabbits and rodents that happen by its lair and, in summer, on fruit and berries.

GRAY WHALE
CI, RW

Seeing whales along California's coast is mostly a chance occurrence, but the gray whale is almost certain to be spotted at Channel Islands and along Redwood's shores if one is patient. This is a spectacular sight, even if it is only for seconds at a time. One cannot fail to be excited at seeing only 2–3 ft. of what is actually a 60–70-ft.-long animal. The gray whale, the one most commonly spotted, journeys south to Mexican waters in the autumn and north to the open Pacific in the spring. In addition to the gray, the goose-beaked whale has been spotted from Redwood; there also have been sightings of the sperm whale and, on very rare occasions, the great blue whale.

LONG-TAILED WEASEL
JT, KC, LV, RW, SQ, YO

Wholly carnivorous, the long-tailed weasel feeds on rats, rabbits, birds, and even other weasels when killing instincts are triggered by the smell of blood. The animal's name is derived from a 6.5-in. brown tail with a black tip. The body is brown with a white chest.

MOUNTAIN LION
JT, KC, LV, RW, SQ, YO

Often called cougar or puma, the mountain lion is a most secretive mammal, living mostly in mountainous areas and seldom seen; it is a rather docile cat, rarely attacking humans, but its scream can be terrifying. Yellowish to tawny, with a long, black-tipped tail, it weighs up to 275 lbs. and measures 5–9 ft., including a 2–3-ft. tail. The mountain lion feeds on deer, coyote, beaver, mice, hares, raccoons, birds, and grasshoppers.

MULE DEER
KC, LV, SQ, YO

The mule deer is a fairly common species of the deer family seen in the western parks, particularly in the early morning and late evening. It is characterized by its large, mulelike ears, from which it gets its name, and white rump, although it should not be confused with the white-tailed deer—also seen in some western parks. It weighs up to 400 lbs.

and stands 3–3.5 ft. at the shoulder. The male loses its antlers in the late winter and is generally solitary in its roamings. The mule deer eats acorns, berries, cactus fruits, twigs, buds, grasses, herbs, tree bark, and mushrooms.

NORTHERN ELEPHANT SEAL CI

Not the prettiest of the seal family, this giant mammal is the largest aquatic carnivore, weighing up to 7,700 lbs. and measuring up to 21.5 ft. Both male and female are a brown or gray color above and lighter shade of either color below. In 1892, as few as 20 elephant seals had survived the massive whaling industry's search for blubber oil. Now more than 65,000 populate the shores of California from Baja to San Francisco. They feed on ratfish, hagfish, squid, small sharks, and other deep-water life, which they can hunt while submerged for 40 minutes at a depth of 200 ft.

NORTHERN FLYING SQUIRREL KC, LV, SQ, YO

Nocturnal and seldom seen, the northern flying squirrel glides from tree to tree by spreading a loose fold of skin between its forelegs and hind legs. It measures 10.5–14.5 in. and is brown above and white below. Like most squirrels, it eats nuts, acorns, seeds, berries, some insects, and, on occasion, vertebrate flesh.

PIKA LV, YO

Sometimes called the "whistling hare," this small furry mammal, which closely resembles the guinea pig, has a pudgy brownish body, is 6.5–8.5 in. long, has short, rounded ears, and lacks a discernible tail. It feeds mostly on green plants and burrows among rocks.

PORCUPINE
KC, LV, RW, SQ, YO

Contrary to legend, porcupines *cannot* throw or "shoot" their quills, although the quills are rather loosely attached and may shake off if the porcupine threshes its tail about in self-defense. Classified as a rodent, it is the only quilled mammal. About 3 ft. long, 1 ft. high, and 35 lbs., it lives mostly in coniferous forests, but may also inhabit brushy areas of the Southwest. It survives mostly on a diet of the wood directly beneath tree bark, although it also eats buds and twigs from a variety of trees and bushes.

RACCOON
KC, LV, RW, SQ, YO

The notorious black-masked raccoon raids garbage cans in national parks just as it does in the suburbs; nocturnal, the raccoon can be seen around park campgrounds. It is reddish-brown with black above and gray below, and measures 2–3 ft., including a 7.5–16-in. bushy tail with alternating black and brown rings. Its diet includes grapes, nuts, insects, rodents, turtles, frogs, and birds' eggs; dens are usually in hollow trees, caves, rock clefts, or culverts.

ROOSEVELT ELK RW

The great Roosevelt elk, taking its name from famed hunter and conservationist President Theodore Roosevelt, is found in only two of our national parks, Redwood and Olympic. It is larger than the familiar Rocky Mountain elk—much broader and more massive. A typical specimen may be 8 ft. long, with a 3.2-ft. antler spread. Primarily grazers, this species, like other elk, feeds on grasses and woody vegetation.

BIRDS

AMERICAN KESTREL
CI, DV, JT, KC, RW, SQ, YO

Until recently, this small falcon was known as the "sparrow hawk." The kestrel measures 9–12 in. from bill to tail and has a wingspread of 22–23 in. It has blue-gray wings and head with a buff breast and nape. The kestrel does not build a nest of its own, but lays its eggs without nesting or borrows another bird's nest in tree holes or building niches. It can be seen perched on trees and telephone poles, from which it swoops rapidly upon its grasshopper and rodent prey.

AMERICAN ROBIN
DV, JT, KC, LV, RW, SQ, YO

Best known of all North American birds, once called "robin," the American robin is gray-brown, with puffed-out, red or orange breast, white throat, and blackish head and tail. It measures 9–11 in. The robin feeds primarily on worms pulled from the ground. In cold weather, the nest is built of twigs and mud and lined with fine material in low, densely leafed or needled trees and bushes; in hot weather, the nest is high in maple or sycamore trees.

BARN OWL
CI, HV, JT, RW

The barn owl is a medium-size owl measuring 14–20 in. The animal has a white heart-shaped face edged with tan; its back is light tan with pearl-gray streaks, and its front is white. The barn owl is often mistaken for the all-white snowy owl when seen in the glare of automobile headlights. It feeds on mice and rats and can be seen perched in trees.

BREWER'S BLACKBIRD
DV, JT, KC, LV, RW, SQ, YO

The male Brewer's blackbird has an iridescent purple-black head, glossy green-violet body, and yellow eyes; the female is a light gray-brown with brown eyes. It is 8–10 in. long and is a very social bird, mixing with other blackbirds, such as the red-winged. Its range is wide, from British Columbia to northern Baja California, and east to the Great Lakes, and it feeds primarily on seeds and insects.

BROWN PELICAN
CI, DV, RW

Though it was at one time near extinction after a history of 30 million years, the brown pelican is making a comeback now that DDT has been banned. Chemical pollutants, absorbed from a fish diet, affected the pelican's calcium metabolism, resulting in thin-shelled eggs that failed to survive incubation. This large, heavy bird with an immense dark bill is easily recognizable as it glides low over the water and then dives to catch fish. It measures 4–4.5 ft. and breeds among the Channel Islands; it can be seen along the coast at Redwood.

CALIFORNIA QUAIL
HV, KC, RW, SQ, YO

Following breeding seasons, this small, plump quail becomes quite social and can be found in large groups in public parks and gardens. Measuring 9–11 in., it has a black forward-curving plume atop a chestnut-brown head; the forehead is creamy and the throat is black, and both are edged in white; the breast is grayish-blue, the back is brown, and the belly is creamy, with brown markings.

CLARK'S NUTCRACKER
KC, LV, SQ, YO

The 12–13-in. Clark's nutcracker is light gray with dark eyes and has a long, sharply pointed bill. Its wings are black, with a patch of white at the trailing edge. It can be found near camp and picnic sites, where it begs or steals food scraps.

CORMORANT
CI, RW

Three varieties of cormorant are found along the California coast: pelagic (smallest, 25–30 in.), Brandt's, and double-crested (largest, 30–36 in.). All three are nearly iridescent black with long necks, and all fly over water; the double-crested cormorant, however, will fly over land to take shortcuts. The bird nests on coastal or offshore rocks and feeds by diving into water for its prey.

DIPPER
KC, LV, RW, SQ, YO

Almost comical as it appears to water-ski over the surface, the dipper really walks in shallow water; in deeper spots, it walks on the bottom with half-open wings while feeding on insects. Uniformly slate-gray, the dipper resembles a wren with a stubby tail and yellowish feet.

GREAT HORNED OWL
DV, JT, KC, RW, SQ, YO

The great horned owl is common to all of North America, from Mexico to the tree line in Canada. It is 1.5–2 ft. from tail to top of head, gray-brown above, with a fine dark-gray horizontal barring below, large yellow eyes, and ear tufts set far apart. It nests in trees, crevices, or cliffs, often in a nest once occupied by a hawk. The owl hunts rabbits, rodents, ducks, crows, and other owls, and it has been seen capturing a skunk.

HAIRY WOODPECKER
KC, LV, SQ, YO

A medium-size woodpecker, but larger than the downy, the hairy woodpecker has a white head with black crown, eyemask, and "whiskers." Male has red patch at base of crown, and black tail with white outer feathers; female has no red patch. Both are 8.5–10.5 in. from bill to tail. It feeds by pecking a hole in tree bark and, with its long, flexible tongue, extracting grubs; it nests in tree cavities.

HEERMANN'S GULL
CI, RW

The Heermann's gull is a medium-size gull, mostly dark, with a red bill and a snow-white head that blends into a gray neck and back; the wings and tail are slate black and trimmed with white. Heermann's gulls follow fishing boats and steal fish from other birds, particularly the brown pelican. They measure 18-21 in. in length and do not nest in either Redwood or Channel Islands.

HERMIT THRUSH
JT, KC, LV, SQ, YO

Some consider the hermit thrush's softly uttered *chup* to be the most beautiful bird song in North America. This little bird measures 6.5-8 in. in length, and is olive-brown with a white, spotted breast and streaked throat.

It flicks its tail and wings in a constant nervous fashion. The thrush nests on or just above the ground in a neat cup of grass, moss, and leaves, and it generally forages on the ground on seeds and insects.

HERRING GULL
RW

This large white bird with gray wings and back measures 22.5-26 in. and populates both the Atlantic and Pacific coasts. Its wing tips are black with white spots, and its bill and eyes are both yellow. A loud *ke-yah* squeals through the air as the herring gull scoops up surface fish and scavenges almost anywhere, from beaches to city dumps.

MASKED BOOBY
AS

The masked booby, largest of the six species of

booby, is widely distributed throughout the tropics in large colonies. About 40 in. in length, the booby has large feet, fully webbed, with four toes. Like all boobies, the masked booby is a superb flier, and it dives into the ocean for prey from a height of 50 feet of more. Its main foods, which it swallows underwater, are squid and fish. The masked booby lays two eggs but raises only one chick. Both parents incubate and feed the chick.

MOUNTAIN CHICK-ADEE JT, KC, LV, SQ, YO

The mountain chickadee is a small, constantly active insect seeker. It is 5-5.75 in. long, gray, with a black cap, white eye stripe, and pale gray sides. The chickadee nests in a hair- or fur-lined natural cavity or woodpecker tree hole.

NENE (HAWAIIAN GOOSE)
HI, HV

The nene, or Hawaiian goose, is Hawaii's state bird. At one time endangered and nearly extinct (as recently as 1951, only 33 or so were known to exist), it is slowly making a comeback on the island of Hawaii, where it nests between 4,000 and 8,000 ft. on Mauna Loa, adapting to life on lava flows far removed from water. The nene (pronounced "ney-ney") is approximately 20 in. tall, is brown and gray with black markings, and resembles its ancestor, the Canada goose, with one major difference: its feet have lost their webbing. The nene is a dryland nester, feeding on berries; because it nests on the ground, it is the prey of the mongoose, and thus its population is constantly in danger.

OREGON JUNCO
DV, JT, KC, LV, RW, SQ, YO

The Oregon junco is the western junco, and its coloring is distinctly different from that of its eastern and northern cousins; this bird has a black hood and a chestnut mantle, with a white chest and buff sides. It measures 5-6.25 in. and feeds on seeds and small fruits.

PEREGRINE FALCON
CI, HV

At one time this bird faced extinction, but experimental breeding is now saving the much prized falcon. It measures 15-21 in. long and has a slate-gray back with a white throat and a finely barred breast. The bird's wingspan can be as much as 40-45 in., as the peregrine dramatically swoops and dives. It nests in a hollow or on inaccessible cliff ledges; in cities it will nest on the ledges of buildings, where it then feeds mainly on pigeons.

PINE SISKIN
JT, KC, LV, RW, SQ, YO

The pine siskin is a small grayish-brown bird that, like the chickadee, will hang upside down to feed on seed pods and catkins. It measures only 4.5-5.25 in., and has a buff breast with yellow on its wings, and a notched tail.

RED-TAILED HAWK
CI, DV, JT, KC, LV, RW, SQ, YO

The red-tailed hawk is one of the larger birds of this genus, measuring 19-25 in. tall, with a wingspan of 48-54 in. It has a dark-brown back, a light-brown chest with a dark belly band, and a finely streaked grayish tail. Frequently seen perched atop fence posts or telephone poles, the bird will sit inordinately still for a long time, then suddenly swoop down on a squirrel or a rabbit, or some other prey.

RUFOUS HUMMINGBIRD
KC, LV, SQ, YO

The male rufous hummingbird is identified by distinctive black throat and white collar below; the female is greenish above, whitish below. Both are 3.5-3.75 in. from bill to tail. It nests in a feltlike cup in shrub or tree, and feeds on insects, spiders, and flower nectar.

SCOTT'S ORIOLE
JT

This bird is at home in pinyon-juniper woodlands, yuccas and palms, and the riparian sycamores and cottonwoods of southeastern California, Arizona, southern Nevada, Utah, New Mexico, and western Texas. It is 7.5–8.25 in. The male, largely black, has bright yellow underparts; the female is yellow with dark streaks on its back. This songbird's diet includes insects, fruit, and nectar.

SPOTTED SAND-PIPER
DV, KC, LV, RW, SQ, YO

The spotted sandpiper is among the smallest of the sandpipers, measuring 7.5-8 in.; it can nearly always be distinguished from other sandpipers by its jerky, uneven flight patterns. In the fall it has an olive-brown back with a white breast, light eyestripe, and, white eye-ring; in the spring, its breast is marked with dark spots.

STELLER'S JAY
JT, KC, LV, RW, SQ, YO

The Steller's jay is common to campsites and picnic areas in parks. The only western jay with a crest, it measures 12-13.5 in. and is blackish on the upper half of the body, including the head, and bluish-gray on the lower part. The eyebrow is oddly and lightly streaked, and the tail has black crossbars. It nests in a neat, twiggy bowl well-hidden in conifers and feeds on seeds, fruits, nuts, the eggs of other birds, mice, and frogs.

TUFTED PUFFIN
RW

The tufted puffin is most commonly seen sitting upright on sea cliffs along the Siberian, Alaskan, and British Columbian coastlines; fortunately, a few nests are found along the California coasts. Occasionally seen off Redwood's shores, it measures 14.5-15.5 in. and is distinguished by its stubby black body, white face, yellowish tufts beside the eyes, and a large orange-red bill. In the winter the bird undergoes some dramatic changes: the colored bill plates are molted and the bill is actually smaller and duller, the face turns dusky, and the tufts disappear. The tufted puffin nests singly or in colonies along vertical sea cliffs and feeds at sea.

AMPHIBIANS, ECHINODERMS, REPTILES, AND SPIDERS

BLOOD STAR
CI

A walk around the tide pools of Frenchy's Cove will reveal many creatures of the sea. The blood star is only one of numerous starfish; 5 stiff, slender, smooth arms have no spines. It generally measures 20-25 cm. in diameter, is usually bright red to orange, and ranges from the intertidal zone to 2,200 ft. out. A tide pool is a collection of tidal water in rocky areas along the shore and is generally filled with life, but inconsiderate collectors are rapidly diminishing these precious life zones. Collecting is forbidden at Channel Islands.

CALIFORNIA NEWT
KC, SQ, YO

The newt belongs to the salamander family and is secretive, voiceless, and lizardlike in appearance. The California newt, found in the Sierra, is about 5-7.75 in. long, rough-skinned, tan to reddish-brown above, and yellow below. During rainy seasons, it is very visible; during hot, dry times, it is mostly in the shadows and damp areas. It preys on insects, mice, snakes, and other small animals.

PACIFIC TREE FROG
DV, KC, LV, RW, SQ, YO

Hollywood filmmakers use the high-pitched voice of the mighty 2-in.-long Pacific tree frog for outdoor night sounds, thus making it famous all over the world. Generally found close to water, the frog ranges in color from green to light tan to black, but it has the familiar black stripe through the eyes and usually a dark triangle between the eyes. It feeds primarily on insects.

SEA BAT STARFISH
CI

This starfish can be found at Frenchy's Cove on Channel islands. It has 5 (sometimes 4-9) arms that are not distinctly separated. The body is fat, with a scaly surface, and its color varies from red to yellow-orange to brown. The sea bat starfish is generally found on mud bottoms and in the sand, although some are found clinging to rocks; the animal ranges from the intertidal zones to 90 ft. out. They are scavengers and congregate in large numbers.

SLATE-PENCIL SEA URCHIN
AS

Globular in shape with projecting spines, this sea urchin lives at the bottom, often in shallow water. It prefers rocky habitats but may be found in sand. The spines are used for locomotion and protection. Moving about with its oral surface downward, it feeds on algae, dead matter, and sedentary animals. The urchin may take two weeks to consume a clump of seaweed.

TARANTULA
DV, JT

These large hairy eight-eyed, eight-legged spiders, when encountered in the United States, may deliver a painful bite. Some species in Latin America carry a lethal venom. Males live only a few years, females to 35 years. Out of sight during the day, they hunt by touch in the darkness. The male's search for a mate may occur in the dim light just after sunset or before sunrise. The body will be 1.4 in. or more, and the legspan may be nearly 6 in.

WESTERN FENCE LIZARD
CI, DV, JT, KC, RW, SQ, YO

One of the most common in the West, this spiny lizard can be olive, brownish, or black, with blotches of wavy crossbars down the back. The undersurface of the legs is generally yellowish-orange, and there are blue patches on the belly. It measures 6-9.25 in. long and is seen year round.

WESTERN POND TURTLE
KC, LV, SQ

The western pond turtle is most commonly seen basking alone in the sun.

It measures 3.5-7 in. in length, and its smooth, broad, low shell is olive to dark brown, sometimes with dark flecks and lines running from the center of scutes or scales. Its home is mostly in still and slow-moving water, sometimes in brackish water, and it feeds on mollusks and other small animals as well as on aquatic plants.

WESTERN RATTLESNAKE
JT, KC, SQ, YO

The western rattlesnake varies in color from cream to black with blotches. It has a stout body and a tapering tail, with a series of interlocking pieces of dry skin at the end commonly called a "rattle." It has vertically elliptical pupils in the eyes when in bright light. A light stripe behind the eye extends to behind the corner of the mouth. Its scales are distinctly keeled. The total length of this snake can run to 5.5 ft. It is primarily found in the foothills, but has been seen at heights of 11,000 ft. This snake dens on rocky outcrops and stream courses, and in northern areas it is found in rock crevices in large numbers. The western rattler eats lizards, birds, frogs, and small mammals.

WESTERN TERRESTRIAL GARTER SNAKE
KC, SQ, YO

There are four subspecies of this garter snake, so the colors and marks vary somewhat. The wandering garter has a narrow, dull yellow or brown back stripe that fades toward the tail; the light areas are marked with small dark spots that are sometimes enlarged, sometimes absent altogether, and at other times fused and mottled. It measures 1.5-3.5 ft. in length. This snake can occasionally be seen basking in the sun during the morning hours. It feeds on tadpoles, frogs, fish, mice, and small birds.

WESTERN TOAD
DV, KC, LV, RW, SQ, YO

The western toad is a large toad, measuring up to 5 in., that is gray to green with a light-colored stripe down its back. Its warts are tinged with red and surrounded by black blotches. It feeds mostly on plants and insects but also eats fruits and vegetables.

FLOWERS, SHRUBS, AND TREES

ARROW-LEAF BALSAM ROOT
KC, LV, SQ

The arrow-leaf balsam root is a nearly leafless stalk with 1 large brilliant yellow flower head growing from a cluster of silver-gray leaves. The flower is 4-5 in. in diameter. The plant grows 8-32 in. in the open. The Indians prepared medicine from these roots.

CAMAS LILY
KC, LV, SQ, YO

Sometimes the common camas lily is so prevalent that it can blanket an entire meadow in blue-violet. This star-shaped flower is generally 1.5-2.5 in. wide, the grasslike leaves 2 in. long; the plant grows to 20 in.

COCONUT
AS

This palm species, *Cocos nucifera*, has a cylindrical trunk of 60–100 feet, ringed with leaf scars. About 25-30 large pinnate leaves, each up to 20 feet long, are clustered near the top of the trunk. Flowers first appear when trees are 7–10 years old. Coconut trees are indispensable to the economy of the tropics; the fruit provides food and a nutritious drink; leaves are made into thatch and baskets; the trunk is a valuable building material; and the fiber is used in brushes and rope.

COLUMBIA LILY
RW, YO

Other names for this large, mostly orange, and immensely popular western wildflower are Oregon and tiger lily. The flower itself measures 2-3 in. wide in 6 petallike segments that curve back toward the stem. The leaves are 2-4 in. in diameter; the plant grows to a height of 4 ft.

COAST REDWOOD
RW
The coast redwood is the world's tallest tree, ranging in height from an average of 200 ft. to the tallest in the park at 367.8 ft. The age of the coast redwood at maturity is 400-500

years, although the oldest recorded through annual rings is 2,200 years. It has a reddish-brown trunk and is quite large at the base, tapering only slightly; the diameter is 10-15 ft. The leaves are needlelike and uneven; cones are .5-1.25 in. long. The genus name commemorates the Indian chief Sequoyah, or Sequoia, inventor of the Cherokee alphabet. This tree has been the source of constant controversy between conservationists and the logging industry throughout the years.

DOGWOOD
KC, RW, SQ, YO

The flower of the Pacific dogwood is larger than that of the eastern or flowering dogwood; the flower is 4-6 in. wide with 4 yellow-greenish petals split in the middle, giving an impression of 8 petals, and has petal-like leaves, all of which make up the "flower." The tree grows to a height of 50 ft. with a dense, rounded crown and horizontal branches.

FOXGLOVE
RW, YO

Spires of hanging flowers all turned to one side and all resembling little bells top tall, leafy stalks that cover the wooded and bushy slopes of the Pacific region. The Latin name is *Digitalis purpurea*; digitalis, the heart stimulant, which is quite toxic when not used properly, is derived from this plant, which is in itself poisonous to livestock. The white-pinkish flower is 1-1.5 in. in diameter, and the plant grows to a height of 7 ft.

GIANT COREOPSIS
CI, JT, LV

This yellow-flowered member of the sunflower family resembles a small tree, with its long leafless stalks that branch at the top. It may grow to a height of 10 ft. in the southern California coastal area, especially on dunes and bluffs.

GIANT SEQUOIA
KC, SQ, YO

This rare species is among the world's oldest trees; among those felled some have been ring-measured at 3,200 years. Almost all of the giant sequoias are protected within 3 national parks—Yosemite, Kings Canyon, and Sequoia—in 4 national forests, and in several California state forests and parks. The sequoia grows to 250 ft. and has a trunk diameter of 20 ft. Its leaves are evergreen (blue-green) needles with cones that are 1.75-3.75 in. long. Many of the virgin trees were lost in the early days of California logging.

INCENSE-CEDAR
KC, LV, RW, SQ, YO

The incense-cedar is a large, resinous, aromatic tree that grows to 150 ft. with a tapering, irregular, 3-5 ft. trunk, and a narrow, columnar and open, irregular crown. Its branches are flat, with

wedge-shaped joints and scalelike leaves; its cones are .75-1 in. in length and are oblong, hanging from a slender, leafy stalk.

LUPINE
CI, DV, JT, KC, LV, RW, SQ, YO

There are several varieties of the lupine in national parks; pictured is the yellow bush lupine, a large, round, bushy plant with tall, 2-9-ft. stands of palmately compound leaves and sweet-smelling, yellow "pea flowers." The lupine was once believed to be "wolflike" in that it devoured the nutrients of the soil; in fact, its name is derived from the Latin *lupus*, or wolf. Actually, the lupine prefers poor soil, from which it draws no further nutrient. The tree lupine grows rapidly, has deep roots, and is excellent for the stabilization of poor or sandy soils, especially along coastlines. Sections of the city of San Francisco, considered sandy and unstable, were once reclaimed by the tree lupine.

MONKEY FLOWER
CI, DV, JT, KC, LV, RW, SQ, YO

The monkey flower is a

leafy plant ranging from spindly and tiny to large and bushy; it can grow to 3 ft. Its yellow bilaterally symmetrical flowers measure .5-1.5 in. on slender stalks, and bloom from March to September.

MOUNTAIN HEMLOCK
KC, LV, RW, YO

The mountain hemlock is a 30-100-ft.-high tree with a conical crown of slender, horizontal branches. Its needles are evergreen and are usually crowded at the end of short side twigs curved upward. The cones are 1-3 in. long and cylindrical; they go from purplish to brown in color. This hemlock provides nesting sites and seeds for birds as well as forage for sheep and goats.

OHIA LEHUA-METROSIDEROS
HI, HV

The most common tree in Hawaii, the ohia lehua-metrosideros consists of a swarm of hybrids; beautiful flowers, mostly red and

yellow, appear throughout the year. It grows from near sea level to about 8,200 ft. On dry lava it will grow 10 ft. tall, but in wetter areas it can grow 20-30 ft. tall. The wood is hard and dark red and was used by ancient Hawaiians for spears, mallets, and idols. Today it is used for the flooring and keel blocks of ships.

OXALIS
LV, RW

The oxalis, or redwood sorrel, is a low plant that grows in patches with 3 heart-shaped leaflets and a funnel-shaped, white or rose-pink flower at the end of each stalk. The flowers are .5-.75 in. wide with 5 petals, sometimes with blue veins. The plant grows to 7 in. and frequently forms a solid carpet beneath the redwoods.

PONDEROSA PINE
KC, LV, SQ, YO

The most widely distributed and common pine in

North America, the ponderosa pine is a large evergreen with a broad, open, conical crown of spreading branches. It is 60-130 ft. high and 2.5-4 ft. in diameter, with stiff dark-green needles and 2-6-in. cones. It is the most commercially valuable western pine.

PUKIAWE-STYPHELIA
HL, HV

Pukiawe-styphelia is an abundant shrub with white, pink, red, or mahogany brown berries that occurs throughout both parks. In Hawaii Volcanoes National Park they are found mostly in the open shrubland along the Mauna Loa Road; at Haleakala, in the crater and along the upper slopes.

QUAKING ASPEN
KC, LV, SQ, YO

The most widely distributed tree in North America, the quaking aspen grows to a height of 80-100 ft. Its leaves are 1.25-3 in. long and nearly round, shiny green above, dull green beneath, and turn golden-yellow in autumn before dropping; the "quaking" comes from leaves that tremble in the slightest breeze. The bark is the favorite of beaver and rabbits; deer, elk, moose, sheep, and goats feed on twigs and foliage.

REDBUD TREE
KC, SQ, YO

The redbud tree is a large shrub or small tree that has a rounded crown of many spreading branches and purplish-pink flowers. It grows to 16 ft. and has a trunk diameter of only 4 in. The Indians once made bows from its wood.

SILVERSWORD
HL, HV

One of the national parks' most unusual plants, the silversword is found only in the two volcanic parks of Hawaii. A lustrous sil-

very down covering thick, daggerlike leaves gives the plant its name. Surprisingly, though it resembles the yucca of the lily family, it belongs to the Compositae family, along with sunflowers, asters, and chrysanthemums. After a growth of 7-20 years, the plant flowers once and then dies.

SNOW PLANT
KC, LV, SQ, YO

A stout, fleshy plant with bright red, corolla bell-shaped flowers, the snow plant grows to a height of 24 in. and flowers from April to July, poking its head through the forest floor just as the snows begin to recede.

SUGAR PINE
KC, LV, SQ, YO

Often called the "king of the pines," the sugar pine is one of the most beautiful of the tall, majestic trees of California. It is a large, tall, 100-160-ft. tree with a straight 3-6-ft.-diameter trunk and horizontal branches that form a high conical crown. The cones measure 11-18 in. in length and have been recorded at 21 in.; they are a shiny, light brown in color. The sugar pine is a major lumber species and played an important role in the building of early California.

WESTERN AZALEA
KC, RW, SQ, YO

This shrub grows from southern California to southwestern Oregon and is generally found in open areas near the coast. The flowers—April to August—are quite fragrant and range in color from white to deep pink. It will grow to a height of 17 in.; the flowers are about 2.5 in. in diameter, and the leaves are 1.25-3.5 in. in length.

PHOTO CREDITS

Page 10: © Gilbert Grant
17, top: American Museum of Natural History
17, bottom: © David Hiser/Photographers Aspen
19: National Park Service Photo by John Brooks
20, 23, 25, top: © Gilbert Grant
25, bottom left: © P. Craig
25, rest, 27: © Gilbert Grant
28-29: © P. Craig
31: © Gilbert Grant
33: © John Brooks
34: © Roy Murphy
37: © Hara
40, 42-43: © Bob Evans/Peter Arnold, Inc.
44: © Robert Gildart
45, both: © Bob Evans/Peter Arnold, Inc.
46, 47, clockwise from bottom left: © Howard Hall/Tom Stack & Assoc.; © Howard Hall/Tom Stack & Assoc.; © Bob Evans/Peter Arnold, Inc.; © F. Gohier/Photo Researchers, Inc.
50-51: © Fran Lanting
52: © Fred Hirschmann
55: © Jeff Foott
59: Death Valley National Park
61, 62, 63, 64-65: © Michael Collier
66-67: © Jeff Foott
69: © Fred Hirschmann
70-71, 72: © Michael Collier
75: © Fred Hirschmann
76-77: Death Valley National Park
78, 79: © Dave Wyman
80: © Fred Hirschmann
81: © Dave Wyman
83: © Jeff Foott
84-85, 87: © Laurence Parent
89, both: © Fred Hirschmann
91: © Donald Young
92: © David Muench
95, 99: Bishop Museum
101: © David Muench
102: © Ed Cooper

104-105: © David Muench
107, 110-111: © Ed Cooper
113: © Werner Stoy/Camera Hawaii, Inc.
114: © Laura Bremner
114-115, 119: © Ed Cooper
120: © David Muench
127, 128: © Tai Sing Loo/Bishop Museum
129: © Ed Cooper
131: © David Muench
133: © Ed Cooper
134-135: © Laura Bremner
138: © Keith H. Murakami/Tom Stack & Assoc.
141: © Ed Cooper
146-147: © Camera Hawaii, Inc.
150: © Werner Stoy/Camera Hawaii, Inc.
153: © Camera Hawaii, Inc.
154, 161 top: © Stephen Trimble
161, bottom left: Joshua Tree National Park
161, bottom right: © Stephen Trimble
163: © Jeff Nicholas
165: © Brian G. Prescott
166-167, 169: © Jeff Foott
173: © Stephen Trimble
174-75: © Jeff Foott
178: © Jeff Gnass
181: © Ed Cooper
185: © Sequoia and Kings Canyon National Parks
189: © D. C. Lowe
190-191: © David Muench
195: © Jeff Gnass
199: © Galen Rowell
200, both: © D.C. Lowe
203: © Manuel Rodriguez
204: © David Muench
210, 211: Lassen Volcanic National Park
213: © Pat O'Hara
215: © Holiday Films
218: © Warren Garst/Tom Stack & Assoc.
221: © Bill Perry
222-223: © Jeff Gnass
225: © David Muench
226: © Jeff Gnass
228, 231: © David Muench
235, 237: Redwood National Park
238: © Rick McIntyre
241: © Stephen Trimble
242-243, left to right: © Gary Milburn/Tom Stack & Assoc.; © David Muench; © John Richardson
246-247: © David Muench
251: © Ed Cooper
252: © David Muench
256-257: © Manuel Rodriguez
259, 262-263: Sequoia and Kings Canyon N.P.
265: © David Muench
266: © Roy Murphy
269, clockwise from top left: © Manuel Rodriguez; © Galen Rowell; © Rod Planck/Tom Stack & Assoc.; © John Gerlach/Tom Stack & Assoc.
272-273: © Jeff Gnass
275, 279: © David Muench
281: © Jeff Gnass
283: © David Muench
284: © Galen Rowell
287: © J. Mark Blackburn/International Stock Photo
291, 294, both: Yosemite National Park
295: © David Sumner
296-297, 299, 300: © Ed Cooper
302, 303, counterclockwise from top left: © Ed Cooper; © John Gerlach/Tom Stack & Assoc.; © David Muench; © Holiday Films; © Tom J. Ulrich/Click/Chicago
305: © Manuel Rodriguez
307: © Galen Rowell
309: © Manuel Rodriguez
311: © D. C. Lowe
315: © Donna Dannen
316-317: © D. C. Lowe
318: © Ed Cooper
321: © Galen Rowell

339

Appendix of Animals and Plants Photo Credits

324, col. 1, top: © E.P.I.
Nancy Adams/Tom Stack
& Assoc., **bottom:** © Roy
Murphy; **col. 2, top:** © G.
C. Kelley/Tom Stack &
Assoc., **bottom:** © Roy
Murphy; **col. 3:** © Roy
Murphy.
325, col. 1, top: © Robert
McKenzie/Tom Stack &
Assoc., **bottom:** © Brian
Parker/Tom Stack &
Assoc.; **col. 2:** © Roy
Murphy; **col. 3, top:** ©
Joe McDonald/Tom Stack
& Assoc., **bottom:** © Gary
Milburn/Tom Stack &
Assoc.
326, col. 1, top: © Bob
McKeever/Tom Stack &
Assoc., **bottom:** © Steve
Martin/Tom Stack &
Assoc.; **col. 2:** © Larry R.
Ditto/Tom Stack & Assoc.;
col. 3, top: © Roy
Murphy, **bottom:** © Rod
Planck/Tom Stack and
Assoc.
327, col. 1, top: © Phil &
Loretta Hermann/Tom
Stack & Assoc., **bottom:**
© Larry Dech/Tom Stack
& Assoc.; **col. 2, top:** ©
C. Summers/Tom Stack &
Assoc.; **col. 3, top:** © Roy
Murphy, **bottom:** © Phil
& Loretta Hermann/Tom
Stack & Assoc.
328, col. 1, top: ©
Christopher Crowley/Tom
Stack & Assoc., **bottom:**
© Stephen Trimble; **col. 2,
top:** © Don & Pat Valenti/
Tom Stack & Assoc., **bot-
tom:** © Anthony
Mercieca/ Tom Stack &
Assoc.; **col. 3:** © John
Gerlach/Tom Stack &
Assoc.
329, col. 1, top: © Len Rue,
Jr./Tom Stack & Assoc.,
bottom: © G. C.

Kelley/Tom Stack &
Assoc.; **col. 2, top:** © Roy
Murphy, **bottom:** © C.
Summers/Tom Stack &
Assoc.; **col. 3, top:** ©
Stephen Trimble, **bottom:**
© Rod Planck/Tom Stack
330, col. 1, top: © John
Gerlach/Tom Stack &
Assoc., **bottom:** © Larry
Ditto/Tom Stack & Assoc.;
col. 2, top: © Alan D.
Briere/Tom Stack &
Assoc., **bottom:** Gilbert
Grant; **col. 3, top:**
Anthony Mercieca/Tom
Stack & Assoc., **bottom:**
© Gary Randall/Tom Stack
& Assoc.
331, col. 1: © Anthony
Mercieca/Tom Stack &
Assoc. **col. 2, top:** ©
Brian Parker/Tom Stack &
Assoc., **bottom:** © John
Shaw/Tom Stack & Assoc.;
col. 3, top: © C.
Summers/Tom Stack &
Assoc.; **bottom:** © Alan
G. Nelson/Tom Stack &
Assoc.
332, col. 1, top: Brian G.
Prescott, **bottom:** Prof. R.
C. Simpson; **col 2, top:** ©
Anthony Mercieca/Tom
Stack & Assoc., **bottom:**
© Kevin Shafer/Tom Stack
& Assoc.
333, col. 1, top: © Tom
Stack/Tom Stack & Assoc.,
bottom: © Roy Murphy;
col. 2, top: © Jim
Yuskavitch/Tom Stack &
Assoc.; **bottom:** © Roy
Murphy; **col. 3, top:** ©
Gilbert Grant, **bottom:**
Joshua Tree National Park.
334, col. 1, top: © John
Gerlach/Tom Stack &
Assoc., **bottom:** ©
Lysbeth Corsi/Tom Stack
& Assoc.; **col 2:** © Rick
McIntyre/Tom Stack &

Assoc.; **col. 3, top:** © Jim
Yuskavitch/Tom Stack &
Assoc., **bottom:** © John
Gerlach/Tom Stack &
Assoc.
335, col. 1, top: © Jeff
Gnass, **center:** © John
Gerlach/Tom Stack &
Assoc., **bottom:** © Gilbert
Grant ; **col. 2 :** © Jeff
Gnass; **col. 3, top:** © Roy
Murphy, **bottom:**© David
Lavender,
336, col. 1, top: © Jeff
Gnass, **bottom:** © Russ
Finley; **col. 2, top:** ©
David Lavender, **bottom:**
© Roy Murphy; **col. 3,
top:** © Ed Cooper, **bot-
tom:** © John Gerlach/Tom
Stack & Assoc.
337, col. 1, top:© Jeff Gnass,
bottom:© Camera
Hawaii, Inc.; **col. 2, top:**
© Manuel Rodriguez, **bot-
tom:** © Stephen Trimble;
col. 3, top: © Ed Cooper,
bottom: © Tom Stack/
Tom Stack & Assoc.
338, col. 1, both: © Ed
Cooper; **col. 2, both:** ©
Roy Murphy; **col. 3:** © Ed
Cooper.

INDEX
Numbers in italics indicate illustrations.